Also by Graeme Gill

Peasants and Government in the Russian Revolution

Twentieth Century Russia: The Search for Power and Authority

The Rules of the Communist Party of the Soviet Union

Stalinism

The Origins of the Stalinist Political System

The Politics of Transition: Shaping a Post-Soviet Future
(with Stephen White and Darrell Slider)

*The Collapse of a Single Party System: The Disintegration of the
CPSU*

*Power in the Party: The Organization of Power and Central –
Republican Relations in the CPSU* (with Roderic Pitty)

Elites and Leadership in Russian Politics (edited)

The Dynamics of Democratization

The Dynamics of Democratization

Elites, Civil Society and the Transition Process

Graeme Gill

St. Martin's Press
New York

THE DYNAMICS OF DEMOCRATIZATION

St, Martin's Press, Scholarly and Reference Division,
175 Fifth Avenue, New York, N.Y. 10010

First published in the United States of America in 2000

Printed in Hong Kong

ISBN 0–312–23171–7 (cloth)
ISBN 0–312–23172–5 (paper)

Library of Congress Cataloging-in-Publication Data

Gill Graeme J.
The dynamics of democratization : elites, civil society, and the transition process /
Graeme Gill.
p. cm.
Includes bibliographical reference and index.
ISBN 0-312-23171-7 (cloth) – ISBN 0-312-23172-5 (pbk)
1. Democratization–History–20th century. 2. Democracy–History–20th century. 3. Elites (Social science)–History–20th century. 4. Civil society–History–20th century. I. Title.

JC421 .G545 2000
320.9'049–dc21   99-056425

Contents

Preface

This book seeks to address one of the most pressing issues of both international politics and the scholarly community, the dynamics of democratization. Its focus is the course of democratization itself and how that process has been analysed and explained. It arose from a general dissatisfaction with the orientation and focus of much of the theoretical literature dealing with this question, and it seeks to point the way to a theoretically more robust method of understanding this process. Its origin and development owes much to discussion with scholars from across the world, most importantly Australia, Europe, North America and Russia. They are too numerous to name, without the invidious result of omitting someone who should be included. My thanks to them generally and individually. However, I must single out Dr Roger Markwick, whose diligence, spark and enthusiasm has been an essential component of the effort which has produced this volume, and Rod Tiffen, who has been a fellow traveller on this journey of investigation from its beginning. I must also thank the Australian Research Council for funding this research, and the Department of Government at the University of Sydney for providing a congenial working environment. And finally, my thanks once again go to Heather, without whose love and support this would not have been possible.

GRAEME GILL

1
Democratization: Economic Prerequisites?

In the last quarter of the twentieth century, the international scene has been transformed by the wave of regime changes that has constituted what one observer has called the 'third wave' of democratization.[1] Beginning with Portugal and Greece in 1974 and rolling through Spain, Latin America and, most spectacularly, the former Communist states of the Soviet Union and Eastern Europe (and Mongolia), and also influencing events in East and South-east Asia, this wave has altered fundamentally the geopolitical map of the globe. Long-standing dictatorships across the globe fell, to be replaced by regimes both professing democratic principles and having considerable success in translating those principles into practice. The political implications of these changes can hardly be exaggerated, with their most important manifestation being the transformation of much of the Communist world which had for so long posed a major geopolitical and ideological challenge to Western capitalist democracy. The misplaced triumphalism of some notwithstanding,[2] it was clear that a major political phenomenon had occurred and needed to be explained. But how was it to be explained?

As the term 'third wave' implies, this was not the first time there has been a significant shift of regimes in a democratic direction. According to Huntington,[3] there have been two prior waves of democratization separated by one reverse wave. The first wave lasted for a century from about 1828 and saw some 33 countries establish 'at least minimal national democratic institutions.'[4] This wave had its roots in the American and French revolutions and included the US, Britain, France, some of the British colonies, some of the smaller countries of Europe and a number of the independent states of South America. In the first reverse wave, many of those countries, especially those which had

1

established democratic regimes just before or after the First World War, saw the re-emergence of authoritarian rule. The principal areas in which this occurred were Central and Eastern Europe, the Iberian peninsula, Japan, and South America. Huntington's second wave of democratization began in 1943 and lasted until about 1962 and embraced many of the countries liberated at the end of the Second World War (although many others, most particularly in Eastern Europe, had authoritarian regimes imposed upon them at this time), a significant number of former European colonies, and a range of countries in South America. Like its predecessor, this wave of democratization was followed by a reverse wave (1958–75), evident in particular in South America and among many of the former colonies. This was followed by the third wave. The metaphor of the third wave[5] highlights the way in which the 1970s and 1980s were not the first occasion on which a large number of such regime changes came about. This has meant that when scholars broached the question that these regime changes raised – why does democracy come about and what makes it endure? – there were already some answers stemming from analysis of the earlier waves.

A number of different approaches to this question had emerged. Prominent among these, and reacting in particular to the failure of democracy in many of the newly-independent former colonies of Asia and Africa, was the argument that the creation of a stable democratic regime was linked to the type of culture to be found in a country. While the most influential of these studies saw a link between a 'civic culture' and democratic forms,[6] others sought to link these with such things as belief in the legitimacy of polyarchy,[7] the rational and individualistic values embodied in European culture,[8] and the presence of Protestantism.[9] This literature was immensely stimulating and often insightful, but ultimately it was unsatisfying as an explanation for the emergence of democracy; it was not clear how culture produced particular, in this case democratic, political outcomes. The focus on culture was more successful in the attempt to explain democratic endurance, with the commonsensical argument that a regime is more secure if its structures and processes accord with popular (and élite) values than if they are in conflict, but even here the link between values and institutions remained somewhat ambiguous.

Another approach, and the one which became the most influential, is that which sought to relate democratization to economic development. This approach to the question was begun with Lipset's seminal article in 1959[10] and his basic finding has been sustained by numerous subsequent analyses,[11] viz. there is a positive correlation between economic development and democracy. In Lipset's words, 'the more well-to-do a nation, the greater the chances that it will sustain democracy.'[12] Lipset's research showed that generally democracies tended to have higher levels of economic development than non-democracies, and despite criticism of his methodology,[13] this basic finding has remained unchallenged. However, further research has shown that this is not a linear relationship: the probability of democracy does not increase automatically as the level of development rises. A number of scholars have pointed to the importance of a middle income range, defined in terms of per capita income expressed in American dollars.[14] It is for countries within this range, neither very poor nor very rich, that the probability of the fall of authoritarian regimes and their replacement by stable democratic regimes was highest. In countries below that range, the establishment of a democratic regime was possible (and did happen), but it was unlikely to endure. In the case of countries above that range, analysts differ. Diamond cites Dahl's argument[15] to the effect that there is an upper threshold beyond which the probability of a democratic regime is so high that increases in wealth have no effect, while Przeworski and Limongi[16] argue that above such a threshold, all types of regimes are better able to stabilize themselves and therefore any authoritarian regimes that survived the 'transition zone'[17] have good prospects of enduring. In any event, all seem to agree that below that upper threshold of the 'transition' or 'middle income' zone, increases in society's wealth increases the probability of democratic rule.[18]

However correlation is not causation. Pointing to the fact that democracies tend to be in societies that are more affluent does not explain why this is the case or why it came about. In principle, it is possible that the direction of causality runs from democracy to affluence (i.e. a democratic political system produces an affluent society), but this is unlikely.[19] It is more likely that affluence leads to democracy, and indeed, this is consistent with Huntington's analysis.[20] The question that remains to be answered is why increased affluence leads to the replacement of authoritarian regimes by democratic.

A number of aspects of the process of economic development have been identified to explain the emergence of democracies.[21]

1. Economic development produces change in the values of the population. Principally as a result of education, the citizenry come to value democracy and become more tolerant, moderate, restrained

and rational with respect to politics and to political opposition. A democratic political culture is thereby generated.

2. Economic development brings higher levels of income and of economic security to the mass of the population, thereby lowering the intensity and stakes of 'class struggle', and enabling the populace to develop longer time perspectives and more complex and gradualist views of politics.

3. Economic development also changes the outlook of those in higher socio-economic strata, encouraging them to see the lower strata as less threatening and worthy of political rights and the opportunity to share power.

4. Increased wealth reduces objective levels of inequality and thereby of class distinctions, and it increases the size of the middle class. The middle class moderates conflict by rewarding moderate and democratic parties and punishing radical groups.

5. Increased wealth and education increase the exposure of the working class to a wide range of different influences and pressures, and thereby makes them less susceptible to the appeals of radical, anti-democratic ideas.[22]

6. The increased wealth resulting from economic development would reduce the premium on political power by reducing the potential costs to groups of the consequences of government activity. If the government sought to implement redistributive policies, the consequences of this would be much greater in poor societies than in rich because groups would have less fat on which to survive. Furthermore, jobs are more plentiful in rich than in poor societies, implying less reliance on the state for employment. Who has power thus becomes less of a crucial issue than it would otherwise have been.

7. Authoritarian structures cannot accommodate the stresses created by the processes of economic development. This involves significant change in the class structure: the growth of a middle class and of a commercial and industrial bourgeoisie, the growth, unionization and increased economic standing of the working class, and the migration of the rural poor to the cities recasts the class structure, in the process breaking apart the clientelistic and feudal rural links typical of the old regime.

8. Economic development leads to the emergence of a large number of voluntary, autonomous social organizations which not only place a check upon government, but also increase political participation, enhance political skills, and generate and diffuse new opin-

ions. Economic development is therefore instrumental in the emergence of civil society.

This checklist would gain wide, although not universal, agreement among scholars as capturing much of the dynamic of economic development which is instrumental in the emergence of democracy. However, these factors need to be examined further.

Most of the factors listed above are essentially enabling or precipitating factors. They may explain why popular sentiment broadly favours democracy, but not why political actors might act to replace authoritarian by democratic rule; they are socio-economic explanations which establish contexts for political action without explaining why particular political actors act the way they do. Changes in values and perspectives on politics are important in telling us why people are willing to accept a democratic system but not necessarily why they prefer it to an authoritarian one (with the exception of point 1 which assumes the generation of a commitment to democratic values themselves). Similarly, the point about the changing class structure may tell us about the sorts of social developments which significantly complicate the capacity of an authoritarian regime to survive, but insofar as democratic transitions are not usually brought about by concerted class action, it does not really explain the dynamics of the transition. To do that, this book will argue, we must turn to the final factor noted above, the development of civil society forces.

A civil society may be defined as a society in which there are autonomous groups which aggregate the views and activities of individuals and which act to promote and defend the interests of those people, including against the state. This implies that there is the public discussion of issues, with questions of public policy being debated widely within the community rather than being decided solely by regime élites. It is through this public discussion of issues in part that autonomous groups act to defend the interests of their respective constituencies. Crucial for the existence of a civil society is that both state and civil society recognize the legitimacy of the other, and acknowledge the right of the other to act unimpeded within certain defined spheres of competence. These spheres of competence must include the political. For a civil society to exist, autonomous groups must be able to defend the interests they embody in the political sphere, as well as more generally in society as a whole. The existence of a network of groups which structures individuals' private lives and their pursuit of their interests in the public sphere does not constitute a civil society unless groups are able to pursue those interests in the political sphere. Most autonomous groups do not act politically, realizing their interests without recourse to political activism, but such political activism is a crucial condition for civil society. Many have failed to recognize this. This point can be clarified by seeing the organization of autonomous activity in terms of three types of groups. First, all societies have a sub-structure of groups through which individuals structure their private lives (e.g. friends, hobby groups). These are limited in their scope, often local in their perspectives, and usually do not interact with the state or political authorities. They also provide a basis upon which second-order groups rest. These second-order groups represent their members' interests in the broader public sphere and are the main currency of civil society. They constitute the dense networks of which the public sphere consists. Although these groups are not specifically political-ically-oriented and rest overwhelmingly on the non-political interests of their members, they may at times have to carry their members' interests into the political sphere. The third-order groups are those which are specifically political in their outlook and aims, seeking to project and defend their constituents' interests in the political sphere. The most important group of this type is the political party. Under an authoritarian regime, it is likely that a wide range of second order groups will be able to exist, but either none of the third-order politically-oriented groups will be tolerated, or they will labour under particularly tight restrictions. But unless such politically-oriented groups are able to function freely, a civil society can not exist. Unless groups are able to defend their members' interests politically, they are not really able to defend them at all.

In cases where there are autonomous groups but a restriction on political activity exists, where autonomous groups can act in defence and furtherance of their members' interests but not politically and cannot place restrictions on the government, those groups constitute civil society forces rather than civil society as such. Until political activity by autonomous groups is accepted by the state, while civil society forces may act independently of the state, the definition of their sphere of activity to exclude the political means that they do not constitute a civil society *in situ*, although they may be seen as constituting the potential for such a society. This distinction between civil society forces which can precede civil society, and civil society, is crucial for the argument of this book.

Civil society has generally been seen as important for democracy because it mediates between the regime on the one hand and the mass of the populace on the other. The changes in values and perspectives on politics noted above with regard to economic development are brought about through the sorts of institutions of which civil society consists. The representation and pressing of interests implicit in much of the above and in an effective democracy is intrinsic to the notion of civil society. And the idea of restraints on government implicit in the above and central to notions of democracy is part of what civil society is about. It is through civil society and its institutions, including political parties and voluntary groups and associations, that the network of popular participation and activism which is the heart of any notion of what democracy means is established. So, in all of these ways, civil society is fundamental for the functioning of an effective democracy, and is instrumental in the generation of those factors identified above as explanations for the link between economic development and democracy.[23] It is the chief thesis of this book that the idea of autonomous self-organization, of independent associative behaviour so linked with civil society and mature democracies, is also crucial for explaining what the purely enabling factors above cannot: how and which political actors mobilize to bring about democratic transition. Civil society forces and the conscious organization they embody constitute the causal connection between economic development and democracy. But this point has generally not been appreciated by students of democratization.

The chief response to the third wave was the development of what has been called the 'transition to democracy' literature, initially embodied in a path-breaking collective study of transitions from authoritarian rule.[24] This approach grew out of some innovative work on regime change in the form of the collapse of democracies[25] and a rejection of the earlier attempts to explain democratization because of their perceived lack of explanatory power. Eschewing the earlier approaches based on cultural factors and economic development, and largely rejecting the importance of notions of civil society for democratic transition, the focus of this work was the activities of political élites and the time frame was the period immediately surrounding the change of regime. The approach was actor-centred and paid no attention to the sort of structural factors intrinsic to both the cultural and economic development approaches. The result has been an extensive and rich literature, but as we shall see, it has been unable to generate a satisfactory explanation of democratization, chiefly because of the exclusion of the notion of civil society. This will become evident as we explore this approach to explaining democratization.

2
The Breakdown of Authoritarian Regimes

The study of the third wave,[1] embodied in the 'transition literature', has conceptualized the course of regime change in terms of three phases: regime breakdown, democratic transition, and democratic consolidation. Breakdown involves the deconstruction and possibly disintegration of the old regime, transition is the shift from old structures and processes to new, and consolidation is when those structures and processes have become stabilized and so embedded in the collective consciousness of the society that they gain normative authority. These phases are logically, but not always temporally, distinct; all three phases overlap, even if the forces driving them are not the same. This is clearest in the case of regime breakdown and transition. With domestic political forces the main actors in the third wave of democratization, that process was a zero sum game; democratic forces could not be successful without the withdrawal or collapse of authoritarian power. This does not mean that the two processes, the collapse of authoritarian rule and the establishment of a democratic regime, are the same; the breakdown of authoritarian rule does not inevitably lead to a democratic polity, and historically most cases of authoritarian collapse have spawned further authoritarian regimes. However, the two processes are closely linked; except in cases when an authoritarian regime has been replaced by a democratic one as a result of foreign invasion or civil war (and both have been rare occurrences), the emergence of a democratic regime must be preceded by authoritarian breakdown. This creates a problem of delineation: when does the breakdown end and the transition to democracy begin? There can be no answer to this question and it makes little sense to seek one because, in successful cases of transition, breakdown is an intrinsic and necessary part of the process while in cases of failed transition, when the regime is able to restabilize itself or is replaced by another authoritarian regime, the question does not arise. The discussion which follows seeks to avoid this difficulty by breaking the analysis into parts. The first part, contained in this chapter, will look at the main elements that recur in cases of authoritarian breakdown as analysed in the 'transition literature'. In looking at the elements which recur in these cases of breakdown, it will ask why breakdown occurred. The second part of the discussion, in Chapter 3, will analyse how democratic transition comes about, discussed principally in the terms of the 'transition literature'.

Explanations of regime breakdown have generally been quite consistent in the components that have been considered important in that process. Breakdown has often been associated with a failure of regime performance, usually in the economic sphere. As economic growth slows, or even stops, the regime is confronted with a policy dilemma about how to respond to the economic difficulties. Within society at large, the slowing of economic growth creates hardship for many sectors of the population, often including those upon which the regime relies for support. As the interests of such groups suffer, mobilization independent of the regime is likely, with its transition into oppositional politics a common development. Confronted with both a policy dilemma and a challenge to its support base, potential divisions within the regime are likely to become manifest. Not only will such divisions focus upon the policy question, but the maintenance of regime control, and possibly also the question of whether the regime should even seek to maintain itself in power, will emerge as crucial issues. The greater the popular mobilization, the higher the costs of attempting to reassert control through forceful means, and therefore the stronger will be the pressures to reach some sort of accommodation through liberalization. Once liberalization has begun, the costs of preventing this from turning into democratization increase dramatically, and it is at this stage that it is probably more useful to discuss the process in terms of transition rather than breakdown. Such an analysis would, in its broad outlines, be acceptable to most students of democratic transition.[2] In seeking to understand the dynamics of this process, we will look at each of its components.

Economic Crisis

An important element in the course of the breakdown of authoritarian regimes has often been economic difficulty. One study of South America between 1945 and 1988 found that no non-democratic regime survived more than three consecutive years of negative growth, while the probability that it would survive three consecutive years of such growth was only 33 per cent (cf. 73 per cent for democratic regimes).[3] In the study by Haggard and Kaufman,[4] of 27 cases of democratic transition between 1970 and 1990, 23 of these experienced declining growth, increasing inflation, or both in the years preceding the transition. In the four other cases (Korea, Chile, Turkey and Thailand), economic conditions at the time of transition were favourable, although there had been periods of difficulty earlier.[5] The experience of these four regimes in weathering economic difficulty and then experiencing democratic transition shows that economic difficulty alone is usually not sufficient to induce regime change. Nevertheless, its presence in so many cases of regime change suggests that economic difficulty can be a very important variable in explaining democratic transition. In some cases economic difficulty amounted to a full-blown crisis, in others the problems were less severe, but in all instances it had an impact upon the capacity of the authoritarian regime to survive unchanged.

Economic difficulty can, if sufficiently severe, create a crisis of economic policy; if the regime is to survive, it must take steps to deal with the economic difficulties before they call into question the regime itself. Consequently, economic difficulties have often had a direct and substantial effect upon both the political élite and the regime more generally. Such crises have often been associated with developments external to the country, as in Brazil and Peru where the oil shock of 1973 was linked with a contraction of international lending facilities resulting in balance of payments problems for these regimes. The balance of payments difficulties usually generated significant fiscal deficits in the economy and increased inflation. Both governments reacted with an adjustment strategy involving currency devaluation, trade and exchange controls, and tighter fiscal and monetary policy. Regardless of the longer-term success of such a strategy, the short-term effect of the crisis was economic slowdown.[6]

But in many cases the principal impetus for economic difficulty was internal, and usually linked with the management of the economy by the regime, although these difficulties were often brought to a point by an unfavourable international environment. The type of crisis and its effects depended upon the nature of the economy, the political economy of the particular type of authoritarian rule in the country, and the policies pursued by the regime. Sometimes, as in Argentina in the early 1980s, it was simply a function of getting economic policies wrong, but at other times, as in Brazil and Chile, it was a case of the economic model being used having exhausted itself. The usual effect of both types of crisis was the same: a recession, with rising prices, increasing unemployment and a squeezing of the business sector. But the economic difficulties were less important for their economic consequences than for their consequences in other walks of life.

This sort of economic situation could have significant ramifications for an authoritarian regime, and not only in the economic arena. Some of the major potential ramifications can be enumerated:

1. Economic difficulty could call into question the credentials and competence of the regime in the economic sphere and, by implication, its right to rule. This might not matter much if the regime was thoroughly in control of the society, but if that control was in any way loose or weak, the regime could find itself confronted by unrest from the popular sector which was suffering as a result of the economic difficulties. Such political mobilization is dealt with below.
2. Economic difficulty could be associated with a policy crisis which the regime must resolve under generally unfavourable circumstances. The leadership must contemplate policy change under conditions which are not conducive to calm, clear reflection or to long time frames. Under such circumstances, the possibility of policy disputes, and thereby of splits within the regime, increase, as the issue of how to handle economic setbacks and to introduce policies which will usually involve penalties to some sectors of society, becomes primary.
3. Economic difficulty could lead to a rupture in relations between the regime and the commercial/industrial sectors of the society. These often serve as the social base of an authoritarian regime, and where they do not, the regime usually needs to keep them on side. Such a rupture can not only undermine the regime's support base, but can significantly complicate its efforts to bring an end to the economic difficulties. This is discussed below.

4. Economic difficulty may have ramifications for legitimation. Most authoritarian regimes have an instrumental notion of legitimation, with legitimation stemming in part from performance, and a perceived decline in performance can throw up questions about the appropriateness of the regime remaining in office. This will be the case particularly when the regime has rested upon the championing of a particular model of economic development, and that model is called into question by the economic crisis. This has been central to the so-called bureaucratic authoritarian model of authoritarian rule.[7]

5. Question marks over legitimation can lead to a crisis of confidence among the rulers about both their capacity and right to rule. This may further complicate policy debate by introducing the question of whether the rulers should attempt to remain in office or seek a way of leaving power.

Economic crisis alone is insufficient to bring down a regime; it is the flow-on effects from the economic crisis which are important. What is crucial is the regime's capacity to manage that crisis and to prevent its politicization. For example, in Argentina[8] economic difficulties at the start of the 1980s led to significant levels of criticism of the government from both business and popular sector organizations and increased disunity within the regime, thereby propelling it in the direction of change. A contrasting example, but one with the same implications, is Chile in the early 1980s when economic crisis did not lead to the collapse of the regime.[9] At this time, the economic model which had been instituted by the Pinochet regime collapsed, creating widespread hardship among the populace in general. This stimulated division and dispute within the élite and within the ruling apparatus more broadly; there was a fragmentation of economic policy-making as different groups within the regime struggled for supremacy. As Pinochet became increasingly isolated, the regime lost a sense of direction and coherence. At lower levels of society, political mobilization occurred, as civil society forces emerged among the capitalist and middle classes and the poor and youth took to the streets to express their disapproval. Political parties, some of which had been able to survive the regime's repression, took a hand in organizing this. The regime's response was to combine severe repression of unrest with some concessions in the formal political realm. This policy was successful, underpinned as it was by the continuing support of the business sector. The regime was thus able to stabilize itself and survive, and when it did give way in 1990, it was in a situation of positive economic performance, and certainly much better than was evident early in the decade.[10]

Short-term economic crisis can therefore be crucial to a regime's ability to sustain itself. Such a crisis poses a challenge both to prevailing policy lines and to the continuing support of the coalitions upon which the regime rests.[11] The onset of crisis demands adjustment of policy, and yet such adjustment may have serious consequences for the interests of those groups which constitute and support the regime. Furthermore, those groups will also be likely to be suffering as a result of the economic crisis itself, so a refusal to implement policy change will not satisfy them either. Where the authoritarian regime relies heavily upon its capacity to deliver material resources to key support groups in order to maintain their support, as authoritarian regimes tend to do, economic crisis challenges the social support bases upon which they rest. This combination of economic and political challenge is likely to engender division and dispute within the regime itself. This logic has been evident in numerous cases of regime change, and is discussed further below.

Political Mobilization

In discussing modern authoritarianism, Amos Perlmutter notes that one of the things upon which such regimes rest is popular mobilization, but a mobilization which is limited, exclusionary and restrictive.[12] It is also a mobilization which is intrinsically non-political. This means that authoritarian regimes seek to involve the population, or at least segments of it, in public life through their participation in official regime organizations and rituals. A range of bodies may be generated to organize and structure public activity, including youth groups, trade unions, women's groups, sporting associations and the like. The aim of such organizations is to keep the populace busy, to involve it in activity which, by its conduct through official structures, is essentially regime-supporting. Similar concerns surround rituals like public demonstrations, meetings, marches, celebrations and elections. The aim is to depoliticize public life, and at its extreme, to make it one great celebration of the regime and its achievements. The crucial element here is to ensure that such public activity is controlled, and to ensure that there is no popular mobilization on an independent basis. Indeed, the obverse side of this sort of popular mobilization is the destruction and continuing suppression of all types of independent organization, especially those which may potentially have a political hue.

Not all authoritarian regimes are equally able to generate the sorts of organizations which will structure and contain popular mobilization. While the capacity of regimes in this regard depends in part upon the quality of personnel holding official positions, structural considerations are also relevant. One significant study[13] argues that military regimes are much less likely than party-based regimes to construct the sorts of organizational channels into society which will enable them to consolidate a popular support base. Military institutions almost inevitably seek to set themselves apart from society and thereby to acquire a special status in the community. Important in this also is the military's rejection of independent political parties as appropriate vehicles for political activity, and the fact that military-dominated parties tend not to be very successful in generating long-term popular support. In contrast, dominant party regimes by their nature seek to embed themselves in society and thereby can act as the connection between regime and society at large.

The problem for authoritarian regimes is that it is very difficult to maintain political passivity without extensive organizational controls and the exercise (or threat) of high levels of coercion. This is particularly the case when societies experience the sort of economic difficulties discussed above. But it is also true when societies undergo (often long-term) socio-economic change of major dimensions. All of the countries experiencing regime change in the third wave were on the margins of the main foci of economic dynamism in the global economy. They were all to some degree in an economically dependent relationship with the major industrial and exporting powers, with their economies structured in part as a result of that dependence. This means that, generally, they were characterized by large agricultural and perhaps commercial sectors and a small industrial sector.[14] These regimes sought to develop industry, sometimes also to change its focus from consumer to producer goods production. Such a policy involved significant shifts within the social structure. Industrialization leads to a downgrading of the importance of primary products in the economy and thereby of the primary producers in the socio-political sphere. This normally means an undercutting of the position of traditional landowning interests. It also involves the promotion of a new class of industrial entrepreneurs whose interests are very different from those of the former land-owners, and who seek to further those interests through alliances with the regime. Industrialization also involves the entry/expansion of financial interests because, if industrial development is to proceed, it requires significant amounts of capital and this cannot be found in regime coffers. Foreign capital may become involved, thereby inserting into the domestic situation a major new international actor. Even if international capital is not a major actor, domestic financial circles will become more important as the need for capital increases.

The new middle class, the industrialists, businessmen and financiers who become important as the economy develops, will seek to pursue their interests not only by operating in the economic sphere, but by applying pressure in the political realm as well. Such pressure can often flow through the regime's own channels; in many cases such groups constitute part of the ruling coalition and can therefore defend their interests and promote their concerns within the regime's councils. But those who lack this entrée must seek other avenues for exerting influence and pressure, for getting their voice heard by the political decision-makers. Even those who do possess entrée into the government can become alienated from it as a result of the sort of economic downturn discussed above. With their interests directly under threat as a result of failing economic performance on the part of the regime, business is more likely to begin to try to seek out alternative forms of political arrangement to those currently prevailing. This often drives them into political activity, into forming their own organizations which will both avoid regime control and place pressure on the regime to bring about policy change; in Brazil, they even pressed for democratization in an endeavour to improve the environment for the realization of their interests.[15]

The splitting of such a group from the regime can be very important. The social support base for many conservative authoritarian regimes has tended to rest at least in part among this section of the population. The industrial/business/commercial sector usually sees its interests as best served by having a passive work-force, and for this the state is a crucial player, possessing the coercive means to enforce such passivity. These groups also often see the state as a source of substantial material support for their economic activities; government policies that favour business are clearly a high priority in the minds of such people, while the sorts of connections we would label as corrupt are also a common feature. For the regime, especially if its legitimation depends upon performance, keeping these groups on side is crucial to economic and therefore regime success. If there is dissent from within this group, the support base of the regime narrows and the likelihood of its increasing isolation in the society grows. Its ability to gauge what is happening throughout the community, and thereby to respond to potential challenges before they gather pace, is thus impaired, and if it does face a challenge, its capacity to meet that challenge successfully declines. Furthermore, the alienation of the business, financial or industrial sector may also deprive the regime of the sort of technical expertise it needs if it is to manage the economy effectively, and thereby increases the likelihood of the regime making policy mistakes. It also discourages continuing investment in the economy on the part of such groups, a development which is likely to increase the dimensions of any economic difficulties the regime may be facing. Such dissent can also lead to splits within the regime, especially when it is a coalition including such interests, and can thus heighten political instability and hasten political change. Even when the regime is not coalitional in nature, the opposition from such groups can stimulate division within the regime by encouraging elements at the top who have doubts or reservations about the course of policy to become confirmed in those feelings. If this major support base is uncertain of the value of current policy, any doubts that exist within ruling circles are likely to be strengthened. This sort of situation is often at the heart of one of the characteristics of many transitions, the alliance between regime moderates and moderates from within the opposition. This will be discussed in the following chapter.

Industrial development also has significant effects at the lower levels of the social structure. It normally involves a process of large-scale population shift from the rural areas into the cities, as people leave the countryside in search of jobs in the new factories. This further erodes the power of rural interests and tilts the balance in favour of the emergent groups in the urban areas. But this mass of new urban inhabitants also constitutes a political problem. Usually living and working in poor conditions, the emergent working class is a force which can develop a sense of consciousness and common purpose, usually under the influence of organizations which can now take advantage of the sort of geographical concentration of people which was absent in the rural areas. Being crowded together in the cities, workers can be better organized than they were when spread between the villages in the rural areas. This group thereby constitutes a new political force with which the regime must cope, and one whose interests and perceptions will often differ substantially from those at the top of the political system. Such differences, and working class opposition, can become significant if the economy experiences difficulties. Under such circumstances, with economic growth slowing, the capacity of the regime to purchase political passivity through the provision of welfare benefits or improving standards of living declines considerably. The emergence of worker leaders and independent organizations can lead to the mobilization of workers against the regime. Strikes, meetings and demonstrations are the main forms of such protest. This sort of activity is most dangerous for the regime when it is accompanied by political demands, principally for democratization, but it can also be a threat when the demands are purely economic. It is a threat in this latter instance not only because it challenges regime policy, but also because by its very existence it challenges the regime's preferred set of societal arrangements. By engaging in independent political activity, it constitutes a rejection of the regime's political model and thereby of the regime as a whole. In practice, mass political mobilization could sweep the regime away. It could destabilize élite politics and thereby lead to its fracturing and subsequent fall, or it could lead to the overthrow of the rulers and their replacement by a new set of personnel and institutional arrangements.

The forms such mobilization will take differ from case to case, but if it is to be successful, it will have to be structured in some way. Instances of spontaneous mass mobilization are alone usually insufficient to bring about the fall of the old order. Some form of organization must be developed to carry the process forward and to give a sense of direction and defined purpose to mass discontent. The two most common types of such organization are political parties and trade unions, and it is often the emergence of these from out of the shadows of the authoritarian state which marks a crucial turning point in the process of regime breakdown. Such organizations may emerge *de novo*, possessing no links with any former organizations of the same type active in the society. Such situations are rare, but the collapse of the Haile Selassie regime in Ethiopia may be a case in point. More usually, such organizations will emerge out of either official structures set up or validated by the regime (e.g. the splitting of the official trade union movement as in the case of the miners in the USSR in 1989 or the rejection of official control by one of the hitherto 'safe' political parties, as in the case of the Peasants' Party in Poland), or pre-authoritarian democratic organisations which were able to survive the authoritarian period may, however weak they may be, constitute the starting point for new and independent mass organisations. The capacity of such pre-authoritarian structures to remain intact will depend upon many factors, including the nature and extent of regime pressure (which is in turn related to the capacity of any civil society that existed to survive – see below), the nature of their own institutional structures, individual personalities, and perhaps luck.[16] Reaching back to a pre-authoritarian history and able to root their origins in a democratic ethos, such bodies are often well placed to direct mass mobilization in an anti-regime direction.

The breakdown of authoritarian regimes therefore usually involves a degree of political mobilization from outside the bounds of the regime élite, often (but not always) stimulated by economic crisis. The form this mobilization takes is also often a function of the changes that have occurred in the society as a result of regime-induced economic development.[17] Sometimes such mobilization signifies the strength of civil society. This will be discussed further below. Such mobilization is usually evidence that the regime is crumbling, at least in the sense that its capacity to exercise continuing control over the popular sector has slipped. While in some instances the regime is able to regain the initiative and restabilize itself, usually through repression but sometimes through policies of limited liberalization, this development often constitutes a source of further pressure on the regime which accelerates the process of breakdown. Often this is manifested through increased division within the regime, and this is discussed below, but it can also act by persuading the regime that it is no longer worth trying to remain in power; the costs of retaining control become prohibitive. Pressures on the regime, and the costs of attempting to remain in control, can also be international in nature.

International Pressure

Studies of regime breakdown have tended to concentrate overwhelmingly upon the domestic sources of such developments. International factors can also contribute to the breakdown of an authoritarian regime, but except in the case of defeat in war, international factors will be likely to be secondary in their effect to domestic factors. It is unlikely that a healthy authoritarian regime not under strain from within could be toppled purely as a result of external factors short of war. Of course, external factors may contribute considerably to the force of domestic factors with, for example, international sanctions contributing to the development of economic crisis within a state, but it is the domestic dynamic which is ultimately likely to bring the regime down. Two types of international pressure have been distinguished in the literature, that occurring as a result of direct and conscious policy from outside the particular state concerned, and pressures which emanate from the structure of the international political economy. The former type is the most obvious and easily observed.

It has been a common characteristic of international politics that states seek to exert pressure on other states through the policies they pursue. Such pressure is usually directed at bringing about some change in the behaviour of the target state, but it can also be directed at encouraging the internal transformation of that state. The most spectacular form of such pressure is military activity, ranging from threats to actual war and invasion, with invasion being significant in the overthrow of a number of regimes and their replacement by ones claiming democratic credentials; wartime Germany, Italy and Japan, and Grenada in 1983 are examples of this. However, the use of force on this scale is rare. More common is pressure applied at the economic and ideological (especially human rights) levels. Many Western states, but most particularly the US, have sought during the post-war period to use their economic strength to exert pressure on other states. Throughout the cold war the US and its allies sought consistently to use their superior economic performance and muscle against the Communist regimes in an attempt to hinder their economic performance and ultimately to bring them down; Reagan's Strategic Defence Initiative, or 'Star Wars', was an explicit case of this. Such weapons have been used widely with regard to other non-democratic states – economic sanctions on post-Gulf War Iraq, trade embargoes on a variety of states in Latin America, including most particularly Cuba, and pressure on international investment in the economies of disfavoured countries, including apartheid South Africa, have been common. Such pressure has often been combined with a high level of rhetorical emphasis on the question of human rights and democracy. Indeed, such issues have often provided the rationale for economic pressure. By appealing to principles of human rights or democracy, by mobilizing international opinion around these symbols and by taking the moral high ground in this way, states have been able to bring to bear the weight of international opinion against regimes perceived to be infringing these principles. Alone, this usually has little effect, but when combined with pressures of other sorts, especially economic, this can be a significant force for change.

Another source of pressure for change emanating from the international environment is non-state organizations. In some specific cases of regime change, such influences have been significant. One organization to which some attention has been turned has been the Catholic Church.[18] There is nothing about the church that makes it naturally a supporter of democracy over authoritarianism. Its own domestic power structure and much of its doctrine are consistent with authoritarian political arrangements. Historically it has also been very close to a wide range of authoritarian regimes. However, it has at times sought to act as a catalyst for democratic change, bringing pressure to bear on authoritarian regimes in Central America and, most spectacularly, in Poland in the late 1980s. Political parties and their supranational organizations, like the Socialist International,[19] have also at times been active in promoting democratic change. The principal form this takes is the rendering of assistance to fraternal parties seeking to bring about change in their own countries; Christian Democrat and Social Democrat parties in Western Europe, especially Germany, were active in parts of the former Communist bloc both before those regimes fell and especially in the aftermath. Such assistance is unlikely to be able to initiate change, but it can help to tip the balance, especially where local independent political forces are in a weak position compared to the regime.

Also important in this process is not just force for change from individual, albeit powerful, actors, but the generation of an international ideology. Huntington's notion of a 'third wave' of democratization has implicit within it the imagery of democratization as an idea sweeping the globe, becoming the dominant paradigm in international politics. We do not have to go as far as Francis Fukuyama[20] to accept that democracy has become the major defining benchmark in international politics; all regimes, now including theocratic Iran, pay some obeisance to the democratic ideal, at least at the rhetorical level. This sort of international environment should foster pressures for democratic change within those states whose practice falls short of the ideal. Of course, some states seek to wall their populations off from such influences; Burma continued to do this with significantly greater success than most for a considerable period of time, but at the cost of economic stagnation. But few have been willing or able to do this, with the result that the international primacy of the democratic ideal has been a favourable context for domestic democratization. In practical terms, the international context has been important in giving succour to domestic democratic forces, both in terms of spiritual reinforcement and of practical assistance; funds, organizational support, the provision of a safe place to meet and organize, have all been important means of rendering such assistance. The international context has also been important through the infection effect[21] whereby the collapse of one authoritarian regime stimulates a similar collapse in other, usually neighbouring, regimes. How infection works is not clear, but it seems to be a combination of the encouragement it gives to would-be democratizers allied to the associated blow to the self-confidence of authoritarian rulers. It is intrinsic to Huntington's notion of the 'third wave'. The clearest recent case was the collapse of Communist regimes in Eastern Europe in 1989, but it may also have been evident elsewhere, as the following dates of regime change suggest: Greece and Turkey (1974), Portugal (1974–75) and Spain (1977), and Ecuador (1979), Peru (1980), Bolivia (1982), Argentina (1983), and Brazil and Uruguay (1985).[22]

But as well as these sorts of international pressures, there are also pressures which stem from the structure of the international political economy. A state's location in the international political economy will clearly have implications both for the structure and health of its domestic economy and for the political implications of this; domestic development will be coloured by international forces. Perhaps the clearest indication of this is the way the oil crisis and the tightening of international credit in the mid-1970s precipitated economic crisis in a number of countries, which in turn triggered pressures for regime change. In an even more fundamentally structural sense, as argued in the discussion on economic crisis, if a regime's rulers decide to try to shift the country's economic base from raw materials extraction or agriculture to industry, they will be faced with the problem that a significant number of states are already established industrial powers which may seek to hinder the proposed course of development. If foreign economic interests are represented in the domestic economy through foreign investment or the involvement of foreign-based firms, this situation may be even more complicated, with such foreign-based domestic interests unenthusiastic about such development plans. Even if the country's economy is able to make this transition, it will still have to compete in order to continue to develop, and in such competition, it may find itself at a real disadvantage. Some argue that it was precisely this problem that was at the heart of the Soviet collapse: the inability of the Soviet production system to compete successfully with that of the West. We do not have to accept all of the assumptions behind the dependency literature to acknowledge that the distribution of power in the international political economy is highly unequal, and that this ensures that the economic performance of many countries is severely and adversely affected by the international system. There are three aspects of this international dimension: economic, political and ideological.

The economic aspect[23] relates to the location of the states undergoing democratization in the global economy as a whole. There have been many attempts to theorize this relationship, including such major schools of thought as world systems theory, dependency analysis and theories of interdependence and globalism. What all of these approaches have in common is the assumption that what happens in these countries does not occur in isolation from the rest of the world, and that the relationship between these countries and the leading centres of economic dynamism (North America, Western Europe and more latterly East Asia) is profoundly unequal. Democratization in the third wave has occurred mainly in countries on the periphery, or margins, of these economically more dynamic centres. The relationship between the central and peripheral countries is unequal in a number of senses. It is unequal in the sense that, through direct economic investment, the involvement of business corporations based in these dynamic centres and often significant aid flows, the economies of the periphery are heavily dependent upon decisions made in the centre. It is unequal in a global economy sense, in that these countries are subordinate participants in the course of the global economy; they are not major industrial powers, or important centres of technological innovation and development, but relatively small and weak economies mainly relying upon primary produce or resource extraction. They lack the economic power to dominate in the global economy, instead having to adjust to developments driven by others. The degree to which such economies are controlled from abroad, although a matter of some debate in the literature, is less important than the fact that local entrepreneurs (and politicians) must act in an environment in which major economic forces are outside their control.

One way of looking at this question is to go back to what was recognized as one of the common elements in explaining regime breakdown, economic crisis. As noted above, economic crisis cannot simply be attributed to mismanagement; it frequently has structural roots also, especially in connection with the drive to industrialize. This drive to foster industrialization may have domestic roots, but it can also have international ramifications. The form industrialization takes will be profoundly affected by the country's subordinate location in the global economy. Guillermo O'Donnell has argued that international location was a significant factor in explaining the attempt by bureaucratic authoritarian regimes to shift from import substitution industrialization to one favouring heavy industry, a shift which disrupted the local ruling coalition and could lead to regime change.[24] The degree to which the local economy is penetrated by international capital, and thereby by actors whose power stems from their international standing, will shape both the course of industrial development and the politics that goes with it. The capacity of the economy to supply its own energy needs will shape its response to things like the oil shocks of 1973 and 1979, while its reliance upon international sources for both finance and markets will determine its reaction to recessions like those of the mid-1970s and early 1980s. The extent to which the local economy is linked into the international economy will determine how vulnerable it is to the ebbs and flows of international financial policy and the sort of financial speculation which has become so common in the 1980s and 1990s.

The political aspect relates to the location of the country in the global geopolitical structure. All of the countries experiencing democratization during the initial stages of the third wave were located in that part of the world which was broadly considered to be within the Western, democratic, camp. Certainly, there were perceived Soviet challenges in Central America, but generally the regions were believed to fall within the Western sphere of influence. This meant that, following the success of the Cuban revolution in 1959, the constraints within which domestic political development was to be allowed to proceed became more clearly defined. In the western hemisphere, any attempt at change which had the appearance of Socialism or which threatened private property would provoke a hostile American response; the history of the Allende regime in Chile and the pro-Castro Bishop regime in Grenada reflects this geopolitical reality. This means that there were clear internationally-imposed limits on the course of political change possible in this region. Similarly in Europe, the tension between the NATO allies and the Warsaw Pact meant that the process of transition in Greece, Portugal and Spain was always going to have international ramifications. It was clear to political actors in all of those countries that the key to the acceptability in the West which they sought was the adoption of a Western-style democratic regime which guaranteed private property rights.

While the end of the cold war removed the main fault line of antagonism and conflict in the international arena, it has not eliminated the geopolitical reality of the predominance of the Western powers. While that predominance remains, and perhaps even when it is gone but while the aspiration remains, the course of political change in these peripheral areas will continue to be shaped in part by larger geopolitical concerns. The Monroe Doctrine predates the cold war, and there is no reason to believe that the US will be any more willing in the future than it has been in the past to give up its role of oversight in Latin America. In Europe, the fall of the Berlin Wall did not extinguish Western aspirations to ensure that acceptable regimes are in power across the continent, notwithstanding West European inaction during the wars of the Yugoslav succession. The logic of the structure of geopolitics, that major states will seek to influence events in less powerful states, will continue to have an important effect upon the course of regime change elsewhere in the world in the future.

The geopolitical aspect is closely related to the ideological. As noted above, the time at which the third wave transitions took place was one when the notion of democracy exercised a form of ideological hegemony at the international level. Even those states which opposed the West, with the exception of Iran, professed to adhere to the democratic creed. This has become even stronger with the end of the cold war, even if much of the rhetoric surrounding this is overblown. The effect of such ideological hegemony is that international acceptance is dependent in part upon public adherence to this ideology, and while there is no necessity for there to be a perfect correspondence between the rhetoric of ideology and the reality of practice, this hegemony does impose a constraint upon domestic actors.

It is clear that there is an important international structural dimension to democratic transitions which much of the literature ignores.

But it is important to recognize that this international dimension does not have a consistent effect on all democratizing regimes. All regimes are involved in the international system in different ways; their means of connection with the international world are different, and they are mediated through varying domestic actors and institutions.[25] It is therefore this pattern of international links and domestic structures which is important rather than international forces by themselves. Unless this pattern of interaction between domestic structures and international forces is understood, analysis of individual cases of regime breakdown and democratic transitions and of the nature of transitions in general will not be understood.

Regime Disunity

A feature of all cases of regime breakdown has been splits within the regime. Such splits have been important in the process of regime breakdown by bringing about the 'narrowing' of the regime and its consequent loss of support,[26] by generating the sort of internal conflict the regime has been unable to sustain or resolve, and by inducing a state of stasis in the functioning of the regime itself. Splits have also been important in structuring the process of transition which has followed. In general, the only cases when splits may not have been instrumental in the process of breakdown was when a regime was pushed from power by military force, and even in these cases the regime was often crucially weakened by internal division. A key question is the source of this disunity, and although the precise details will differ from case to case, common elements can be found.

One potential source of disunity is the institutional structure of the regime. In those regimes where a personal dictator or even a single prominent leader is not to be found,[27] rule tends to be in the hands of a group of people who represent, or at least come from, different institutional structures in the society. Institutional differences will also occur where single leaders are prominent. In many single-party regimes, rule has effectively been shared between the party and sections of the state machine, with the Communist party-states being the best example.[28] Most military regimes also included some civilian involvement, although instances differed markedly in terms of the scope and importance of this.[29] In some cases, such as Peron's Argentina and Franco's Spain, this coalition comprised people from a political party, the military and sections of the state machine with, in the Spanish case, membership of Opus Dei adding an extra dimension.[30] Sometimes technocrats from the state machine (and possibly from big business also) are allied with the military, with senior positions being shared between these constituencies. This sort of arrangement has been typical of the bureaucratic authoritarian regimes, including pre-1974 Brazil,[31] and also of what Gillespie referring to Uruguay called a 'collegial military–technocratic' regime.[32] Even in those military regimes where civilians played a minor role, institutional divisions could be salient. The split between military as government (and thereby guided by considerations of regime continuity and success) and military as institution (and thereby guided by considerations of the best interests of the military) has also been important in some instances, including Chile under Pinochet in the 1980s. There could also be differences between the various arms of the military (army, air force, navy, special forces) as in Greece, or between the military and security services, as in Venezuela in the mid-1950s. Factionalism within the individual structures has also been a common cause of disunity. Sometimes such factions may be organized around individuals, but more usually they rest upon group interests of some sort. Whatever the lines of division, the search for advantage and for the defence of institutional interests and prerogatives will always be potential sources of division and conflict. The April 1974 coup in Portugal by leftist junior and middle-ranking officers against the civilian-led government supported by the military top brass was a good instance of this.[33]

The military and security services are particularly important when a regime is primarily civilian in nature. A civilian authoritarian regime must take special care to ensure the compliance of the military and security services. In a party-dominated state, and even a traditional autocracy like that of Haile Selassie's Ethiopia, the rulers will be concerned to ensure that the coercive arms of the state, or at least the most powerful sections of it, are on side because this is the institution whose command over armed force poses a major potential threat to the longevity of their rule. The military/security apparatus for its part will be inclined to look to the government because this is the source of funding and therefore the key to institutional maintenance and aggrandizement.

Institutional difference and strain can therefore be a potent source of conflict and dissension within a regime. Structural strains will also be evident in those regimes where a single dictator is promi-nent.[34] No dictator can stand alone. All dictators rely on some form of organizational structure, be it formally constituted like a party or military, or more informal and resting on a social movement or a clientelistic basis. In the case of a dictator resting on an organiza-tional structure of some kind, there is likely to be tension if the leader seeks to consolidate and strengthen his personal position, because this will involve a weakening of the position or lessening of the importance of his organizational support base. It may even be seen as a positive danger to or attack upon the institutional preroga-tives of that institution. In either event, it is a threat to the personal positions of leading members of that institution. Such a support base will inevitably, through its continuing operation and functioning, develop a vested interest in the maintenance of its power and posi-tion and will be likely to seek to check any growth in the power or authority of the individual leader. For example, in Chile virtually from the outset, there was tension within the regime between ten-dencies toward personalized power on the part of Pinochet and toward a more institutional arrangement embracing the military establishment collectively. Ultimately this debate seems to have been resolved with the 1980 constitution which consolidated Pinochet's personal power and enshrined a more personalist arrangement than had been evident before.[35] In Portugal, the fear was not that the leader would increase his power at the expense of the military, but that he was unable to defend its interests, or even appreciate what those interests were. This led to the defection of the middle-ranking officers and undermined the basis of the regime.

The potential problem of the relationship between individual leader and support organization often becomes manifest at times of leadership succession. The question of succession not only brings personal ambitions into play, but can also trigger institutional com-petition. A clear instance of this is where rule is in the hands of a junta which consists of different arms of the military. Even where a mechanism may have been set in place to rotate leadership between the chiefs of the different military institutions, periods of succession can witness the overthrowing of such rules or arrangements. A similar instance of a collective personal leadership being instituted which came under strain as a result of personal and institutional ambitions was post-Tito Yugoslavia. Succession can throw open the whole political game, causing rules of political procedure to be abandoned in the struggle for temporary political advantage.

Another potential source of division within authoritarian regimes relates to the aims of those regimes, and in particular the tension between the view that the regime constitutes a viable long-term system for the country and that it is merely an interlude before a (re)turn to democracy. The Fascist wartime regimes and their paler Spanish and Portuguese survivors were examples of the former. So, too, were the Communist regimes and the sort of theocratic regime established in Iran in 1979. All of these sought to base their rule on foundations other than a commitment to democratic principles, be this a national zeitgeist, a class-based view of the future, or militant Islam. All sought consciously to offer a model of rule, and indeed a model of community, which espoused values and reflected principles that clearly contrasted with the liberal democracy that sought global ideological hegemony in the post-war period. They set out to build enduring political, social and economic structures that were to last their communities into the foreseeable future, and although they may have utilized democratic trappings, the essence of their sense of self-legitimation was rooted in ideological assumptions very different from those of liberal democracy. As such, these regimes did not see themselves as a temporary interlude before the installation of democratic rule, but as a viable alternative to Western liberal democracy. A similar view has been held by a variety of other regimes which are claimed to have instituted a form of government particularly suited to their national characteristics but which in practice differed little from more traditional forms of authoritarian rule. The appeals to Arab tradition to buttress rule in countries like Kuwait and Iraq, and the attempt to generate an imperial tradition in places like the Central African Empire (under Bokassa, 1976–79) are examples of this. In contrast, many post-war authoritarian regimes, particularly those of a military persuasion, have sought legitimation through the claim that they are in power to clean up the mess left by the former regime, and that once the political system and community more broadly have been cleansed from the unhealthy consequences of such rule, the regime will step back and allow a democratic system to take over. They thus present themselves as preparing the way for the (re)establishment of democratic rule.

These differing perceptions of the purpose of the regime can be the source of disunity and division within regime ranks. For those regimes whose legitimation is instrumental and dependent upon the promise of the future transition to democracy, the issue is when have the conditions that will permit democratic rule been created. Uncertainty about this will exist not only because regimes rarely spell out in detail upon what conditions they will relinquish power, but also because there are no objective criteria for determining when conditions exist that will facilitate democratic rule. This must therefore be a matter of judgement and, potentially, disagreement on the part of leading figures of the regime. This issue is complicated, particularly in cases of military rule, by concerns about the impact continued ruling can have upon the institution itself. With military involvement in political life comes at least a degree of politicization within the military. This has effects which run directly counter to the ethos of professionalism which is such a strong part of the military establishment, and thereby in the eyes of many military figures poses a direct threat to the continued institutional integrity and health of the military as an institution. This is a clash between the principles of the military as government and the military as institution. This sort of concern, which was evident in both Brazil and Chile, increases pressures within the military to get out of political life, and thereby strengthens the likelihood of conflict between those who wish to see the military return to the barracks and those who want to hang on to power.[36]

Those regimes which do not see themselves as acting as preludes to the return to democracy do not have implicit in their perceptions of their roles the same sort of potentially divisive issue as when their rule should end. By seeing themselves as building the future without any definite end point, the question of the continuation of the system and structure need not arise, unless it is brought onto the agenda by developments outside the top levels of the regime. If this occurs, it will create the same sorts of tensions, divisions and arguments as in those regimes which saw their role to be strictly as an interim administration.

Regime disunity is often also generated by substantive policy difference. In any regime there will be policy differences because of the varying outlooks and perceptions of individual political actors and the institutions of which they are part. Such policy differences can often be institutionally defined; for example, in bureaucratic authoritarian regimes, military concerns over security may not be consistent with technocratic priorities for economic development. In coalition regimes, it is possible that different segments of the coalition may have very different priorities and strategies, which can give rise to dispute and disagreement. Even when the regime is not coalitional in nature, such differences can emerge among factions, groups and/or levels of the regime. Such disputes are likely to be more serious when the regime encounters a setback; economic crisis and political mobilization are common causes of disunity within regimes. Economic crisis in particular can generate policy disagreement, because the onset of the crisis will be interpreted by many as illustrating that policy must be changed.

But as well as disagreements over substantive policy issues, such crises can also provoke conflict over the regime's general survival strategy. Indeed, it is differences of this type upon which many writers on transition focus. Essentially, the dispute concerns how the regime should best respond to challenge: should it seek to liberalize in an attempt to assuage opposition and re-consolidate its base, or should it seek to strengthen its control, possibly including the use of force to suppress the opposition? The terms that writers use to refer to the protagonists in this sort of dispute – reformers vs. standpatters, softliners vs. hardliners, liberalizers vs. conservatives – reflect the tactical rather than substantive nature of these differences. They are not about substantive policy issues, or whether the regime should be maintained or ended, but about the best means of ensuring the survival and continued power of the regime. Nevertheless, this issue can paralyse a regime or, what may be worse, result in wild swings in policy as first one tactic then the other is tried.

These potential sources of disunity, regime structure, regime aims, policy difference and survival strategy, are not unique to authoritarian regimes nor to the period immediately preceding regime breakdown. But what makes these sources of disunity difficult to handle is the unitarist nature of the regimes themselves. By unitarist is meant a structure and an ethos which makes no provision for opposition and dissent. It is not that the regime is not characterized by disagreement, but it makes no provision for the adequate expression of that disagreement or for a mechanism for finally resolving it to the satisfaction of all parties. There are no channels within the regime for disaffected groups to air their views and feel that those views have been taken into account, to believe that by expressing their opinions they can have an impact on the decisions made at the upper levels of the system. Representation of institutional interests rarely occurs on a regularized basis through formal and effective institutional fora, but usually relies on the activism and contacts of individuals and groups. This creates a sense of arbitrariness, even when there has been some effort to create some regular-ization of procedures, because the resolution of issues is seen to rely more on the whim of those at the top than on the careful and structured working through of the issues at hand.[37] This means that when decisions are made, this is not accompanied by a satisfaction on the part of those whose views did not prevail that their views had been given fair consideration. By failing to acknowledge dissent and opposition as an intrinsic part of politics, and thereby not providing channels for its airing and resolution, authoritarian regimes have usually set up a situation which allows frustration and resentment to grow.

Without an institutional means of raising differences and resolving disputes within the regime, the options for regime leaders are limited. If there is no room for disagreement and opposition, then any manifestation of these is by its nature anti-systemic. One response is to use force to deal with the dissidents, with the waves of purges running through some regimes a manifestation of this sort of reaction. A forceful response to dissident activity can, if conducted on a sufficient scale, effectively push dissent out of the political arena, at least for a time. But all it does is to suppress dissent and prevent its appearance; it does not prevent dissent from developing. It thus tends to be only a short-term palliative, potentially storing up problems for the regime in the future. The other response is to do nothing: allow those who disagree to remain part of the regime and continue to carry out their functions, perhaps making minor concessions to them while continuing to reject any major criticisms. Successful pursuit of this tactic depends upon how serious the dissent is, in terms of its nature (is it restricted to one or a few policy areas or is it more all-embracing?), the size and importance of those adopting dissident positions, and the tactics they choose to follow. Regardless of which tactic is adopted, dissent and how it is to be handled will remain a problem.

Another factor which can make disunity difficult to deal with is the likelihood that its dynamics will not continue to be determined by the causes which generated it initially. In particular, given that disputes within the regime potentially can have very significant consequences for the actors involved, those actors are likely to remain sensitive to the shifting patterns of élite interaction. Alliances may remain weak and volatile as individuals and groups seek a strategy which will minimize the risks of failure and maximize the chances of success.[38] The effect of this sort of attitude is to increase the unpredictability involved in élite disunity and thereby increase the importance of the voluntarist aspect. Clearly there have been cases of such behaviour, when individuals and groups act on a purely opportunistic basis according to how they believe they are most likely to emerge victorious. But most people are unable to act in a purely opportunistic way. They are inhibited by past positions and associations, by existing sources of support and opposition; they cannot respond purely to the vagaries of the cut and thrust of political conflict. Underlying structural elements will continue to operate, and while a high level of uncertainty is possible in conflicts within the regime, the impact of structural factors should not be underestimated. Such factors will include regime structure, as noted above, but are not restricted to this. Coalitions with social forces can also be important (see below).

So, while all types of political system experience disunity at various times, the danger for authoritarian regimes is that the weakness of institutional procedures for resolving disputes creates significant potential for instability. This problem is exacerbated by the implications such disputes can have for legitimation.

One of the difficulties posed by disunity is symbolic. Authoritarian regimes usually come to power with a rhetorical emphasis on unity. Ideology and military ethos are often cited as the wellspring of such an emphasis. In those cases where a democracy has been supplanted, following the division of the community that is claimed to have resulted from the democratic system of government, the authoritarian successor regime promises to bring about the unity of society and the overcoming of all divisions. This is a rationale for the claimed attempt to replace politics by administration in society; politics is portrayed as divisive and not in the community's interests, whereas the rational and unbiased exercise of administration will restore order to the body politic. The ideology of unity can only be maintained if the regime itself remains united, at least to outward appearances. Thus the emergence of disunity within regime ranks threatens the basis of legitimation of the regime. Not only does it call into question the capacity of the regime to govern, but it may cast doubt over the entire project in which it claims to be involved.

The question of legitimation is raised by many scholars trying to explain the fall of authoritarian regimes. The basic argument is that the disappearance of a regime's legitimacy removes the basis upon which it rests and thereby leaves it vulnerable. But does this argument carry any weight? According to Przeworski,[39] it is greatly exaggerated. He argues that legitimacy alone is not essential to regime survival; a regime may maintain itself in power despite lacking popular legitimacy simply because of fear. What is important for Przeworski is the presence or absence of preferable alternatives to continued authoritarian rule; if the populace see that there is a clear alternative to continued rule by the incumbent regime, they are more likely to transfer their allegiance to it and thereby leave the regime bereft of popular support, or at least with weaker support than that possessed by the alternative. At one level, there is clearly something to this argument; in principle, people may prefer one system to another without either appearing illegitimate. But how realistic is such an approach in practice? Do people sit down coolly and with rational detachment add up the pluses and minuses of various alternatives and come up with a preference for one over the other? Rarely would questions of regime change be resolved in this way. What is more likely is that potential alternatives to the status quo do not emerge as serious contenders for power unless there is already a question mark over the legitimacy of the existing regime, at least in the eyes of significant groups within the populace. Unless there is already a perception that the existing regime's right to rule is eroding, and often this is related to perceived failures in performance, it is unlikely that any possible alternative will emerge as a genuine contender for power. This means that legitimacy will remain important for mass acceptance of the existing regime.

Legitimation may also be important in another respect. Crucial to the maintenance of any political system is the continued confidence of the rulers not only in their ability to rule, but in their right to rule. While their belief in their right to rule remains intact, their confidence to continue ruling remains unimpaired. Thus, while they see their position, and thereby the whole structure, as legitimate, they will seek to continue to rule. However, should that belief in their right to rule be shaken, the whole regime will be rendered vulnerable. That belief could be shaken by a range of different factors: failures in performance, erosion of ideological belief, and defeat in war have all been catalysts for the growth of élite self-doubt, and when combined with heightened criticism from below, can fuel a crisis of confidence within the élite. The consequent loss of a sense of their own legitimacy may contribute to the rupturing of élite agreement, which leads to the sort of disunity discussed above. With this in mind, it would be unwise to dismiss legitimation as a factor in regime change.

It is one thing to isolate these four factors, economic crisis, political mobilization, international pressure and regime disunity, as crucial elements in many cases of regime change, but this does not really get us very far in trying to understand the actual dynamics of the erosion of authoritarian rule and its transformation into democratic power. If we are to theorize regime breakdown, we must see whether these factors interact in a consistent fashion across different cases. If consistent patterns of causative relationships can be demonstrated to exist between these factors, the basis exists for a theorizing of regime change which can have a high level of explanatory, and perhaps even predictive, power. The looser the relationship, the less the predictive power, although this will not necessarily affect the explanatory capacity to the same extent.

A survey of major cases of transition in Latin America and Southern Europe suggests that there is no clear pattern of relationships between these variables. In all cases, economic crisis, political mobilization and regime disunity were evident, suggesting that these were an intrinsic part of the process, whereas international pressure was less direct and was in many cases a second-level factor. Accordingly, the subsequent analysis will focus principally upon the three main factors. But even given that these were evident in all cases, there appears to have been no clear and unambiguous relationship between them that applied across all cases. For example, in Bolivia regime disunity preceded political mobilization which preceded economic difficulties, while in Brazil the order could be said to have been political mobilization, economic crisis and regime disunity. Part of the problem is knowing where to begin. Put simply, when do the processes which ultimately lead to regime change begin? This is not a pedantic issue, because different points at which the analysis begins may give temporal primacy to different factors. For example, an analysis of the Greek experience that began with the economic difficulties of the early 1970s, the political mobilization in 1972–73 and the attempted liberalization of 1973, and the regime disunity in 1973–74 and concluded with the restoration of civilian rule later that year, would miss the split within the military between the army on the one hand and many navy and air force officers on the other during the late 1960s.[40] Yet the May 1973 attempted coup against Papadopoulos and his attempt to establish a Greek republic emanated from this split and was based among pro-royalist naval officers. A starting point of soon after the colonels' coup in 1967 would therefore see the seeds of decline in the initial presence of regime disunity, while a beginning in the early 1970s would see such disunity as following political mobilization and economic difficulties. Or to take the Argentine case, with cycles of political mobilization alternating with regime strategies of liberalization and crackdown from the 1950s, where one began the analysis would determine how important each of these components appeared in driving the process as a whole.

Of course, the difficulty here is that one can get into the problem of ever-receding starting points. Clearly the roots of developments in one period can be found in earlier periods; even when there is a major rupture with the past as in a full social and political revolution,[41] continuities with the former period remain to help structure contemporary development. Indeed, except for those of a deterministic cast of mind, it is clear that the roots of a variety of different sorts of developments can be found in earlier periods, so that the task is less discovering those roots than explaining why particular lines of development prevailed over others. The key to this is not discovering a temporal relationship between the variables, but a structural relationship, and the key to this is the nature of the regime and the relationship between it and society.

Authoritarian regimes are, by definition, not accountable or responsible in any direct, institutional fashion to the populace over whom they rule. But this does not mean that they exist in a vacuum, isolated from the population and not linked with it in any way. Every regime, except perhaps the short-term conquest state, seeks to consolidate its position by embedding itself within the society. It does this by creating links with segments of society which are sympathetic to it or which see their interests as being best served by association with the regime. The segment of society that is most often seen as crucial in this regard for virtually all regimes, regardless of their nature, is the business sector. The importance of this sector lies in the role it plays in fostering economic development. All regimes desire economic growth; for most, this is at base the key to ensuring social passivity. The continuing provision of economic goods and services is a means of buying off the populace, with economic well-being compensating for political influence. This has sometimes been seen in terms of a putative 'social contract' between regime and people. Even predatory states like Mobutu's Zaire which evinced no concern for the economic well-being of the populace, seek economic growth if only to swell the coffers of the rulers themselves. Conversely, business is usually keen to influence the rulers.

At a minimum, business will seek security from the state for their property and operations, but usually their aspirations will extend to seeking economic advantage from their governmental links. Subsidies, state contracts, protection from foreign competition, benign regulation of the market and ensuring a passive labour force are the sorts of advantages business hopes to gain from association with the rulers, in addition to the regular and more mundane construction and maintenance of basic facilities (like roads, ports and communications). The right-wing or conservative disposition of most authoritarian rulers has strengthened this sort of alliance.

In many states characterized by authoritarian rule there has been another segment of society in which ideological outlook could constitute a basis for regime-social segment alliance. This is the traditional right. In many countries that have experienced regime change, including many in Latin America, this traditional right has consisted primarily of the old landowning class. In other countries, it has also comprised groups clustered around the monarchy, sometimes, as in the Greek case, including groups within the armed forces as well as traditional landed or aristocratic interests. The regime may see the traditional right as being important principally because, if there has been only limited land reform, this group may have significant power over the peasant population, and association with them (even cooptation of them) may be the key to preventing rural mobilisation. But the traditional right is also often important in terms of legitimation, by providing a basis of legitimacy for the authoritarian regime. This was clearly an important issue in Greece. The traditional land-based right is often sympathetic to the authoritarian rulers because its own economic position is under threat as a result of industrialization and/or international economic competition and they see the regime as a potential buttress for their position. However, for a regime looking for economic growth, an alliance with the traditional right is not a long-term proposition.

The largest part of society is the so-called popular sector, principally the working class but also the peasantry. Although there have been some regimes which have sought to rest upon the systematic mobilization of the popular sector, with Peron's Argentina a noted example, most authoritarian regimes have seen this sector of society as something to be excluded from politics rather than as a reliable and viable support base. However, complete exclusion has not always been possible. Continuing suppression of a population is both very expensive and difficult to achieve, and it contradicts the democratic ethos which has been globally hegemonic and which most regimes attempt to use in an instrumental fashion to shore up their own legitimacy. Under such circumstances, most regimes attempt to coopt at least the leading sections of the popular sector, usually through a process of limited mobilization. The generation of a wide range of regime sponsored organizations, including trade unions, youth groups, cultural and sporting bodies, and perhaps even political parties and pseudo-parliaments designed to structure (and restrict) the activity of the masses, has been a common regime response to the problem of controlling the popular sector. The regime will seek to suborn any civil society forces that emerge and thus provide the semblance of participation while robbing it of any political efficacy. They are a means of giving a sense of involvement without power, thereby blunting popular resentment at their effective political exclusion.

In the policies it follows, the authoritarian regime is usually therefore more constrained than is popularly appreciated. Popular passivity and compliance are best facilitated through policies ensuring economic well-being; if people experience a good or improving standard of living, they are more likely to be content with their political masters than if they experience the reverse. But the regime must also satisfy that sector of society upon which it relies for positive support, the business sector. Satisfaction of that sector is usually heavily dependent upon continuing economic good performance, an outcome to which business has much to contribute. Indeed, economic growth is usually fundamental to the satisfaction of all segments of society. But alone, it is insufficient. Whether economic growth ensures the satisfaction of the interests of all sectors of society depends not only upon the levels of that growth, but upon how its fruits are distributed. A booming economy in which there is a highly unequal distribution of wealth, which is usually the case, will not necessarily contribute to general social harmony or regime support. Regime policy, if it is to contribute to regime longevity, should thus be designed with an eye to maximizing its levels of support in society. This equation will be different for different regimes, depending upon their particular circumstances; a regime with a highly efficient coercive apparatus will be better able to ignore the population at large and direct more of the rewards to its particular supporters in the business community than will a regime whose access to coercion is more limited. In any event, economic management is clearly crucial for the regime's ability to maintain itself with regard to the broader society within which it is found.

It is this relationship with society and the different sectors of it which gives economic crisis its potency. Economic crisis, and some-times even more minor economic setbacks, can have serious conse-quences for authoritarian regimes. Where regime support and general popular passivity rest principally upon instrumental consid-erations of economic welfare, disruptions to that can have serious ramifications for the regime. It is at such times that the regime and its links with society come under strain. While the different sectors of society are likely to respond in different ways to the economic downturn, what will be crucial for the regime is the state of its link-ages with those sectors. While business remains wedded to the regime, seeing it as the best guarantee of its future regardless of current, and in their view hopefully temporary, economic difficul-ties, the prospects for regime survival are improved. However, if those links are strained excessively or even broken, and the business sector deserts the regime and perhaps even takes up an oppositional political position, prospects for regime survival are reduced. Under such circumstances, the regime must either restore those linkages or seek another support base. The traditional right may be a possible source of support in this sort of situation, but it cannot provide a long-term solution to the regime's problems.

The difficulties confronting the regime will be exacerbated should popular mobilization on a political basis eventuate, perhaps in response to the economic downturn, perhaps stimulated by other factors. Independent popular mobilization by its very existence chal-lenges the regime because it constitutes a rejection of the institu-tions the regime has set in place to structure popular activity. It is a concrete manifestation of the weakness, or perhaps circumvention, of the institutional linkages the regime has sought to use to tie the masses to it. If popular mobilization is allowed to continue, the danger is that it will grow and so erode the regime's moral authority, that its capacity to continue to rule will be fatally undermined. Once again, crucial here is the strength (and flexibility) of the institutions that the regime has designed to structure popular activity. If they are able to maintain control over the populace and to divert pressures for independent political activity into safe channels, if they can stifle the emergence of the tertiary civil society forces noted above, the prospects for regime survival increase. If not, those prospects accordingly decrease; the transformation of the regime (as opposed to a simple switch of leaders) is more likely if actors outside the regime rooted in society become directly active in political developments.

It is clear, then, that crucial to a regime's capacity to survive a challenge is the state of its linkages with society more broadly. Different types of regime will have different types of linkages. Military regimes with little or no civilian component are likely to be the most isolated from society. The strong emphasis upon military professionalism and the conception of the military itself as a closed structure with its own ethos, standards and principles all hinder the easy establishment of institutional linkages with society at large. Certainly the military as an institution will be connected with the society more broadly through the personal connections of individual members of that institution with the society, but these rarely are transformed into the sorts of institutional structures which can establish affective, and effective, bonds between regime and society. The linkages that may exist between society and the military as institution cannot always easily be transferred to the military as government.

Purely civilian regimes and those involving a coalition between civil and military components (including bureaucratic authoritarian regimes) are generally better placed to establish significant channels of linkage. The civilians in the regime usually lack the institutional barriers which prevent the military from generating effective ties into the populace. More importantly, they often remain active in non-regime circles, continuing to pursue business activities despite holding public office being one of the most common forms of this. Furthermore, lacking the institutional and ideological baggage that goes with a military establishment, such people are more likely to remain sensitive to the need to meet the demands emanating from society, and are more likely to be seen as 'their' representatives in the regime by the social groups from which they come. Civilian regimes generally tend to be better at building strong, institutional linkages which can mediate between regime and society than are military regimes. This means that civilian regimes, or those with substantial civilian elements, are more likely to be able to weather a crisis than those of a purely military nature because they are better connected with society and can better retain the support of crucial power groups within that society.

But the health and nature of regime–society linkages is not the only factor in the ability of a regime to survive a challenge. As argued earlier, the internal unity of the regime is also crucial. In general terms, the basis for unity is stronger where there are fewer institutional interests represented in the regime and where the individuals involved have been long associated together. If there is a prevailing ethos of discipline, as characterized military establishments and Communist parties, discipline is also likely to be easier to achieve. But in practice, the more important consideration is not whether unity is always present, but when disunity occurs, whether there is an effective mechanism for resolving it quickly. This often amounts to the presence or absence of effective mechanisms for coordinating the diversity of interest and opinion found within the regime. If the regime can act quickly and efficiently to restore unity when it breaks down, its chances of survival will be much enhanced. In contrast, if there is no means of resolving differences, and in most authoritarian regimes there is no effective means of achieving this short of force, regime flexibility and survival prospects are reduced.

The important point about the breakdown of authoritarian regimes is that these different elements can fit together in a number of different patterns. Economic crisis may induce popular mobilization which, together, may lead to splits in the regime. Or popular mobilization could develop on the basis of a particular grievance, leading to splits within the regime which in turn stimulates disagreement over policy, including economic policy, issues and subsequent economic crisis. Or economic crisis could of itself generate regime disunity. Or splits could occur within the regime, for example over succession, the sharing of power, or simple personality incompatibilities, encouraging popular leaders to seek to use mobilization in order to take advantage of the regime's current weakness; or individual regime leaders could themselves even seek to mobilize popular forces in an attempt to strengthen their positions in the élite conflict. There is therefore no set order or relationship between these variables. Each can stimulate any of the others, depending upon the specific circumstances of each particular case. But, given the relationship between the internal character of the authoritarian regime and the weakness of its mechanisms for conflict resolution on the one hand and the regime's relationship with society as a whole on the other, the emergence of any of these elements is likely to stimulate the emergence of others.

An important factor here, and one which cannot be foreseen, is the nature of the individual personalities and personal relationships involved. The importance of individuals cannot be exaggerated. The strong leader who is able to stamp on dissent and carry his leadership colleagues with him will have a profoundly different effect upon a situation of regime crisis than a leader who is less decisive and more willing to compromise. Similarly, the strategic skills and personal qualities of potential popular leaders can greatly influence the form and outcome of popular mobilization. The impact individual personalities can have is increased in times of crisis by the way in which the regularized rules of politics possess less normative impact as a result of the perception of the crisis situation and the consequent need for extraordinary measures to cope with it.

But while the role of individuals may be very significant, it cannot adequately be theorized. This is because of the essential voluntarism which is at the heart of personal activity. However, some approach can be made to theorizing the structural factors within which individuals act, because even powerful individuals function within an institutional context. If we can approach the theorization of these structural factors, we can also approach a theorization of regime breakdown. Based upon the sorts of structural considerations discussed earlier in this chapter, a number of principles can be identified which can constitute the building blocks of a theorization of regime breakdown.

1. The stronger the unity, or the mechanisms for maintaining unity (including resolving succession issues) and coordinating interests, within the regime élite, the greater the prospects for regime survival.
2. The greater the diversity of institutional interests represented in the regime, the more difficult the maintenance of unity will be, and the greater the likelihood of difference emerging in times of pressure on the regime.
3. The better the links between the regime and the business sector, the greater the likelihood of the regime surviving economic difficulty.
4. The more effective the regime's links with the popular sector, the less likely popular mobilization is to escape regime control. Alternatively, the greater the degree of independent organization in society, the stronger the civil society forces, the less secure the regime's control.
5. The more effective the regime's coercive apparatus, the less likely popular control is to slip.
6. The better the élite's control over the coercive apparatus, the more secure its position.

7. The better the regime's economic management skills, the more likely it is to survive economic difficulties.
8. The stronger the regime domestically, the better able it will be to survive externally-induced setbacks. This is why external factors are usually of secondary importance in explaining regime change.
9. The stronger the regime, the better able it should be to manage events, including the circumstances of the transition to democracy should it occur.
10. The stronger and more independent the civil society forces, the more likely political difficulty is to lead to regime transformation rather than simple leadership change.

The reverse of all of these also applies. Put together, these do not provide a coherent theory of regime breakdown, because the list does not have embedded within it any causative or relational principles linking these different elements. These elements will be linked in a variety of different ways in different instances of regime breakdown. In practice, what this constitutes is a list of principles which can be applied to different cases of regime breakdown in an attempt to understand the course of that process. These principles are, of course, also relevant to the process of democratic transition. It is also in this context that the role of civil society forces is most clear.

3

Elites and Transition

The breakdown of an authoritarian regime does not always lead to a democratic outcome. It could, and historically in most cases has, led to the replacement of one authoritarian regime by another. However, particularly in the last quarter of the twentieth century, many cases of authoritarian breakdown have been part of a shift to democratic rule. The dynamics of this shift are more complicated than those involved in regime breakdown more narrowly considered because, as well as involving all of those forces which contributed to that breakdown, new elements will also usually play a part in structuring the change. This also means that there is more scope for transition to be derailed, and increases the level of potential uncertainty.

The emergence of this wave of transitions to democracy in the latter part of this century led to the emergence of what has been called 'transition literature'. This body of writing has been very influential in shaping our understanding of the process of regime transition. One of the earliest, and most important, works of this type was by Dankwart Rustow.[1] His model comprises three 'phases' and a 'background condition'. The background condition is national unity, which means that there is agreement among the citizens of the putative democracy that they all belong to the same particular political community. In practice, this means that the aim is democratization of the existing political system rather than secession from it and the creation of a new system based upon a different conception of the political community. The first phase is the 'preparatory phase' and this is characterized by 'a prolonged and inconclusive political struggle'[2] between protagonists representing well-entrenched (usually class) forces over issues which they hold dear. A polarization of political life results. The second, 'decision', phase sees the leaders of these groups accept that a diversity of views will exist, and thereby seek to institutionalize 'some crucial aspect of democratic procedure'[3] to structure and channel this diversity. In this process, 'a small circle of leaders is likely to play a disproportionate role.'[4] Finally the 'habituation' phase sees political leaders learning from the successful resolution of some issues and thereby placing their trust in the new rules and procedures, new politicians ushered into the new structure, and the mass of the populace linked into the structure by effective parties. This model, which assumes sequential development of the phases, was important both in stimulating further thought on the question of the origins of democratic regimes as well as emphasizing the key role played by élites.

While this latter, élite, focus became the principal concern of the writing which followed Rustow, that writing gave much less attention to the sorts of factors identified by Rustow as part of his preparatory phase, especially the presence of long-term conflict over central issues by established political actors. Instead, the principal focus was on the dynamics of élite interaction during the process of transition. This focus has yielded a rich and interesting literature, but by its downplaying of non-élite, and in particular civil society, actors, its explanatory power has been impaired. This is clear when we look at the explanations of transition emerging from this school. The path-breaking, and paradigm-setting, work in this regard was the collective study edited by Guillermo O'Donnell, Philippe C. Schmitter and Laurence Whitehead.[5]

For these authors, transition is that 'interval between one political regime and another',[6] and its chief characteristic is uncertainty. This uncertainty relates not simply to the outcome of transition, which may lead to a democratic polity but which may also result in another form of authoritarian rule, but more importantly to the process itself. Transitions are characterized by 'insufficient structural or behavioral parameters to guide and predict the outcome',[7] leading to uncertainty and indirection. Structural factors may help shape the process of transition, but they are much less salient than in normal circumstances. Instead, there is a 'high degree of indeterminacy embedded in situations where unexpected events (*fortuna*), insufficient information, hurried and audacious choices, confusion about motives and interests, plasticity, and even indefinition of political identities, as well as the talents of specific individuals (*virtu*), are frequently decisive in determining the outcomes.' In such situations, 'it is almost impossible to specify *ex ante* which classes, sectors, institutions, and other groups will take what role, opt for which issues, or support what alternative.'[8] During the process of transition, the rules of the political game are uncertain, but so too may be the identity of all of the main actors, their motives, and the likely courses of action they will pursue.

This emphasis upon uncertainty creates an analysis which is essentially voluntarist. The main focus of study is the various élite actors whose manoeuvrings and relationships constitute the dynamic of the transition process. Crucial for the authors is division within the authoritarian regime, which they see as being at the root of every transition. [9] This split, which usually stems from domestic rather than international causes, will create openings for other political actors to become involved. The form the split usually takes is over the question of whether to liberalize or to try to tough it out, and the task for those favouring change is to try to ensure that opponents within the regime do not feel so threatened as to act to halt this process. Pacts are an important means of doing this,[10] although they are also acknowledged as intrinsically undemocratic. Some scope for non-élite, popular, involvement is provided, in that the authors argue that the split in the regime can be followed by a general mobilization of the population. The people can also participate through involvement in 'founding elections', which may be important for the development of parties. However they argue that popular mobilization is shortlived, and the populace becomes demobilized as democratization proceeds. The opening of negotiations between regime reformers and opposition moderates is important in bringing this about.

The key elements in the approach of the O'Donnell/Schmitter volume are its élite (even at times individual) focus and the emphasis upon uncertainty. The two things go together. If structural factors are assumed to be weak from the outset, uncertainty will doubtless result and a premium will be placed on the decisions and actions of political élites; if nothing else imposes restraints on the developing situation, it will be determined overwhelmingly by the preferences and actions of the political actors. Or, put the other way, if all depends on those personal preferences and actions, the result is bound to be societal uncertainty. This sort of approach makes it impossible to theorize. If all depends upon the whims of individuals and groups, the large-scale theorization of social and political change is impossible. Change is rendered contingent in a way which cannot be overcome, and therefore theorization of change is impossible through this approach.[11]

Despite these problems, discussed further below, the O'Donnell/

Schmitter/Whitehead volumes stimulated a whole literature on democratization. Much of this literature constituted a refinement and further discussion of the chief elements in the O'Donnell/ Schmitter/Whitehead analysis, or a picking up of elements which were either downplayed in or omitted from this seminal work, but chiefly in the form of a discussion of individual cases of transition rather than any attempt at generating a theoretically grounded explanation that went beyond the categories of explanation used by O'Donnell, Schmitter and Whitehead. In the absence of a worked out theory of democratic transition, the best means of understanding the dynamics of that process as understood by the transition school is to investigate the categories of explanation they used. The chief categories are liberalization, regime disunity, pacts, civil society, international influences, and the role of the individual.

Liberalization

One of the crucial stages identified by most writers when analysing the transition process is that of liberalization. The notion of liberalization that is to be found in much of the transition literature is essentially spatial in nature. It envisages a process of winding back state control in order to leave room for autonomous action on the part of the population or a segment/s of it. O'Donnell and Schmitter have tended to see liberalization principally in terms of rights.[12] In their words:

> By liberalization we mean the process of making effective certain rights that protect both individuals and social groups from arbitrary or illegal acts committed by the state or third parties. On the level of individuals, these guarantees include the classical elements of the liberal tradition: habeas corpus; sanctity of private home and correspondence; the right to be defended in a fair trial according to pre-established laws; freedom of movement, speech, and petition; and so forth. On the level of groups, these rights cover such things as freedom from punishment for expressions of collective dissent from government policy, freedom from censorship of the means of communication, and freedom to associate voluntarily with other citizens.

Liberalization, for O'Donnell and Schmitter, means making

progress in the achievement of these rights. The conception of liberalization in terms of the guaranteeing of rights does capture one possible part of this process. If such rights were guaranteed when formerly they were not, this would constitute a genuine advance in a liberalizing direction; it would mean creating space for people to act when such space was not present before. But by discussing such a development in terms of rights and guarantees, this conception is overly legalistic. If firm guarantees are to be present, these would appear to have to be couched in terms of legal rights, duties and prohibitions for this conception of liberalization to apply. However, if people are able to act as if they had such rights without those rights being formally embedded in law, with the regime now accepting something which formerly it would not, this could be classed as a form of liberalization. Legalization may come later, but it need not be an intrinsic part of liberalization from the outset. The O'Donnell/Schmitter emphasis on legal factors reflects their view of democratization as being bound up with citizenship.

This definition of liberalization is deficient in another respect also. It assumes that liberalization constitutes a defence against acts by the state which are 'arbitrary or illegal'. One problem here is, illegal according to whose laws and arbitrary in whose eyes? In practice, many authoritarian states act in a quite regularized fashion in their relationship with their subjects. Many of their actions are not illegal according to their own systems of laws nor arbitrary in the sense of irregular or conducted at whim. But their law and their *modus operandi* may be so extensive and intrusive that little or no scope is left for individual action on the part of the people. The extent of regime control may be such as to be restrictive and oppressive while being neither arbitrary nor illegal.

One of the contributors to the O'Donnell, Schmitter and Whitehead collection offers a different view of liberalization. According to Luciano Martins,[13]

> [t]he liberalization of authoritarian rule can therefore be defined as the adoption of formal democratic institutions and the simultaneous exclusion of the four principles which give to such institutions their true democratic content: consensus concerning the rules of the game, political accountability of the rulers, the right to ample political representation, and alternation in power.

Once again this captures what may be one form of liberalization, but it seems excessively restricting to argue that liberalization only exists when democratic institutions are formally adopted but their essence is missing. Often the formal adoption of such institutions occurs only part way through a process of liberalization. State controls are often rolled back leaving *de facto* room for independent popular activity before formal adoption of democratic forms. Indeed, such a development often provides the impetus which produces the democratic institutions, and to leave liberalization dependent upon formal action would omit so much that is important in explanation of this process as to be seriously misleading.

A better approach is provided by Huntington. In his view,[14] liberalization

> is the partial opening of an authoritarian system short of choosing governmental leaders through freely competitive elections. Liberalizing authoritarian regimes may release political prisoners, open up some issues for public debate, loosen censorship, sponsor elections for offices that have little power, permit some renewal of civil society, and take other steps in a democratic direction, without submitting top decision makers to the electoral test.

This conception of liberalization[15] is valuable because it captures the two essential aspects of the liberalization process: the opening of the political system to enable independent activity on the part of the citizenry or segments of it, and the limited nature of the process. What is important about liberalization is that while it does constitute a partial rolling back of state activity and control in some sectors of life, it does not challenge the continuing control of the authorities. It does not alter the authorities' ability to rule or to change particular outcomes; even in those spheres of activity from which the authorities withdraw, they are still able to intervene to reverse an outcome they did not favour.[16] Despite concessions at the edges, the essential power structure remains intact.

This emphasis upon the way in which the capacity of the authorities to continue to rule remains unimpaired by the process of liberalization is important. It explains why sections of the regime, when under pressure, see liberalization as a possible way of easing the situation, of enabling their critics to let off steam without fundamentally affecting their continued capacity to rule. It is this restriction of liberalising measures to areas which do not bring about a change in the fundamental power structure which is what distinguishes liberalization from democratization. The latter is a process which involves making the governors accountable to the populace. It thereby involves a fundamental transformation of the power structure and how it operates. Thus in principle, there is a clear difference between liberalization and democratization, but in practice the two often shade into one another. Liberalizing moves may become radicalized and thereby transformed into forces for democratization. A press which has some of the shackles removed from it, may become more assertive and achieve true independence. A tame legislative assembly may become more vocal and critical, giving voice to discussion of public policy and thereby driving the political agenda in a democratising direction. Permission to hold popular meetings can turn into oppositional rallies. There is no inevitability about this. Liberalization does not automatically spawn democratization. But once a regime embarks upon a programme of liberalization, it will usually be faced with pressures to expand it. Whether such pressures are successful is contingent upon the circumstances of each case. However, what is clear is that if liberalization does not necessarily lead to democratization, democratization cannot occur without liberalization, except where it comes from a rapid and probably violent rupture of the political process.

The usual response to a policy of liberalization is the proliferation of autonomous organizations within society. But such organizations cannot be accommodated within the existing institutional contours of the regime, with the result that either those contours will be changed or, if this does not happen, the new organizations must seek to realize their interests through popular mobilization. If this happens, liberalization is on the way to escaping official control and being turned into democratization. This can lead to the halting of the liberalization process, or to liberalizers becoming even more radical and powerful within the regime.

What factors affect this question of the transformation of liberalization into democratization?

Regime Disunity

Regimes usually resort to liberalization when they are under pressure and when they are internally divided in the way discussed in the previous chapter. Such division may be important both in terms of the origins of liberalization and of its effects. If the regime remains united and it does not come under pressure (for example, as a result of economic crisis), it is unlikely to opt for liberalization. This generalization is subject to a qualification. Those regimes which really see themselves as temporary, as restoring the system to health before withdrawing to enable a competitively-based system to take over, may embark upon a process of liberalization not as a strategy to hold on to power, but as one designed to surrender it to others. If the belief in their own provisional nature is widely shared within the élite, then that élite might decide to seek ways of withdrawing from power. Such a situation has not been uncommon with military regimes, many of which have explicitly seen their term as being limited and temporary. Of course, such initial convictions are often transformed into an unwillingness to surrender power once it has been gained, but the fear that continuing to rule will have adverse effects upon the military as an institution has also been a strong theme. Such a belief has been the stimulus needed to persuade the regime that it should set in motion processes to withdraw from power; Brazil in the 1970s is a case in point.

But more common has been regime disunity and splits, with O'Donnell and Schmitter's so-called softliners favouring liberalization and the hard-liners opposing it. Such a situation is normally the result of disagreement between these two groups over what is to be done about the crisis confronting the regime, as discussed in Chapter 2. For the hardliners, the crisis is seen as not being of sufficient magnitude to warrant the political risks involved in any partial or controlled opening of the regime. They believe that the existing structure, perhaps with a reinforcement of coercive capacity, will enable the regime to ride out the difficulties. In contrast, the softliners believe that the crisis poses a real danger to the regime and that unless it acts to broaden its support base by giving the people some part to play in political life, they will be vulnerable to popular unrest. Liberalizing measures are thus seen by this group as a means of stabilising the regime by involving the populace (or segments of it) in political activity which will have no practical effect on the basic power structure; seeking some form of electoral validation is a common tactic to achieve stabilization. By keeping these measures under control, the softliners believe that they can maintain their power and the position of the regime as a whole. This means that liberalization is seen not as a step on the path to the passing of power to others, but a means of attempting to re-consolidate authoritarian rule.

In those cases when the softliners actually see liberalization as a prelude to transferring power to another set of rulers, or when liberalization escapes from their control, the situation is most dangerous. Either of these eventualities could provoke a backlash from the hardliners if they are not in agreement about the need to transfer power; a coup is a likely response, with the abortive Greek coup of mid-1973 and Bolivia in November 1979 cases in point. Softliners clearly want to avoid such an outcome. So, too, does the opposition within society. It is this fear of provoking a violent response by elements opposed to the liberalization process, that is often important in creating the conditions favourable to the making of pacts (see below).

Different patterns of regime disunity, and their interaction with opposition forces, characterize different types of transition. This is outlined below. An important element in this equation is the attitude within the regime to the possibility of withdrawing from power. Some work has been done on the military in this situation, and one scholar[17] has identified six factors which help to determine whether senior officers will seek to extricate the military from political rule:

1. Perception of the strength and commitment of the opposition, especially those elements close to the regime.
2. Calculation of the choices available to the military and the costs and benefits of these. Considerations of the military's institutional integrity and prestige will be relevant here.
3. The balance between those within the military seeking a political opening of the regime and those seeking to obstruct it.
4. The pattern of societal cleavages and the degree to which they are represented by different political forces that have become mobilized and involved in the political process.
5. The substantive programmes of the opposition, especially in terms of the presence or absence of a project that could legitimize a new regime.
6. The presence of actors antagonistic to the military. In practice, the military has usually sought to exclude such actors from participation in the transition.

Although explicitly associated with the military, this checklist would be applicable to those elements in all sorts of regimes confronting the prospect of a transition to democracy. All people placed in such a position will be concerned for the implications of such a change both for them directly and for the institutions within which they are located. They will do calculations designed to evaluate the implications of likely changes. Under such circumstances, their capacity to negotiate an agreement with their opponents will be an important consideration.

Pacts and Pacted Democracy

Central to the process of transition have been notions of negotiation between the main actors. However, such negotiation can be said to be common to virtually all cases of transition only if that term is defined sufficiently broadly to encompass all sorts of dialogue between the actors and not only direct face-to-face discussion; the public expression of positions, the making of demands, even the conduct of internal party debate can be part of this dialogue. Participation in such dialogue and the outcome of it will be dependent upon a range of factors, including the strength and unity of the regime on the one hand and the opposition on the other, and the nature of the role played by forces in the society more generally.[18] When such negotiations result in an agreement between the actors on, for example, the conduct of an election or the terms under which the regime will leave power, this is usually referred to as a pact. For much of the literature, pacts are central to the smooth course of the transition process.

A pact is defined by O'Donnell and Schmitter as 'an explicit but not always publicly explicated or justified, agreement among a select set of actors which seeks to define (or, better, to redefine) rules governing the exercise of power on the basis of mutual guarantees for the "vital interests" of those entering into it'.[19] At the core of a pact 'lies a negotiated compromise under which actors agree to forgo or underutilize their capacity to harm each other by extending guarantees not to threaten each others' corporate autonomies or vital interests'.[20] Pacts are an attempt to provide a greater degree of certainty during the transition by guaranteeing the interests of major parties and thereby assuring those parties that the transition will not have significantly adverse consequences for them. In the view of O'Donnell and Schmitter, pacts may be of specified duration and seen as temporary, and may therefore need to be renegotiated (e.g. when the situation changes, or new actors enter the process) although some elements may become institutionalized in the transition arrangements and thereby become continuing features of the system. But there is a paradox about pacts: they move towards democracy by undemocratic means. They are negotiated by a few actors, they reduce competitiveness and accountability, they attempt to structure the agenda of policy concerns, and they distort the principle of citizen equality.[21] O'Donnell and Schmitter identify three possible types of pacts: a pact governing military withdrawal from politics, a political pact involving the gradual extension of political rights (often through the medium of political parties) and of inclusiveness, and an economic/social pact to facilitate the making of hard economic decisions.[22] Most pacts involve agreements over interim institutional procedures, although more substantive questions may also be addressed.

The notion of a pact is a recognition of the crucial dynamic at the heart of the transition process. In the words of Huntington:[23] 'Negotiations and compromise among political élites were at the heart of the democratization processes. The leaders of the key political forces and social groups in society bargained with each other, explicitly or implicitly, and worked out acceptable if not satisfying arrangements for the transition to democracy.' This sort of pact is usually seen as a four actor pact. It implies that the regime is divided into hardliners and softliners and the opposition into moderates and radicals. The pact is an agreement between the softliners and the moderates whereby they try to work out some of the details of transition, but each must be careful not to antagonize and provoke the other part of their sides; softliners must not compromise so much that they upset the hardliners and push them into acting, while the moderates must ensure that they do not give away so much that the radicals seek to upset the process.

Huntington, like O'Donnell and Schmitter, sees these sorts of agreements as being of different types and covering different things. He argues[24] that in Brazil, Peru, Ecuador and Bolivia understandings involving mainly procedural (especially electoral) rules for the transition were arrived at between the opposition and an official caretaker coalition. In Colombia and Venezuela in 1957 and 1958 explicit agreements were negotiated between interested parties, while in Spain government and opposition reached agreement on the constitutional framework for the new democracy and, through the Pact of Moncloa, on a range of economic measures. In Uruguay military and party leaders agreed on the Club Naval Pact in August 1984, while 'round table' agreements between government and opposition were a feature of many East European transitions at the end of the 1980s. As well as such formal pacts, in many cases agreements also included the leaders of major social and institutional forces in the society, such as labour unions, the church and the business community.

Terry Karl[25] has discussed what she calls 'foundational pacts'. These set out the rules of the game on the basis of mutual guarantees for the vital interests of those involved, and have three essential components:

1. They are comprehensive, including virtually all politically significant actors. Only if all such actors are included can vital interests be protected. The pact is therefore usually a series of agreements that are interlocking and dependent upon each other, e.g. between the military and civilians, political parties, and state and public bodies.
2. Initially they are principally concerned with procedural, or rule-making, issues, but will also address substantive questions. They are different from 'managerial accords' which are 'partial rather than comprehensive, exclusionary rather than inclusionary, and substantively-oriented rather than rule-making in content'.[26]
3. Although inclusionary, pacts restrict the scope of representation so as to reassure traditionally-dominant elements that their vital interests will be respected. Such restriction may come about through restricting contestation, as when the Colombian parties in 1958 agreed to alternate in power regardless of the outcome of elections, restricting the policy agenda, as when the Venezuelan parties agreed in 1958 to implement the same economic programme, or restricting the franchise, as in Chile in 1874.

Pact-making is facilitated when a number of conditions are satisfied. Important here is a situation in which each party to the agreement depends upon the other/s. If one particular group is in the position to achieve what it wants without compromising, there is little incentive for it to seek agreement Or, put in a slightly different fashion, the chances of pact-making are increased when groups are not characterized by widely divergent political resources. This need for mutual reliance is reflected in the circumstances of some transitions. Where the process was dominated by military leaders, as in Brazil and Peru, civilian political leaders had little choice but to accept military demands. Where the relative power of both sides was more equal, as in Uruguay, military demands were modified during the course of the negotiations. Where overwhelming power lay with the civilians, as in Argentina and Greece, the military's requests were rejected and they had to accept what they were given.[27] Successful pact-making is also facilitated when the negotiations which go into making that pact can be conducted in private with a limited number of partners. The more discussion occurs in public, the less room for manoeuvre leaders have and the less likely they are to accept the sorts of concessions that may be necessary for a successful pact to be completed. And the more public the discussion, the greater the number of participants and thereby positions, and therefore the more difficult it is likely to be to obtain compromise. Furthermore, pact-making can only succeed if leaders are able to ensure the obedience of their followers; unless all parties to the negotiations have confidence that their partners can ensure that their own followers will abide by any agreements reached, and that confidence is well-founded, stable pacts are unlikely. This is a major problem for pacts and those who design them: agreement may result in widespread opposition, alienation and disillusionment among the followers, which may in turn lead to the breakdown of the whole transition process as it is wrenched out of the hands of political élites and seized by their erstwhile followers. But this danger is one which, for Huntington, must be faced: 'democracies were often made by leaders willing to betray the interests of their followers in order to achieve that goal'.[28]

One of the compromises often involved in the structuring of the process of transition is what Huntington called 'the trade-off between participation and moderation'.[29] This involves a commitment to widen the boundaries of participation in the political system, thereby enabling formerly excluded political forces to have a voice, in return for a shift away from their most radical positions on the part of those forces. This occurred in many of the transitions occurring in the last quarter of the twentieth century. In Argentina the formerly proscribed Peronistas were accepted back into the system by the military establishment. In Greece in 1974 and Spain in April 1977 the respective Communist parties were legalized. In Uruguay the Broad Front was legalized in August 1984, while in Brazil the ban on the pre-1964 political leaders was lifted in 1979 and in 1985 the Marxist parties were legalized. The Chilean Communist party was legalized in 1989. In return for such inclusion, the leaders of these political forces offered moderation at both the tactical and policy level. This involved a commitment to work through the established, mainly electoral, channels rather than direct action, and the acceptance of a capitalist economic (and ownership) framework. The left-wing parties referred to above virtually all moved towards the centre of the political spectrum, shedding their radical visage and appealing to the mass of the populace.

Another aspect of pact-making and successful transition is 'exit guarantees'.[30] These are sometimes seen as techniques used by the opposition to induce segments of the supporters of the old regime to desert that regime and swing their weight behind change. This is how Dix sees exit guarantees. However these can also be crucial aspects of the negotiating process which culminates with pacts. They are assurances given to elements in the old regime that their interests will not be crucially affected by the transition to democratic rule. Such guarantees are often extended to sections of the military, and involve guarantees against prosecution for any actions undertaken during authoritarian rule. This is particularly important in those cases where the military in power has been engaged in violent action against civilians, as in the so-called Argentine 'dirty war'. Guarantees also often take the form of an offer of immunity from reprisals as long as the principals retire and do not seek to play any part in public life. Such guarantees may also safeguard the institutional integrity and honour of particular institutions, usually the military.

Pact-making will also be affected by the identity of the governing authorities with whom the opposition seeks to negotiate. What is important here is that the negotiators are sufficiently distant from those who run the old regime that they can gain the confidence of the opposition, and yet close enough to the regime to be able to reassure the former rulers that the process will not escape control and become dangerous to their interests. This is one reason why a caretaker transitional administration often oversees the transition to democracy. Similarly, it also helps to explain why particular leaders of the opposition movement are able to push themselves to the fore: Karamanlis was a moderate conservative who was acceptable and reassuring to the anti-Communist Greek military, Soares was a moderate Socialist who appealed to some elements of the radicalized Portuguese military, Juan Carlos and Suarez had solid conservative Francoist credentials in Spain, while the Chilean Christian Democrat Aylwin was sufficiently conservative for sections of the military to trust.[31] This sort of situation, with conservative or centrist political leaders playing a leading role in guiding the transition process, is an important further guarantee for the rulers that they will not be exposed to significant danger and therefore should encourage them to enable the process to continue.

The key to pacts is that they limit the uncertainty associated with democratic transition, and thereby give some guarantees to those who potentially have a lot to lose as a result of transition. Pact-making is a form of conflict resolution. But it does have a cost in the form of constraining further democratization, marginalizing those seeking greater change (i.e. it is exclusivist as well as inclusivist), and demobilizing the populace. Pacts give guarantees to established interests, often in the form of guaranteeing property rights, marginalizing radical challengers, and slowing future development. Thus, while pacts may facilitate the process of transition by moderating the course of potential élite conflict, they do so at the expense of the mass and of the pressing of more radical social and economic agendas.[32] In this sense it may be that the unleashing of mass activity and consequent significant radicalization of the process, occurs only when pacts are not reached, when pact-makers cannot ensure that they are supported by their followers, or when leaders with authority among the populace are excluded from the pact-making process. But the exclusion of popular leaders will not inevitably lead to mass activism. According to O'Donnell, at least in Latin America, pacts are facilitated when civil society, and especially its popular sector, is weakly organized and politically inactive, or when the levels of social organization and political activation are high but these are accompanied by a strong representative party system. When civil society is weakly organized and politically inactive, narrow exclusivist élite agreements are likely to emerge. When there are higher levels of organization and activation, more comprehensive compromises are likely between institutionalized political actors, with the parties gaining access to electoral competition and/or administrative posts in exchange for guaranteeing their supporters' commitment to the agreement.[33] The general point O'Donnell is making here is that the mass will be excluded from the pact-making process if its leaders are not seen as being at the head of a constituency which cannot be excluded from that process.

Sometimes in the literature there is some ambiguity or uncertainty in the way the notion of a 'pact' is used. In those cases where there is an actual meeting or meetings between the representatives of different groups and an agreement with clear points issues from that meeting, as in the Pact of Moncloa in Spain and the Naval Club Pact in Uruguay, then it is clear that a pact has been devised. However, when there is no conscious act of agreement between different parties with a reasonably clear conception of the items of agreement, it is more difficult to say that a pact has come into existence. If we talk about some sort of implicit pact reflected in a series of actions taken by the regime which will meet some of the demands of the opposition, without some sort of concrete agreement, how are we to distinguish this from a regime-sponsored policy of liberalization? It is not enough to assume, as some seem to do,[34] that all transitions involve secret or implicit pact-making, and that the terms of the compromise must be deduced from analysis of the reforms adopted during the transition. A pact must have at least two parties; if measures are adopted only by one side, they may be better seen either as a policy of liberalization by the regime or concessions by the opposition.

If pacts are distinguished from liberalization and concessions by the agreement of the various sides, they are also usually distinguished by their component elements. According to Ethier,[35] when negotiations are undertaken, the regime usually presses four demands: an amnesty for any offences committed by officials, exclusion of radical parties from future government, continued repression of 'disloyal' forces, and the postponement of radical economic reform and acceptance of the liberal capitalist model. In return for such guarantees of security, the opposition will seek expanded rights and opportunities in the political sphere. This sort of compromise sets the broad rules for the transition and creates the basis for the subsequent installation of democracy. Although in practice, of course, the terms of a pact may not always be observed; when the sides no longer need each other, the incentive to abide by the agreement is weakened.

Civil Society

Although a significant concept in social science and referred to at times in the transition literature, civil society has remained a concept little utilized in a systematic or analytical fashion by the transition school. Certainly, the transition literature recognizes that the mass often plays a part in the structuring of democratic transitions through popular and radical mobilization. Support for the opposition (thereby affecting the balance between regime defenders and challengers),[36] the outbreak of strikes, demonstrations, riots and revolts can all be significant in stimulating this process of democratization. But such mass action is often not the crucial factor in advancing the democratic cause; according to Huntington, although some form of mass action occurred in almost all cases of third wave regime change, it was central in only about six (replacements in the Philippines, East Germany and Romania, and extrications/transplacements in South Korea, Poland and Czechoslovakia) of a total of about 33.[37] In the other cases, although some mass action did occur, this was background noise, or merely added to the effect of factors promoting regime change. This view of the role of popular action is the reverse side of the transition school's focus upon élite activity as the key factor in democratic transition.

The approach to civil society in the transition literature was to see it generally as a residual category; it was a term used to refer to mass action or activity by a few civil society forces, but it was never a concept that was allowed to engage with the élite focus to explore more fully the dynamics of transition. This not only ignored the real value the concept has had in social science analysis,[38] but it undercut the aspirations of the transition school adequately to explain the course of democratic transition. As will be argued below, such an engagement between élite and civil society foci is crucial to an understanding of transition.

As defined in Chapter 1, civil society exists when there is a sphere of activity outside direct state control, in which the citizenry may organize to pursue their own interests and concerns in their own way (within limits). Most importantly, the activity of these organizations and the public sphere within which they operate is not only independent of state control, but is recognized as legitimate by the state and includes acceptance of the right to pursue interests through political activity.[39] If there is no recognition of this legitimacy, then civil society does not exist. This means that for some regimes, usually labelled totalitarian, the emergence of civil society forces is itself part of the process of liberalization and, perhaps, democratization. But for the vast majority of authoritarian regimes which did not seek the sort of all-encompassing control which would have denied the very possibility of civil society, liberalization could take the form of an expansion of the boundaries of acceptable activity by civil society forces. Legalization of political parties or labour unions, permission for strikes or rallies to take place, the lifting of press censorship, all involve an expansion of the vehicles for participation and of the boundaries of civil society. The expansion and strengthening of civil society can clearly have a major impact on the chances for regime restructuring, if for no other reason than that it provides vehicles through which political actors can seek to exercise power and to influence the rulers. The degree to which civil society forces have been able to maintain themselves under authoritarian rule is therefore a significant factor in structuring the course of and prospects for democratization.[40] In those countries where civil society forces have not been destroyed by authoritarian rule, the chances of a rapid transition to democracy are much greater than where such forces have either been crushed or lacked vigour to begin with. Where civil society forces were able to retain their integrity and therefore the basis for a civil society remained essentially intact, as in Southern Europe, popular pressure was more significant as a factor than in those areas like Latin America where civil society forces were less established.[41] The presence or absence of vibrant and vigorous civil society forces can thus be central to the prospects for regime change and democratization (see below). Without a perspective which gives serious attention to the shape and contours of the potentially emergent civil society, the explanation of transition will be incomplete.

As argued above, the transition literature generally eschews systematic analysis of the notion of civil society. Recognizing that political parties and factions within parties have had a role in bringing about democratic transition and have been more important than populist movements and spontaneous mass activism in this regard, the transition literature has usually been content to discuss civil society purely in terms of this particular type of civil society force, the political party. Parties have not played a central role in all cases of democratic transition, but usually the main interlocutors with the authoritarian regime have rested upon party foundations. What has given the standing to many of these people to negotiate with the rulers has been their positions of leadership in major parties. This has not only provided them with a sense of legitimacy, since parties are seen as essential to democracy, but it has also been a source of power. It has been a source of power in two senses. First, parties possess political resources which they can mobilize into the struggle for democracy. Such resources may comprise international support (particularly important for Social Democratic and Christian

Democratic parties), media outlets, funds, organizational structure and capacities embracing wide parts of the country, and a history or tradition which encourages popular support. In a sense, they are often the best placed organizational vehicles for confronting and negotiating with the rulers because of their capacity to mobilize popular support, to get people out onto the streets, and to win their votes in elections. Second, this power stems from the fears of the incumbent rulers. If those rulers seek to negotiate exit guarantees, they want to be certain that they can come to agreement with people who can make that agreement stick. Given that elections will normally be an important part of the transition process, including a means of deciding, or at least ratifying, the identity of the future governors, it is logical for authoritarian rulers to seek those guarantees from party leaders.

Another reason why parties so often play a central role is the nature of transition itself. At the heart of the transition process is the negotiation of rules of the game to provide structuring to that process and some degree of certainty to the actors. Such rules are for the most part procedural in nature, and therefore impinge directly upon the normal activities of parties. The growth of a stable party system is important to the successful establishment of a democratic regime, and therefore a prominent role played by parties is a logical, if not essential, aspect of the transition process.

Of course ultimately the power, and role, of parties stems from the popular support they can generate or, at certain times, from the popular support the authoritarian rulers believe they can generate. It is concern about the populace, its mood and potentialities, which persuades authoritarian rulers to embark upon the course of liberalization and democratization. If they were not afraid of popular retribution, they would be unlikely to seek to change the regime, regardless of how difficult the circumstances had become. It is the knowledge that political parties are better placed than the regime to tap into this popular sentiment which propels the parties to centre stage. But where such parties either do not exist or are very weakly rooted, this role of mobilizing the populace is rendered difficult to achieve. Labour unions can play such a role, but they are often not well suited to it being sectoral in nature and sometimes regionally constrained. A social movement is possible, but the loose structure of such bodies makes it difficult for leaders to exercise the sort of control over their followers which would encourage rulers to negotiate with them or enable them to give the sorts of guarantees which would be acceptable. A populist individual leader is also a possibility, but such, possibly charismatic, individuals are not frequent occurrences and in any case suffer the same shortcomings as the social movement. However, it is clear that without organization, mass activism is unlikely to be sufficiently sustained or focused to be able to contribute substantially to the democratization process. And it is this weakness which has encouraged the transition school to focus on élites and to view parties primarily through the élite rather than the civil society prism and to thereby underplay the importance of civil society forces to the transition process. This will be discussed further below.

International Influences

The principal dynamic identified by the transition school in the transitions they have studied has been internal, arising from the contradictions, tensions and forces within the respective societies, rather than from external factors.[42] However, external factors have also been significant in some cases of democratization. The most obvious form in which external factors have been important has been foreign invasion and the installation of a new, democratic regime. Alfred Stepan has discussed some of the different forms in which this can occur.[43] Post-war Germany, Italy and Japan are the most obvious instances of this,[44] but perhaps Grenada in 1983 would also be a case in point.[45] Defeat in war can also be significant, even when it does not result in a victor imposing democratic forms on the defeated, with the Greek setback in Cyprus in 1974 and Argentine defeat in the Falklands/Malvinas dispute in 1982 being cases of this. But even in those cases when internal factors have been paramount, external factors have sometimes played a part. One of the most important aspects of this question is the structural location of the country and its economy in the world system, but this has received little attention in the transition literature[46] (see Chapter 2 above). The transition literature has, to the extent that it has taken account of international influences, focused upon less deeply embedded factors and the role they have played.

One such factor has been the hegemonic ideology prevailing in the 1970s and 1980s. Although many of the cases of democratization upon which the transition literature has been based occurred before the end of the cold war, and therefore while the ideology of capitalist democracy was still confronted by that of Marxist socialism, all the cases of transition occurred in parts of the world solidly located in the Western political sphere and where capitalist democracy prevailed as the generalized overarching principle. Although the leading states (and in particular the US) did not always act to realize the coincidence of the capitalist and democratic parts of this ideology, it would have been difficult for countries in this part of the world to have changed regimes in the name of principles other than capitalist democracy, even if, as in Nicaragua, the result of regime change may have fallen short of democracy.[47] Even if reversion to authoritarian rule occurred, it was justified in the name of economic stability, and thereby securing capitalism, or of removing unhealthy features in order the better to stabilize democracy. A regime could not hope easily to establish a sense of its legitimacy unless it publicly adhered to these principles of democratic capitalism. This principle also applied to the later cases of regime change in the Communist world, many of which were conducted at least formally under this rhetoric. Thus, this international yardstick was an important, if intangible, factor favouring democratization. But alone, it could not produce regime change; it required the domestic generation of opposition before it could take effect.

Hegemonic ideology is most effective if underpinned by the reality of political action, and in many cases this reality was evident. In the post-war period, the US was not an unambiguous supporter of democracy throughout the globe despite the claims of its rhetoric. In many cases the Americans clearly preferred stability and dictatorship to what they perceived to be the potential instability accompanying regime change and democracy. Nevertheless, there were times when American influence was important, especially in Latin America. Similarly in the Southern European transitions, the influence of the EC was an important factor.[48] Such influence could take a number of forms:

1. Pressure exerted by the regional power on the old regime in an attempt to induce change or strengthen democracy.[49] Such pressure could be economic, in the form of sanctions or, more usually, the granting or withholding of economic (aid, trade and investment) privileges; the use of human rights[50] as a touchstone for the granting of most-favoured-nation status is one such common tactic. There have also been attempts to provide direct assistance for the consolidation of democratic institutions

and procedures through the provision of specialized (e.g. electoral) assistance.[51] Other forms of pressure could include public statements of support for democracy and opposition to authoritarian rule, threats of international isolation, veiled warnings about support for the overthrow of the regime should its rulers not change their behaviour, and the possible ending of arms supplies. This last was often a potent weapon when dealing with military regimes, and could be influential in stimulating a split within military ranks.There have also been instances of the mobilization and deployment of the military short of invasion in an attempt to exercise influence through this not very subtle form of sabre-rattling; US deployment of naval vessels off the Dominican Republic at the time of the counting of votes in the 1978 election and overflights in support of Aquino in the Philippines are two examples of this.

2.   Direct support of those forces seeking change. Such support has been of a variety of types. Most notoriously it has included armed support for 'freedom fighters' waging conflict against the regime, as in US support for the Contras in Nicaragua in the late 1980s.[52] But more usually the support has been in terms of resources, material and rhetoric. Foreign countries have often provided the safe havens within which opposition leaders and parties could establish themselves and continue to play a part in politics at home, as in the cases of Wilson Ferreira in Uruguay, Mario Soares in Spain and Constantine Karamanlis in Greece.[53] They have been the location for crucial meetings of opposition figures in which agreements could be reached regarding the future course of the struggle, as in Venezuela in 1957. But they have also been the source of material, like paper for printing, organizational experience and talent, and, most importantly, funds, as in the case of the Portuguese Socialist Party in 1975 which received considerable funds from the German SPD.

3.   The general promise of benefits in the event of a democratic outcome. It is clear that in the Southern European cases, entry to the EC was an important stimulus for democratization because membership was dependent, *inter alia*, upon democratic political forms.[54] In Spain, business circles were convinced of the need for entry to the EC and realized that this could be achieved only if the country was democratic in form, with the result that a reactionary alliance between business and sections of the military was stillborn. Analogous circumstances

existed in Portugal and Greece. But this question of benefits may be even more important once the transition has been achieved in the way it can strengthen the newly-established regime. For example, entry to the EC involved the incorporation of the new members into a wide range of structures and processes which reinforced the newly-established democratic contours of the regime and inhibited any tendency to back away from them.

Governments are not the only possible sources of influence; non-governmental organizations have also been active. Laurence Whitehead shows how the Socialist International was particularly intent on trying to foster democracy in Latin America.[55] Political parties abroad have often sought to assist their counterparts in the struggle for democratization,[56] while organizations like Amnesty International have added their voices to concerns which have fed into the democratization process. In some cases the churches, too, have played a role, even if the attitude of the Vatican under John Paul II has been more concerned with stability than democracy in Latin America; the reverse priority applied in Eastern Europe.[57]

Another type of influence is the contagion or snowball effect. This occurs when the successful replacement of an authoritarian regime, or even significant action against it, stimulates similar activity in other states.[58] While the actual dynamics of how this works are unclear, it is likely that success elsewhere encourages would-be democratizers to press their case at home. It may also discourage authoritarian rulers in the face of such pressure. Crucial to the operation of this sort of effect would appear to be the media, which is the means through which news of the developments elsewhere is brought home. Nevertheless, despite the way a globalized media can transmit images from the other side of the world, it is probable that the effect of developments in neighbouring countries is much more potent than what happens at a greater distance. Immediate neighbours are likely to be the yardsticks whereby the domestic situation is evaluated, even if only because more is known about them and they are more familiar. Moreover, the closer the geographical proximity, the greater the opportunity for direct assistance. The clearest case of such diffusion is Eastern Europe in the late 1980s, discussed in Chapter 6. There may also be a variant of this, called by one author[59] the demonstration effect. This is when the image of democracy, usually presented in terms of an affluent

Western lifestyle, is projected into non-democratic countries and undermines the basis of the existing regime, which is perceived as being incompatible with such an image. Unlike contagion, this is not linked to territorial contiguity, but relies overwhelmingly on the media.

It is clear that there have been cases where the course of transition has been consciously affected by similar developments elsewhere. In Argentina Alfonsin sought to legitimate his actions through 'extensive use of the Spanish "metaphor"', the prosecution of some officers in Argentina persuaded sections of the Uruguayan military to go back on their commitment to withdraw from power, and in Korea public reference was made to the role of the church in the fall of Marcos in the Philippines.[60] Both would-be democratizers and opponents seek to learn lessons from attempts at democratization elsewhere, avoiding those strategies and tactics which fail and seeking to rework and adopt those that are successful. In this sense, past heritage and common cultural roots can be important; the democratization of Portugal and Spain were very significant for Latin America because of the role of these two states as former colonial powers and cultural wellsprings. But this also means that international influence can be important not only in stimulating the turn to democratization, but in helping to structure that process once it is under way.

The role of international factors in helping to structure the course of transition may be more important in the models and guidance they can offer than in terms of any direct intervention by external actors. Those domestic actors playing a part in transition will look to the experience of other countries in the hope of learning from them. Such experience may be most important in the choices élites make about the institutions the new democracy will have, where choices about such things as electoral systems and presidential versus parliamentary regimes may be influenced by external experience. It is this role which has led some to argue that international influence is stronger during the process of democratic consolidation than transition.[61]

Role of the Individual

O'Donnell and Schmitter emphasize the fluid nature and relative weakness of longer-term structural factors in determining the course of transition. The corollary of this is the increased scope for a significant role to be played by individual actors. Clearly, in a situation of regime transition, established rules will lose much of their authority and dominant individuals will become increasingly important. The qualities such individuals possess will be even more relevant than usual. For example, in the Spanish transition, the difference between Navarro and Suarez was important. Navarro appeared as a representative of the past, of the Franco regime in which he had held high political office, whereas Suarez lacked ties with the civil war and the foundation of the regime and appeared as a young franquist bureaucrat, capable and forward-looking rather than reactionary and tainted by the past. His franquist experience made him appear trustworthy to the remnants of the regime; his youth, ability to discuss questions with people of diverse ideological commitment and his political style connected him to the opposition.[62] Similarly Karamanlis in Greece had this combination which enabled him to gain the trust of both regime and opposition. Acceptability to both sides was therefore an important consideration in the capacity of an individual to act as intermediary for the introduction of a new set of political practices. In some other cases, such as Chile, an individual has, through strength of personality and resources available to him, been able to stamp his imprint decisively on the course of transition. Clearly, individual actors have at times been very influential.

These, then, are the principal elements of the transition school of explanation: liberalization, regime disunity, pacts, civil society, international influences and the role of the individual. This style of explanation is overwhelmingly elitist in focus, with the attention given to civil society essentially residual. The whole process is explained through the perspective of the élites. This is clearly demonstrated when looking at the typologies of transition that have emerged from this literature.

Forms of Transition

The notion of transition covers a diversity of types of regime change, including virtually all except those resulting from revolution. However, the transition literature assumes that this diversity obscures a considerable degree of commonality in the paths of political change evident in the countries experiencing such change. Certainly O'Donnell believes that once a certain degree of 'stateness' and of socio-economic complexity has been achieved, there is a high degree of commonality in the process of change from one regime to another, regardless of the original regime type.[63] Clearly, at one level there is significant commonality in contours and processes such that, generically, many forms of regime change may be labelled transition. However, we need also to be aware that there are different modes of transition.

In analysing transition, writers have come up with a confusing array of names to refer to essentially the same processes. Confusingly, some writers have also not been consistent in the names they have used at different times. The typology given below is based principally upon that of Donald Share and Scott Mainwaring,[64] substantially supplemented by that of Samuel P. Huntington.[65] Huntington distinguishes between four modes of transition from authoritarian rule. One of these, a result of foreign intervention,[66] will be excluded from the subsequent analysis because it is the result of external supplanting of domestic processes. Three main forms (both in terms of our focus of concern and numbers of states experiencing them) of transition, remain.

Transition Through Transaction

This occurs when 'the élites in power took the lead in bringing about democracy.'[67] They institute liberalization and thereby initially shape the process of transition; it is a process of transforming the existing structure with incumbent élites playing a leading part.[68] This is the equivalent of Linz's 'reforma', Huntington's 'transformation',[69] Stepan's 'redemocratization initiated from within the authoritarian regime',[70] and the Linz/Stepan 'reforma-pactada, ruptura-pactada'. According to Huntington, the largest number of cases of democratization in the third wave were characterized by transaction. These are said to include Spain 1976–79, Chile 1989 and Brazil 1985–88. Transaction requires the government to be stronger than the opposition, and often has five phases:[71]

1. The emergence of reformers within the authoritarian regime. This constitutes the splitting of the regime discussed in the previous chapter, with one group believing that movement in a democratic direction is necessary.
2. The reformers achieve power in the regime.
3. Attempts at liberalization fail, instead stimulating demands for

democratization among some and the desire for repression among other members of the regime.

4. Reformists move against conservative elements in the regime, but selectively so as not to provoke a backlash. In addition, the reformers sought to reassure the conservatives by seeking to legitimize the new order through reference to the old, e.g. emphasis upon the dominance of procedural principles arising out of the past, what Huntington calls 'backward legitimacy'.
5. Coopting the opposition, usually through negotiations and the formation of pacts.

Transition Through Extrication

This occurs when the regime is weakened, seeks to extricate itself from power, but is in a weaker position to be able to dictate the terms than in cases of transaction. Thus, although negotiation occurs, the relative power of regime and opposition is tilted more in favour of the latter than during transaction.[72] For Huntington, who called this 'transplacement', it 'occurred when democratization resulted largely from joint action by government and opposition groups', while Ethier refers to it as transition by transfer of power.[73] Linz has no equivalent. Huntington believes it to have occurred in eleven out of 35 cases of third wave democratization and to have constituted the second largest category of regime change. Among the countries said to experience this type of change are Bolivia (1979–80), Uruguay (1982–85) and South Korea (1985–87).[74] The essence of extrication is negotiation between regime reformers and opposition moderates, with both realizing that neither can achieve democratization alone. There is often a distinct sequence of steps:[75]

1. The regime engages in liberalization, and begins to lose power and authority.
2. The opposition exploits this to intensify action in the hope of bringing down the government.
3. The government reacts forcefully to contain this.
4. The leaders of both sides see a standoff emerge and begin to explore the possibility of a negotiated transition.

This process often goes in cycles of protest and repression before the stage of negotiation is reached. Both sides will be divided and there will be a high degree of uncertainty about how to proceed.

Before negotiations can begin, each side must grant a degree of legitimacy to the other, while each will also have an interest in strengthening their negotiating partners against the radicals on either side. The negotiations will involve the extension of guarantees.

Transition Through Replacement

This 'occurred when opposition groups took the lead in bringing about democracy, and the authoritarian regime collapsed or was overthrown.' This is Huntington's term, and it is equivalent to Linz's 'ruptura', Share and Mainwaring's 'transition after regime break-down or collapse', Share's 'transition through rupture',[76] and Ethier's 'transition through abandonment of power'.[77] It is said to have occurred in Portugal (1975), Greece (1974) and Argentina (1983). Replacement has been most common in the third wave movement from personal dictatorship. Democratic reformers have been less important in this type of transition; reformers within the regime are weak, and the impetus for democratization comes from the growing strength of opposition allied to the increasing weakness of the regime. This process sees no emphasis upon procedural continuity and backward legitimacy, with the new leaders seeking to justify their actions and positions in terms of what they sought to achieve in the future. There are usually three phases to replacement:[78]

1. The struggle by opposition forces to produce the collapse of the regime;
2. The actual collapse;
3. The working out of processes of democracy-building, which may involve disputes between the former oppositionist forces.

In practice, the distinction between these modes of transition will not always be easy to see. The principle which underlies the distinctions is the comparative roles played by regime and opposition in the process: where elements within the regime play the leading role in structuring the course of change it is transaction, where the opposition and the regime both play prominent roles it is extrication, and where the regime plays little role it is replacement. Conceptually these differences are easy to see, but in practice these modes are not clearly distinct. Some transitions that begin as one form turn into another; it has been common for transitions seeming to take the course of transaction and extrication to turn into replacement, as the initial moves on the part of a government to liberalize are overrun by pressures released from below by this process. However, in Huntington's view, although all historical cases 'combined elements of two or more transition processes ... [v]irtually every historical case ... more clearly approximated one type of process than others'.[79] But regardless of the mode of transition, the essence of this process involves interaction between government and opposition, the dynamics and forms which this takes.

Although the transition school has identified the categories discussed above as the principal elements in the process of democratization, these categories have not been fitted together to provide a coherent theory of democratization. In different cases of regime change these various elements have interacted in different ways, and in some cases, not all of them have been present. But this does not mean that the relationship between them is either completely random or arbitrary; while the process may not be highly structured, nor is it completely unstructured. One way of seeking to bring some sense of structuring to this has been through the notion of path dependency.[80] The strength of the path dependency approach is that it escaped from the focus on an essentially contingent situation to make provision for the structuring effects of both the legacy from the past and of decisions by the contemporary actors on the course of future options and development. Path dependency recognized that when actors made decisions, it was in a context structured by a combination of legacies from the past and their own decisions. This shift away from an essentially contingent analysis in principle made theorization more possible.

Path Dependence

The most important theoretical work on democratization to appear since the O'Donnell/Schmitter/Whitehead volumes is that by Juan J. Linz and Alfred Stepan.[81] As the authors correctly claim, this is the first book that covers a range of different cases of democratization yet speaks with a 'single authorial voice'; it is not a collection of case studies by different authors, but an attempt to theorize various aspects of the transition process and demonstrate the utility of this by application to various cases, all of which are written by the volume authors.

The Linz/Stepan approach constitutes a significant advance upon that of O'Donnell/Schmitter/Whitehead because it seeks to do what many writers have called for[82] and which the earlier work did not do: to relate the strategic choices that élites make (and upon which O'Donnell/Schmitter/Whitehead concentrate) to the structural constraints within which they must act. Linz and Stepan begin from what they see as essential to the establishment of a consolidated democracy. Accepting Rustow's point[83] that a precondition for democratization is national unity, in the sense that the population broadly accepts the existing state as constituting the relevant political unit for their future, Linz and Stepan see five interacting and reinforcing arenas as crucial to consolidation:

1. A free and lively civil society 'where self-organizing groups, movements, and individuals, relatively autonomous from the state, attempt to articulate values, create associations and solidarities, and advance their interests'.[84]
2. A relatively autonomous and valued political society. This is an arena within which the polity organizes itself to exercise control over public power and the state apparatus.
3. The rule of law 'to ensure legal guarantees for citizens' freedoms and independent associational life'.[85]
4. A state bureaucracy which can be used by the democratic government; this is important for making the government effective and thereby generating a support base.
5. Institutionalized economic society, meaning a set of norms, institutions and regulations that mediate between state and market. A legal and regulatory framework instituted by the government is the most common form this takes.

When these five arenas are highly developed, the situation is most favourable for successful democratic consolidation, and the less work the democratizers have to do to achieve that end. The weaker these arenas, the more difficult consolidation becomes.

These five arenas are also linked to the question of transition and how that process unrolls. Linz and Stepan discuss this through an analysis of the way regime type affects transition. Many writers have argued that the form and contours of the non-democratic regime will affect both the process of transition and of the subsequent post-transition regime,[86] and Linz and Stepan agree with this view. They argue that there are basically four types of non-democratic regime which can succumb to democratization:[87]

1. Totalitarianism. This is characterized by the absence of any social, economic or political pluralism, by an elaborate and guiding messianic ideology, continuing extensive and intensive popular mobilization (i.e. embracing most areas of life), and a leadership which rules (often charismatically) within undefined limits and with great unpredictability for both members of the regime and ordinary citizens. This is viewed as an ideal type, and therefore never realized in its ideal form.
2. Post-totalitarianism. This is characterized by limited but not responsible social, economic and institutional pluralism but almost no political pluralism, a guiding ideology still formally in place but to which actual commitment has waned, routine mobilization without the commitment and enthusiasm, and a leadership concerned for its personal security and operating in a more routinized fashion. The authors distinguish between three types of post-totalitarianism, which they see in terms of a continuum[88]:
   (a) early post-totalitarianism, which is 'very close to the totalitarian ideal type but differs from it on at least one key dimension, normally some constraints on the leader';
   (b) frozen post-totalitarianism 'in which, despite the persistent tolerance of some civil society critics of the regime, almost all the other control mechanisms of the party-state stay in place for a long period and do not evolve';
   (c) mature post-totalitarianism 'in which there has been significant change in all the dimensions of the post-totalitarian regime except that politically the leading role of the official party is still sacrosanct'.
3. Authoritarianism. This is based on Juan Linz's classic discussion of Spain[89] and is a system characterized by limited but not responsible political pluralism and often quite extensive social and economic pluralism (sometimes including some space for semi-opposition), no elaborate and guiding ideology but with 'distinctive mentalities', no continuing popular mobilization (although it could occur on an episodic basis), and a leadership operating within formally ill-defined but actually quite predictable parameters.

4. Sultanism. This is a system characterized by the fusion of private and public power in which the leader may interfere arbitrarily in all areas of life. There may be economic and social pluralism, but it is subject to despotic and unpredictable intervention, there is no ideology but glorification of the leader and the manipulation of symbols by that leader, no continuing popular mobilization although it may occur on an episodic basis, and leadership is highly personalistic and arbitrary.

The five arenas can be related to these four regime types: all arenas will be at a low level of development under both totalitarian and sultanist regimes, and at higher levels under post-totalitarian and authoritarian regimes, with the precise levels differing according to the circumstances of the case (e.g. the authors' distinction between 'early', 'frozen' and 'mature' post-totalitarianism).

Linz and Stepan try systematically to relate these regime types to transition paths,[90] attempting to show how the contours of the latter are shaped by the conditions of the former. They identify four main paths of transition, plus a residual set of regime-specific circumstances:

1. 'Reforma-pactada, ruptura-pactada', or pacted transition. A pacted transition is impossible under totalitarianism and most forms of sultanism because there is no room for either a democratic opposition or a moderate wing of the leadership. This may be possible under mature post-totalitarianism, and is possible under authoritarianism, where leadership tends not to be unitary and monolithic and space exists for opposition forces.
2. Defeat in war. In the cases of totalitarianism and sultanism, this could lead to a democratic outcome only under external supervision and guidance. A similar situation would apply to many post-totalitarian regimes, although the mature post-totalitarian regime may be closer to the authoritarian regime in this regard. Defeat of an authoritarian regime in war (or its collapse as a result of war) could lead to a democratic transition if democratic opposition forces were able to assert themselves; the regime would have a weak negotiating position.
3. Regime overthrow followed by interim government. Given the absence of political society and the weakness of civil society under totalitarianism, an interim government is unlikely, but should one occur, there would be little substantial pressure for

elections. The government may therefore seek electoral legitimation, but this would not ensure democratization. The overthrow of a sultanist regime could result in groups around the former leader claiming power on the basis of their support for the rising and the weakness of alternative political forces, and postpone democratic change in the name of pressing domestic reform. The best chance for democratization following the fall of sultanism is if the rising is supported internationally and led by democrats who set a date for elections and allow free contestation for power.[91] In the case of early and frozen post-totalitarian regimes, with weak civil and political societies, regime overthrow could lead to élites close to the former regime gaining power and legitimating this electorally; in cases of mature post-totalitarianism, opposition activists could form an interim government and move toward election. In the case of authoritarian regimes, oppositionists could demand early elections and thereby move the society along the path of democratization, but if the pressure for elections is weak, an interim government may seek to postpone elections and consolidate its own rule.

4. Extrication from rule by hierarchically-led military as institution. This path is not available under totalitarianism, post-totalitarianism and sultanism because these forms of rule deny the possibility of military rule. Under authoritarianism, if the 'military as institution' feels under threat, it may pressure the 'military as government' to withdraw and hold 'extrication elections'. The severity of the perceived threat and the strength of democratic forces in civil and political society will determine the length of transition and the concessions the military can gain as part of the price for withdrawal.

As well as these four paths, Linz and Stepan identify a number of other regime-specific circumstances. These too relate to the structure (broadly interpreted) of the regime. They can be expressed in terms of general principles:

1. A totalitarian leadership could split, opening the way for popular mobilization which could lead to either a reimposition of totalitarian controls by force, or the transformation of the regime to a post-totalitarian one.

2. If a totalitarian regime is supported by an external hegemon

which withdraws its support, domestic power relationships can change, with an increase in both popular mobilization and the costs of repression. If the regime falls, the weakness of civil and political society can result in control by people connected with the old regime.

3. If a post-totalitarian regime is confronted with a crisis, it could collapse, leading to a non-democratic takeover by alternative élites, democratization or chaos.

4. If a post-totalitarian regime is supported by an external hegemon which withdraws its support, it could collapse. If an 'early' post-totalitarian regime, it is likely control will be taken by people connected with the old regime; if it is a 'late' post-totalitarian regime, leaders could come from civil society and institute free elections.[92]

5. If an authoritarian regime led by a non-hierarchical military (i.e. by a group of military officers but not by the military as institution) collapses, the imposition of civilian democratic control and of trials on the military will be easier than if the regime had been led by an hierarchical military, i.e. military as institution.

6. If a civilian-led authoritarian regime initiates democratization, any agreements made will be only as powerful as the electorate and elected officials allow them to be. The new government will have more freedom to do what it wants than had the authoritarian regime been led by a hierarchical military.

7. In a sultanist regime, the death of the leader will usually lead to attempted succession by a family member. If successful, no transition will occur.

8. If a sultan is supported externally, withdrawal of that support can lead to the collapse of the regime, or to the sultan seeking to gain a form of electoral validation. The role of the external patron will be important in structuring this process.

9. The most likely domestic cause of the fall of a sultanist regime is domestic revolt, thereby activating path number 3 noted above.

These residual circumstances are not analytically as significant as the four paths to transition discussed by Linz and Stepan. They are really codicils to the broader categorization, acknowledging that a schema of regime categorization of this sort may be useful for the broad brushstrokes of interpretation it generates, but cannot capture the nuances of transition in all individual cases. This is also recognized by the way in which Linz and Stepan discuss a series of variables, leading to what they call 'middle range propositions', which affect transition.[93] They discuss two actor-centred variables, the institutional structure of the non-democratic regime and who initiates and controls the transition, and three contextual variables, international influences, the political economy of legitimacy and coercion, and constitution-making environments.

In discussing the institutional structure of the non-democratic regime, Linz and Stepan identify four basic types:

1. Hierarchical military. This type of institutional configuration in power is only possible in Linz and Stepan's authoritarian type of regime. In this, the officer corps sees itself as part of the state apparatus with interests and functions that transcend the interests of the government of the day, and if they believe that the costs to the military as institution of remaining in power are too great, they favour the passing of power to civilians. The more hierarchical the military, the weaker the civilian forces and the less they are forced from power, the better able the military will be to shape the terms of its withdrawal.

2. Non-hierarchical military. If the regime is led by a non-hierarchically led military (e.g. a regime of colonels and majors) and it encounters difficulties, the military as institution may be encouraged to restore hierarchy by supporting or waging an extrication coup. This would be easier than if it was a hierarchically-led military regime. This also makes it easier for the subsequent regime to conduct trials of former military governors since these are not seen as constituting a trial of the military as institution.

3. Civilian leadership. A civilian leadership is more likely to initiate and participate in democratic transition than a military leadership because its members tend to be more able and willing to negotiate complicated reform pacts, possess closer links with society, and are more likely to see themselves as potential winners from the transition process. But civilians may also be better able than the military to introduce liberalization and stop it short of democratization without undermining their position.

4. Sultanistic leadership. The greatest chance for democratization is the death of the leader because this can cause the regime to collapse given the fusing of personal and political power. But

given that there is little space for democratic oppositional activity under sultanistic rule, the overthrow of the regime usually occurs through popular unrest, assassination or revolt, leading to an interim government.

In the discussion of who initiates and controls the transition, Linz and Stepan argue that transitions initiated by hierarchical state-led or regime-led forces do not lead to interim or provisional governments, while those sparked by popular revolt, regime collapse, armed revolution or non-hierarchically-led military coup tend to facilitate the emergence of an interim government. Whether such a government will pursue democratization depends upon its nature and perceptions. Elections are seen as being crucial for the furtherance of democratization, because these are the main means for new political actors to emerge and gain democratic credentials and for democratic structures to form. Elections are most likely when civilians form the core of the interim government, least likely when this role is played by the military.

The international influences identified by Linz and Stepan are foreign policy, zeitgeist and diffusion, and these are discussed in the same way as these factors have been discussed above. The contextual variable they call 'the political economy of legitimacy and coercion' refers to the way in which poor economic performance can undercut the legitimacy of authoritarian regimes, but in their view this becomes a real crisis only when popular blame for the situation is directed at the regime and an alternative is popularly evident. The third contextual variable, constitution-making environments, mainly refers to regime consolidation, although it is possible to argue that non-democratic rulers may be more willing to accede to democratic demands if they perceive some protection for what they hold dear to be enshrined in the constitution.

The Linz-Stepan discussion provides a very rich analysis of the ways in which the patterns of transition are shaped by various factors, especially regime type. Their propositions are empirically testable and add considerably to our capacity to think about transition in a systematic fashion. But, despite the richness of the analysis and the suggestiveness of many of its arguments, the overall schema is very difficult to apply in a way which will produce generalizations about transition that can be applied broadly. This is due, in part, to the complexity of the schema. Linz and Stepan talk about five arenas crucial for consolidation, four regime types (with some sub-types), four transition paths, nine regime-specific circumstances, four institutional structures of regimes, and three contextual variables. Although they suggest systematic linkages between some of these (most particularly regime types and transition paths), there is no explanation of how they all fit together. If these variables do not relate in a systematic and regular fashion, but can instead link together in a wide variety of patterns, effective generalization is rendered impossible. This is shown by the effect the nine regime-specific circumstances have on the relationship between regime type and transition path. These regime-specific circumstances are meant to account for variations in the relationships between regime type and transition paths that Linz and Stepan draw, but their effect is to call into question the basic patterns they identify: if so many regime-specific circumstances are necessary, how valid are the basic structures of the theory, the relationships between regime types and transition paths? The schema thus has such a bewildering array of paths, arenas and contingencies and generates so many variables and possible combinations, that it is virtually impossible to get any sense of predictability or consistency, or of a pattern of the general dynamics of regime change.

The Linz/Stepan schema has two more problems. First, its explanatory core is regime types, and yet one of these, the authoritarian, is so broad that a variety of different institutional configurations can be accommodated within it. And yet, as the Linz/Stepan discussion of the institutional structures of the regimes demonstrates, the precise institutional configuration can be crucial in structuring the subsequent course of development. This suggests that this category of regime type requires greater refinement if it is to be useful as an explanatory variable. Second, the focus on regime structure tends to obscure the role played by non-regime actors. As is argued in Chapter 4, this is a crucial gap in all of the transition literature. Thus despite the sophistication and innovativeness of this schema, it does not enable the sort of broad generalization essential for adequate theorization of regime change. For this what is required is a schema with fewer explanatory variables and which gives greater scope to non-regime civil society actors.

4

Beyond the Elites?

The dominance of the élite focus in studies of democratic transition was a reaction to the failure of the earlier attempt to identify prerequisites for democracy discussed in Chapter 1. But the shift away from a search for prerequisites seemed to bring a downplaying of all notions of structural considerations as being of any relevance to the explanation of transition. Not all authors writing on transition have eschewed structural factors (for example, in the O'Donnell/Schmitter/Whitehead collection the studies of Venezuela and Brazil give some attention to structural factors underpinning the respective transitions[1]), but the overwhelming emphasis of this school of analysis has been upon contingent choice and the role of élites. In the words of one critic of this approach:

> the dynamics of the transition revolve around strategic interactions and tentative arrangements between actors with uncertain power resources aimed at defining who will legitimately be entitled to play in the political game, what criteria will determine the winners and losers, and what limits will be placed on the issues at stake.[2]

Transition is explained in terms of the changing relationships between different élites or sections of élites. The balance between hardliners and reformers in the regime and between moderates and radicals in the opposition, the ability of the reformers and the moderates to come together in agreement and thereby to manage a measured shift towards democracy; these are the principal sorts of considerations for writers of the transition school. The strategic choices made by these groups and by individuals within them are the main currency of the transition. The process is thereby fundamentally shaped by the perceptions, beliefs and actions of the élites, and it is the acknowledgement of this which enables one author (Samuel P. Huntington) to prescribe checklists of the sorts of actions which would-be democratizers should follow.

This focus on individual choice, élites and decision-making is linked to two elements of this scholarly endeavour, the definition of its boundaries and an assumption about the nature of the process being studied. The definition of boundaries refers to the way in which the focus of study is usually defined very tightly in terms of the period of the actual transition from one regime to another. Most studies begin with the emergence of splits in the old regime and end with the establishment of a democratic successor, although precisely when these occur remains uncertain in many cases. What is important about this focus is that it encompasses only a very short period of time. Sometimes it is less than a year, rarely is it more than five years. This short time span (and even five years is a short period of time) by definition obscures the operation of longer-term trends, and although it does not necessarily mean that the results of such trends cannot be appreciated, it does encourage an emphasis upon the more immediate. Within a short time period, what is most apparent is the activity of political actors, the course of day to day and month to month manoeuvring, not the structuring impact emanating from forces external to that time period. Because of this focus on the immediate, it is the short-term tactical manoeuvring which fills the canvas, the sound and fury of élite conflict and compromise, and the political posturing of the main actors.

The other element linked to this focus is the assumption that what characterizes these periods of regime change is uncertainty. In the words of O'Donnell and Schmitter, transitions are characterized by 'insufficient structural or behavioral parameters to guide and predict the outcome'[3] and there is a 'high degree of indeterminacy.'[4] The process is seen as being one in which rules are few, predictability is low and the outcome therefore always uncertain. Such an assumption encourages the focus on immediate actors and their actions. If the situation is uncertain, it is useless to look for underlying structuring principles (although this does not prevent authors from offering a series of prudential rules for would-be democratizers) or factors which might generate some consistency both within specific cases and across cases. If everything is uncertain, actors have complete freedom of action, and if this is the case, the only logical focus is upon those actors.

However, the problem with this sort of focus is that it is in danger of degenerating into a form of voluntarism, where everything is pliable and subject to shaping by individual or collective political actors. If individual actors are omnipotent, then not only does this render attention to others than these actors irrelevant, but it also makes the task of theorizing change well nigh impossible. Any approach which assumes the potency of individual action within a context of a high level of uncertainty by definition makes sustainable generalization and substantive theorization impossible. The best that can be done is the drawing of prudential rules designed to achieve a successful outcome of democratization based upon analysis of precedents, but these are very different from the sorts of generalizations necessary to sustain theoretical explanation. They are principles of action which, in the eyes of the analyst, contributed to the success or failure of previous attempts at democratization. They are not underlying explanatory principles which contribute to an explanation of the dynamics of the whole process. Indeed, while the level of analysis remains at that of individual actor contingency in a context of uncertainty, such explanatory principles cannot be found. The problem is that this mode of analysis, which is essentially the application of the rational actor model to regime change,[5] can only produce probabilistic analysis of the type which may be able to define what a rational person would do in such circumstances but cannot provide an explanation which will stand up to the complexity of real life. The focus must be widened in order to make the generation of theoretical explanatory principles possible, and by so doing, recognize that the individual actors do not act upon a blank sheet of paper nor in accord purely with calculations regarding different actors' preferences, comparative power resources and opportunity costs. They are constrained, shaped and influenced by factors which, if a satisfactory explanation is to be obtained, must be included in the analysis.

One consequence of the élite focus of the transition literature is the low profile of the mass of the population and non-political élite actors in these explanations. Few studies make no reference to the masses, but rarely are they a central part of the explanation. The discussion by O'Donnell and Schmitter which seeks to draw out conclusions from the case studies[6] does include some acknowledgement of possible mass involvement. They acknowledge that mass mobilization may occur from within civil society and that some groups in particular may organize to press their interests, with the result that democratization may be pushed further than it otherwise would have been. They also recognize that elections can be an important part of the democratization process, and this of necessity gives the populace a role to play. But the overwhelming emphasis is upon élite political actors, both as the crucial actors in the dynamics of democratization and as those best placed to ensure a democratic outcome; it is assumed that such an outcome will be more likely if managing the democratic transition is left in the unhindered hands of the élites.[7] But this sort of approach seriously underemphasizes the role of the masses who, even when not consciously mobilized into the political process, may play a significant part in structuring the unrolling of regime change.[8] Indeed, their role is implicit in much of the élite-focused analysis of the transition writers.

Most discussions of democratization begin with the breakdown of the old regime, but, as argued in Chapter 2, little attempt is made to theorize this. While one might not expect such an attempt from individual case studies, such collective endeavours as those of O'Donnell, Schmitter and Whitehead[9], and Baloyra[10] might have been expected to present an attempt to theorize about the circumstances and processes of breakdown more systematically. Certainly the general principles of the process as they see it are clear: usually a performance failure generates a crisis within the regime, leading to a split between different elements of that regime, one of which then seeks to follow a path of change in order to stabilize the regime and is opposed in that by a group which sees a further consolidation or tightening of rule to be the answer to the problem. Such an explanation is fine as far as it goes, but the problem is that it does not go far enough. No attempt is made to explain why some performance failures bring on regime crisis and some do not. Nor why in some circumstances a regime will split and in others it will not.[11] Nor is any systematic attempt made to compare the way different types of regimes respond to such crises. While admitting the mass of the populace (and its relationship to the government) into the analysis would not resolve all of these questions, it could assist the analysis both in terms of answering these questions and creating the basis for a more consistent process of theorization, generalization and comparison. How can the admission of the masses into the analysis help achieve these ends?

Any attempt to explain regime crisis and the subsequent dynamics of how the regime responds to such a challenge must involve analysis of the nature of the regime itself, its basis of legitimacy, the structures and strains within it, and the dynamics whereby it functions. But also central is the relationship between the regime and the society at large. Is the regime autonomous from the society over which it rules, or is it deeply embedded within that society? Are there clear channels of access into the regime on the part of the populace, or are the regime-mass linkages purely means of exercising control from above, i.e. mobilizational rather than participatory? The closer a regime is to autonomy, the less influence the society can exercise on it and its functioning. As a corollary, the more embedded the regime is in the society, the greater the influence on the regime and its contours exercised by that society. In practice, very few regimes are sufficiently autonomous from society that they can afford totally to ignore the views and feelings of the populace over whom they rule; even the Soviet regime, usually acknowledged as one in which the populace exercised very little influence in policy terms, maintained an economic policy involving massive budget subsidies to living standards, which ultimately proved crippling, at least in part to ensure popular passivity. Unless it seeks to rule principally through terror, a regime must always remain sensitive to what its subjects will accept. This will enable it to maintain the fiction of consent as well as greatly reducing the direct costs of maintaining its rule through the deployment of substantial force. None of the regimes which fell as part of the third wave (including the former communist regimes) had sought to rely overwhelmingly upon overt force, although of course all had the option of the use of force in their armoury. As a result, all were characterized in part by concern for popular attitudes. This can have direct implications for a regime. A number of aspects of this are important.

The most obvious way in which popular attitude could be significant relates to the implications of failings in regime performance. All sorts of regime performance failures could have reverberations within the populace at large. Most directly, failures in economic performance (which seem to have been a high proportion of those types of failures which have brought on regime transitions) can have an immediate effect on the populace and its standard of living. Even failures in foreign policy, such as the Cypriot affair for the Greek government and the Malvinas conflict for the Argentinian government, can have popular effects. Not only can such developments give rise to popular resentment because of the sullying of national honour they are thought to bring on, but they can also lead to popular recognition that the regime is itself deficient, if not in the formulation of appropriate policy, then in its implementation. Such things would not matter were it not for the potential power that is seen to lie within the populace. When the regime recognizes that, ultimately, its capacity to rule rests upon popular acceptance, or at least an absence of popular opposition, it must do all within its power to ensure that that opposition is not aroused. Consequently it needs to respond when performance failures become apparent. Thus, while regime breakdown may not be brought about by popular action, it is very often the worry that such action may begin which pushes the regime to seek to meet the problem through liberalization. Indeed, there would be little reason to pursue a path of liberalization unless it was to meet concerns about popular, or popularly-based, opposition.[12] In this sense, the crisis of the regime manifested in the split over how best to stabilize its rule and ensure that it can continue, often assumes a fear of popular opposition and recognition of the need to offset it. Thus, even if popular activity was not a direct cause of regime breakdown, fear of the response of the populace is usually a factor in shaping the nature of the regime's response to its problems.

Popular involvement is also important during the phase of transition following the breakdown. Even when the populace was not a direct actor in the circumstances of the breakdown of the regime, the loosening of political control and erosion of rules of the game central to the transition means that the capacity for popular involvement is increased. What is crucial is how that involvement manifests itself, and it has been here that the transition literature has been especially deficient. For all of its passing acknowledgement of the possible importance of civil society and of elections, and in some of the case studies of the role of particular groups (such as in Cardoso's study of entrepreneurs in the Brazilian case[13]), the transition literature has tended to see the potential role of the populace principally in terms of street demonstrations, strikes, riots and mass movements. Thus, in Maxwell's study of Portugal,[14] the role of the peasants in taking direct action and thereby radicalizing the agenda is noted, but in those cases where no similar sort of mass mobilization occurred, little attention is given to the people. The result is that élite interactions are portrayed as taking place within a rarefied arena, isolated from the populace and society within which it is ultimately encapsulated. Politics is thereby divorced from its social moorings, with all participants somehow disconnected from the broader social and economic milieu.

The clearest indication of this problem is the way the transition literature treats potential vehicles for mass participation in politics, especially labour unions and political parties. Historically both have been important mechanisms for structuring and organizing mass mobilization in political life. They have not only been means of organizing popularly-based protest activity, but have acted as channels for the transmission of popular views into the political process. Notwithstanding the applicability of Michels' thinking to such organizations, they have been able at times to bring a non-élite view to bear on the course of political discussion and negotiation. Yet the transition literature rarely looks at this side of their activities. When party leaders or the heads of labour unions are shown as participants in the process of transition, they are almost invariably portrayed as élite actors having little connection with their mass base. And while it may be appropriate to see them as élites, the question needs to be asked how they attained such status. The answer must lie in their relationship with their putative mass base. If they are outsiders to the regime, taking part in negotiations not because they are a fraction of the regime itself but because they are head of a party or union, then the only reason they have been included in the negotiation is because of the potential power their support base represents. Their political capital lies in the popular energy they could bring onto the streets if they needed to. Indeed, the whole notion of a pact, so central to much of the transition literature, makes no sense unless this relationship between leaders and at least a section of the populace is assumed: those with whom the pact is agreed must be able to carry their followers with them because if they cannot do this, the guarantees intrinsic to the pact are meaningless.[15]

The failure to see such organizations as unions and parties, the classic linkages between regime and society, in this way and thereby as reflective of the importance of the élite–mass relationship, is not compensated for by the sort of references to civil society evident in the transition literature noted above. All such references do is provide a convenient framework within which various groups of the population can be noted and said sometimes to be influential in the transition. But such references are no substitute for the detailed analysis of society and of the sorts of organizations which may emerge within it to exercise pressure in favour of democracy. It is such organizations, and the culture which sustains this type of organization, which is often fundamental for progress toward democracy because it gives substance to the democratic aspirations of the populace and thereby represents the sort of moral pressure which is often influential in helping to structure the way élites act. But it is not enough simply to assume that civil society is there or to use it as a bland formula to cover all the sorts of social forces which method- ologically have no part in élite-focused analysis. If such forces are to be admitted into the explanation in a theoretically-informed way, civil society must be demonstrated to exist by sustained analysis of the structures and processes at work within society at large and how they are linked to élite politics. The notion of civil society must become an analytical tool, not a means of avoiding such analysis. This leads to two observations, the first concerning the nature of democracy, and the second on how these structures and processes may be studied.

Implicit in the transition school's approach is a conservative con- ception of democracy. Most scholars writing on transitions adopt a purely procedural definition of a democratic system, usually relying upon notions of popular contestation and control exercised through the electoral process. This type of definition is a legitimate one to adopt, and it is defensible given that what is needed is a reasonably clear set of criteria whereby one can judge whether a system is democratic or not (even if it is not always clear that those criteria have been adequately applied). However, if scholars restrict their conception of democracy to merely procedural principles, not only are they working with an impoverished notion of democracy, but there are also clear problems for their analysis. One consequence of this approach is that democracy is something which is to be achieved through the exertions of élites acting in ways which will ensure the continuing stability of the system. The achievement of democracy is seen to be a matter of designing the right rules of the game, of constructing institutions which will ensure a system emerges which meets the minimum procedural principles identified. In achieving this, primacy should be given to those who can work together cooperatively, reaching agreements which will ensure a democratic outcome while safeguarding major interests in the system. Democracy is thus something to be achieved by anti-democ- ratic means; indeed, some even come close to saying that it cannot be achieved when there is significant mass involvement.[16] This sort of emphasis is also apparent in most of the literature on the consoli- dation of democracy. The élite focus is reflected in the way in which much of the discussion concerns the most appropriate form of insti- tutional mix, the relative virtues of the presidential and parliamen- tary systems and the most appropriate type of voting system.

Certainly the references to voting systems and to the creation of party systems acknowledge that the mass of voters do have a role to play in the political system, but the concern is with the stability of the system rather than the realization of democratic values.

The stripping of democracy of its normative ideals and reduction of it only to procedural principles[17] facilitates the rational actor paradigm in explaining transitions, but it also makes democracy out to be a second best, and perhaps even temporary, solution.[18] As political élites sit down rationally to work out how the regime is to escape its crisis, democracy shorn of its ideals becomes simply one of a number of possible options they could choose. But is it really like that? Is the global ideology of democracy, which rests on the attractiveness of its ideals, of no relevance in this sort of situation? Is democracy seen in the same light as a different form of authoritarianism to that from which they are escaping? The sort of enthusiasm with which popular movements and some political actors embrace the democratic solution suggests that it is seen as not just another set of institutional arrangements. If the transition literature does not recognize this normative aspect of democracy, it cannot explain the appeal of this form of government except through the terms of the rational actor seeking personal advantage, an explanation which does not fit well with the enthusiasm often evident at this time. Furthermore, unless there is a recognition of these normative aspects of democracy, the rational actor approach cannot explain why individuals and élites commit themselves to institutionalized compromise, accommodation and mutual guarantees,[19] especially when by its nature even a procedural definition of democracy means the likelihood of a loss of power for some of the political élites. Why will people restrict their possible future power and privileges? Perhaps it is because they know that they must make some accommodation with rival élites if they are to retain any of their past power and position, but if the aim was to do this, a democratic outcome would not be the sort of scheme one would expect them to choose. Certainly self interest will be an influential factor here, but alone it is insufficient; it may explain élite accommodation, but not the sort of accommodation that is reflected in a democratic outcome. To explain why élites would opt for such a system, even when the strongest proponent of the rational actor school acknowledges that its greatest feature is uncertainty,[20] reference to the normative implications and attraction of democracy is essential. Without it, the explanation is incomplete.

Turning to the question of how the structures and processes at work in society which then influence democratization are to be studied, we need once again to widen our focus far beyond that evident in the work of the transition school. It is clear that in seeking to understand the dynamics of a process of democratization, strategic choices made by political élites are important. An approach which focused solely upon structural factors like class, industrialization, international location or institutional configuration cannot explain the process of democratization satisfactorily; it may tell us why pressures for democratization mounted, but it cannot explain why a shift towards democracy occurred at the time it did, nor can it tell us about the precise course of that shift. What such an approach does is to illuminate the structural constraints and opportunities within which political actors act, but in doing so recognition of the role of those actors is essential for adequate understanding.[21] But, similarly, the sort of account offered by the transition school focusing upon individual volition is incomplete unless it takes into account the structural constraints and opportunities within which political actors must act. Such actors do not play out their roles in a vacuum, but in a context consisting of the structures from the past continuing into the present. They must deal with the legacy of what has gone before rather than create their own environment *de novo*. Entrenched social, political and economic structures are important in shaping the actions of political élites. In the words of Terry Karl,

> the decisions made by the various actors respond to and are conditioned by the types of socioeconomic structures and political institutions already present. These can be decisive in that they may either restrict or enhance the options available to different political actors attempting to construct democracy.[22]

Strategic choice must be related to the structural constraints and opportunities confronting political élites; indeed, the definition of 'strategic', and the identity of different relevant élites, will in part be determined by those constraints and opportunities.

The way in which this legacy of the past has usually been approached by those few looking at democratization who accept its importance has been through the notion of path dependency. The quotation from Karl above is a classic, simple statement of the essence of path dependency: contemporary choices are structured by the legacies of former choices. The influence of the past on the present can appear to be highly determinative, as in the formulation that a route of development chosen earlier tends to re-establish itself over time by shaping choices for future development,[23] or it can appear to be more contextual, subtly shaping the arena of events and the choices which appear relevant to contending élites. It is this latter approach which is most useful, recognising that political élites do have a degree of autonomy of action, but that they also must act within certain constraints. However, the danger of the path dependency approach, especially in the hands of those whose concerns are intellectually shaped by a focus on the immediate, is that this can lead to a static analysis; the past legacy is taken as a given and conceptualized in narrowly contemporary terms, with no attention devoted to the longer term historical dynamic of which it is part. In this approach the focus is on the structures as they are at the immediate time of analysis, with no attention given to how they developed or the dynamic balance of forces within them. This is the essence of the criticism of path dependency that it cannot explain how a particular model of development came to be locked in to a particular society.[24] This criticism may be thought to be less important than it appears, because those who seek to use path dependency to explain contemporary instances of democratization are not interested in understanding the longer-term course of historical development of the society concerned. But unless a longer-term perspective is adopted, there is no way of knowing the strength, importance or dynamic structure of the socio-historical forces which constitute the legacy from the past and help to shape contemporary options.

Longer-term socio-historical factors can manifest themselves in three main forms: institutional structures, actors and culture. The types of institutions which exist at the time of transition are a function of the course of development which preceded that point in time. Those institutions may be newly formed, emerging under the authoritarian regime currently experiencing pressures for democratization, or they may stem from some period before that regime came to power. In either event, the impetus intrinsic to them should ensure that, in the absence of conscious action to eliminate them, they will continue on through the transition period and thereby help to structure the dynamics of that process. They will have interests to protect and advance, and simply by being there may be important forces which political actors must take into account. Similarly, the actors who are present at the time of transition, or who emerge as part of that process, will have their roots in the past, the same as the institutions. Indeed, it is often the nature of the institutions which determines the identity of the relevant actors. The clearest case of this is the nature of the regime (see below); military élites tend to be much more important in the exit from a military regime than they are when it is a civilian system which is experiencing change. Culture relates not simply to the generalized culture of the society, but to the organizational and élite cultures which encapsulate the activity of political actors. These, too, are related to the course of past development, and particularly to the institutional structures which have been able to sustain themselves. While in many respects intangible, the cultures are carried in the collective consciousness of the élites and in the behavioural patterns which are generally accepted as defining appropriate behaviour. In combination these three manifestations of socio-historical constraints, institutional structures, actors and culture, significantly shape the options confronting political actors and help to structure the course of democratic transition.

A crucial structuring element in the course of transition is the nature of the authoritarian regime in power at the time transition begins. The type of regime will help to shape a variety of aspects of the transition process, as Linz and Stepan have argued. These include the identity of the main political actors in that process and some of the sorts of resources which they can bring to bear as they seek to realize their aims. Attempts to design typologies of authoritarian regimes have been legion, but what is important for our current purposes is the combination of elements that together constitute the contours of the regime. In principle, there are two main types of component of such regimes, with each component including a number of sub-categories. These components are:

1. Military. The military as institution is not a monolithic body even though it is usually characterized by significantly higher levels of discipline than civilian organizations. Lines of potential fracture in the military follow divisions between the different arms of the military establishment (army, navy, air force, palace guards, security apparatus, etc), the strongly hierarchical rank nature of the institution, and regional differences. If one arm of the military is traditionally dominant, and usually this is the army, it will be likely to lead the military government; if not, a military junta including the heads of the different sections will be likely to be the ruling institution.
2. Civilian. In principle, the range of civilian organizations is

greater than that within the military. Different bases upon which such organizations rest can be identified, reflecting the different nature of the organizations themselves. One relevant distinction is that of political party, whereby party élites participate in the ruling councils of the regime. In the case of single-party regimes, such élites may completely dominate political power, but even when a party is not dominant, representatives of such organizations often can be found within the regime's power structure. Another type of division is that of bureaucratic or technocratic interest, whereby the upper echelons of the regime are dominated by representatives of major bureaucratic hierarchies. Government departments are often the major players here, but also important could be business and industrial organizations. The corporatist state is a common form of this type of regime.

The balance between these different sorts of components determines the contours of the regime. All regimes will contain such a balance: even strict military regimes usually contain a civilian component[25] while most civilian regimes will seek to ensure military support, and this often means some form of military involvement. Perhaps the sort of system where the military (as opposed to a militarized style) has been least in evidence has been the Communist single-party states, yet even here, especially in the last years of Communist rule, the coercive arms of the state (especially the security apparatus but also the military) have had a prominent place in some governing circles; Poland has been the clearest example.

Sometimes the balance between these types of institutions is obscured by the dominance of a single leader, as in Spain under Franco, Portugal under Salazar, Argentina under Peron and Chile under Pinochet. Under such circumstances where the single most important dynamic within the regime is individual leadership, the institutional balance between the various types of bodies may appear less important. However, the leader does not rest on thin air. He requires an institutional structure upon which to stand, and although this may be provided in part by his personal entourage, he also has need of solid institutional supports if his rule is to be stabilized and sustained over a long period of time. Furthermore, the onset of pressures for democratization is often associated with the death of the dictator, thereby leaving the remaining institutional structures as the major organizational legacy of the regime.

The precise institutional configuration of the regime has implications for the transition. The balance between different institutions within the regime will shape the major players in the transition. When the military constitutes the major component of the regime, the internal state of that institution is decisive; if the split in the regime includes division within the military, the prospects for transition will be improved compared with a situation where there is a split between a united military and the civilian components. Even when the military is not the dominant element in the regime, its stance may be decisive; if it remains united and opposed to regime change, successful pursuit of democracy will be more difficult than if it either favours change or remains neutral.[26] Similarly, the more involved the military has been in the ruling of the country, the greater the likelihood it will have to be involved in the negotiations regarding the shift toward democracy, and the greater the effect its presence will have upon that shift. Adam Przeworski argues[27] that where the military remained cohesive and autonomous (as in the 'paradigmatic' Chile and Poland, but the same occurred in Spain, Brazil, Uruguay and South Korea), the process of extrication from the authoritarian regime overshadowed that of the constitution of a democratic one, while in those cases when military cohesion was weak due to foreign adventure (as in Greece, Portugal and Argentina) or the military was clearly under civilian control (as in Eastern Europe except for Poland), the processes of extrication and consolidation were combined. Karl and Schmitter[28] draw a contrast between Latin America and Eastern Europe. They argue that in the former, the role of the military stemming from the nature of the civil–military relationship was important, with participants in the process seeking to act in a way designed not to provoke a military coup; the overriding issue was removing the military from power without provoking it to react aggressively. In contrast, they argue that in Eastern Europe the main concern focused on civilian bureaucrats and in particular the party-state apparatus, with the main worry of participants in the transition whether that apparatus was going to sabotage that process. Thus, the identity of the main actors in the process, and some of the concerns with which they have to deal, will be shaped by the contours of the former regime.

But it is not only the contours of the regime that are important. So, too, is the regime's relationship with society. This relationship may be conceived of in a variety of ways. A common approach to this question has been to discuss the relationship in terms of state autonomy, but the problem with this sort of approach is that it focuses upon the society's impact upon the state rather than vice versa. What is of interest here is the state's impact on society, and in particular the degree to which state control has prevented the emergence of civil society forces, of potential pro-democratic political actors in society. This raises the issue of state penetration, the degree to which the state has been able to penetrate the society and to establish its control over all parts of that society. In principle, the greater the extent of state penetration and control, the less opportunity for independent actors to emerge either while the regime remains in place or when it begins to falter. In contrast, the weaker the penetration of society, the greater the possibility of independent forces developing.

As well as capacity, regime intention is also important. If a regime has the capacity thoroughly to penetrate society but seeks only to exercise overall control, then room may be left for autonomous forces predating the authoritarian regime to retain their institutional independence and a degree of coherence. However, if a regime is able to penetrate society and seeks to bring about transformation on a significant scale, the ability of pre-existing forces to retain their independence and capacity will be limited. This has implications both for the identity of actors who can play a part in the transition, and the strategy of transition that is possible. If a regime seeks (or is able) merely to control the society but not to transform it, then pre-regime political organizations may be able to sustain themselves during the regime's rule and to re-emerge onto the open political stage at the time of transition. Political parties are the most common types of such organizations[29], but labour unions too may be significant. This may be seen as civil society forces retaining their integrity in the face of authoritarian rule. In contrast, if a regime wishes and is able to implement policies of transformation, the capacity of pre-existing bodies to survive is reduced, and such survivals from the past are likely to be correspondingly less important in the course of the transition. The effect on the strategy of transition can also be considerable. According to Baohui Zhang[30], pact-making during transition is facilitated by the autonomy of the various élites during negotiations and the ability of those élites to enforce the terms of the pact upon their followers. This assumes strong societal institutions that provide for social representation and control. Zhang argues that corporatist authoritarian systems make provision for such institutions while the Communist states, with their much more extensive penetrative activities and capacities, effectively destroy such bodies. As a result, 'contemporary pacted transitions have so far only occurred in corporatist regimes.'[31] While it is not clear that this conclusion is beyond dispute (see below), the logic of the argument is clear: the structure of the regime and its relationship with society is an important influence upon the shape taken by regime transitions.

But the relationship of regime and society should not only be seen in terms of the penetration by the former of the latter: the nature of the latter in itself is important. The aspect of the society which is of most relevance here is the way in which its development produces interests which have a stake in the working out of future political arrangements and are able to play some role in this. Such interests occupy different locations in the society; some may be dominant or central, others subordinate or marginal. They will possess different types and amounts of resources which they can utilize in the polit- ical arena. And the motivations to enter that arena will differ, depending *inter alia* upon perceptions about how their interests may best be advanced and the opportunities for doing so. None of these are the result purely of immediate historical conjunction, but of the earlier course of societal development. Recognition of the impor- tance of the development of such interests has been a major concern of scholars for some time.

Scholars have long recognized the importance of longer-term his- torical analysis in understanding the genesis of such interests. This has often taken the form of study of the path to Western liberal democracy, sometimes in terms of questions about 'the rise of the West' or the positing of some sort of 'European miracle'.[32] Indeed, before the transition literature, this constituted the major alternative mode of analysis of the emergence of democracy to the search for economic prerequisites discussed in Chapter One. But it has also been approached more directly. One of the most stimulating and fruitful attempts to do this has been the work of Barrington Moore Jr;[33] stimulating because of the range of questions generated by his work, fruitful because of the extent of commentary and of concep- tual advance generated.

The approach adopted by Moore was very different to that used by many writers from the modernization school which was promi- nent in political science at his time of writing. Many of these people focused their attention on the newly-emerging independent post- colonial countries of Asia and Africa and the problems these countries had in stabilizing both political authority and democracy. Their analysis usually involved a counter-posing of the problems of backwardness, often associated with the perceived legacies of the precolonial traditional society, with the difficulties of establishing a stable democratic political structure. Implicit in this sort of approach, and sometimes even explicitly, this involved a checklist of preconditions for democracy. Such preconditions were usually a combination of cultural, structural and economic factors, and were drawn overwhelmingly from assumptions about the way modern democracies functioned and what underpinned their survival. This sort of approach did produce some insights into both the nature of pre-colonial regimes and of contemporary democracy, but it was essentially static. It gave no sense of how the contemporary situation was arrived at nor, by lifting the perceived preconditions out of their cultural context, was it sensitive to the effect of cultural and historical differences. Moore's approach, and the associated results, have been very different.

Moore defines his task as follows:

> it is an attempt to discover the range of historical conditions under which either or both of these rural groups [the landed upper classes and the peasantry] have become important forces behind the emergence of Western parliamentary versions of democracy, and dictatorships of the right and the left, that is, fascist and communist regimes.[34]

However, this description, while capturing the essence of the problem as Moore sees it, is narrower than the result of Moore's endeavours. In seeking to describe the class constellations that made these different types of political outcome possible, Moore's analysis must embrace a broader range of political actors. Consequently, a large part in his analysis is played by the state, referred to by Moore as the monarch but actually including the growing state bureaucracy, and the emergent urban bourgeoisie. Moore's basic assumption is that the different patterns of relationship between these four actors (landed upper classes, peasantry, state and bourgeoisie) create different paths to modernity, and resulting different political outcomes. While these different paths could constitute alternative routes and choices, Moore sees them much more as historical stages with, accordingly, a limited determinate relation to each other. The methods of modernization chosen in one country change the dimensions of the problem for the next countries who take the step.... Without the prior democratic modernization of England, the reactionary methods adopted in Germany and Japan would scarcely have been possible. Without both the capitalist and reactionary experiences, the communist method would have been something entirely different, if it had come into existence at all.[35]

This perception of the nature of these paths means that Moore does not see them as blueprints which subsequent political forms must follow. They are not checklists of preconditions, but explanations of the constellations of forces which brought about particular political outcomes in the form of democratic, Fascist and Communist regimes.

Moore's analysis is rooted in a close study of the history of the societies with which he is concerned. This means his analysis has a level of detail and specificity which, while it may be necessary to give historical weight to the patterns of relationships which he is intent on drawing, is unnecessary for an application of those patterns to other historical circumstances. The broad class configurations can be extracted from the historical detail, and their utility for an understanding of the process of democratization discussed, without becoming caught up in that historical detail.

Moore outlines three paths to modernity, plus one path into the contemporary world which stops short of modernity. These paths can be outlined as follows:[36]

1. The democratic-capitalist route occurs when there is a rough balance between the state and the landed upper classes and when a strong and independent urban bourgeoisie is thereby able to establish its control over national policy, either by winning over the landed élite or by destroying its position. The commercialization of agriculture is sponsored by the bourgeoisie either in alliance with the landed upper classes, as in England, or by destroying the economic power of the latter, as in France.

2. The route to Fascism comes about when the landed upper classes sponsor agricultural commercialization through a tightening of controls over the peasantry exercised in part through the repressive apparatus of the state. The urban bourgeoisie is

politically and economically weak, relies on this conservative alliance between landed upper classes and state, and fails to exercise any significant independent influence on national life.

3. Communism is the likely outcome where the urban bourgeoisie is weak, the landed upper classes do not promote agricultural commercialization, but market relations intrude into the countryside. If the peasantry is cohesive, the connection with the landlord is weak (e.g. in the case of absentee landlords) and the peasants can find allies with organizational skills, peasant revolution is likely to lead to a Communist outcome.

4. The cul-de-sac occurs when the urban bourgeoisie is weak, the landed upper classes do not engage in the commercialization of agriculture, and the peasant community lacks the cohesion necessary for effective political action.

The key to the process implicit in these paths is the commercialization of agriculture.[37] When this involves a strong, independent bourgeoisie, the balance of power shifts from the rural areas to the city as the dominating role of the landed upper class wanes and the peasantry as a class is destroyed as a major political actor. In England, agricultural commercialization involved the enclosures movement and the transformation of part of the peasantry into an urban proletariat and part into independent farmers. Commercialization began under the influence of an increasingly commercially-minded landed class which, instead of opposing the emergence of the bourgeoisie, allied with its nascent elements in the struggle against the power of the state represented by the crown. In France, the landed upper class did not seek to sponsor commercialization, but instead to profit from it by increasing traditional repressive methods of extracting the surplus from the peasants. This meant that by the time of the French Revolution, with the capacity of the government effectively to handle the strains produced by commercialization clearly under challenge, the peasant demand for property added fuel to the fires coming from the revolutionary sentiments of the urban lower classes. When increasing radicalization of the revolution threatened to call into question the gains made by the peasants, they acted as a brake on this process, thereby paving the way for Thermidorean reaction. However, this was not before the power of the landed upper classes had been destroyed and the peasants had been turned into farmers. In America, Moore's third case of capitalist democracy, there was no peasantry, but there was a conservative landed upper class in the South resting upon labour-repressive plantation agriculture. However, the power of this group was destroyed by an alliance between the Northern industrial bourgeoisie and Western independent farmers. The crucial point about these three patterns of reaction to agricultural commercialization is the destruction of the conservative power blocs based in the countryside: alliance between bourgeoisie and already commercially-minded landed class leading to the transformation of the peasantry, destruction of the landed class by peasant revolution which also transforms the latter into a class of farmers, and the overthrow of a landed upper class by a bourgeois–farmer alliance.

The key to the non-democratic paths is the failure to destroy such power blocs.[38] The basic underpinning of the power of the rural landed upper classes is a labour-repressive form of agriculture. Moore acknowledges[39] that all forms of agricultural labour may be classed as repressive, but he is distinguishing between the use of political mechanisms and of the labour market to ensure an adequate labour force and the continuing production of the surpluses necessary to maintain appropriate levels of consumption. A landed upper class seeking to maintain its dominance without engaging in broad-ranging commercialization must use labour repressive methods to at least maintain and hopefully increase production levels. This may take the form of the so-called second serfdom in Eastern Europe, or slavery in the American South. In either event, the landed upper class needs the power of the state to validate and ultimately enforce the system of labour repression. Hence the alliance between conservative landowners and the state. Furthermore, if the interest of the landowners lies in repression of peasant workers and the interest of the emergent weak bourgeoisie is also seen to lie in repression of the urban counterparts of the peasants, then the basis exists for an alliance between these two groups: Moore's notion of the 'marriage of iron and rye'. Thus, in Moore's view, the maintenance of the power of the rural upper class in alliance with the state and perhaps the weak urban bourgeoisie lies at the heart of the paths to Fascism and Communism. In Germany and Japan the landowners sought to intensify traditional methods of agricultural exploitation, and in so doing allied with state and bourgeoisie in an arrangement which effectively excluded the lower classes from being able to enter the political arena in an organized fashion. The outcome was a political system fashioned from above, emphasizing property rights and, at least in part as a justification for militarism and an attempt to gain the ideological commitment of the lower classes, hypernationalism. In Russia and China the landowners also sought to intensify labour-repressive methods, but in doing so the peasant community was not destroyed and when the state's failure to maintain its authority became manifest, that community rose up and threw off landlord control. The result of this was a system fashioned out of popular revolt in which the traditional power-holders were swept away.

The other aspect of this was the fate of the peasantry. Where that peasantry either did not exist (America) or was transformed into a class of independent farmers and urban proletariat (England and France), capitalist democracy ensued. Where that peasantry was maintained as a servile agricultural class, rural power structures were not transformed and the basis for non-democratic rule continued. Whether that structure was gradually transformed from above through class alliance (Germany and Japan) or was shattered from below by peasant rebellion (Russia and China) depended upon the continuing power of the repressive apparatus wielded in the interest of the upper classes by the state and the capacity of the peasant community to act collectively in pursuit of its interests.

The destruction of the power of a conservative landowning class, and associated impossibility of an aristocratic–bourgeois coalition against the lower classes, is also an intrinsic part of another aspect of Moore's argument: the need for a revolutionary break from the past. Moore argues that in all three cases of the path to democracy, there was a revolutionary break from the past which had the effect of destroying the power of those elements which potentially would have stood in the way of democracy. In France, the revolution broke the power of absolutist monarchy and of the conservative landowners, while in the US the civil war resulted in the decline of the Southern white plantation owners as a politico-economic force. In England the civil war undercut aspirations toward absolutism and reduced the political power of the state compared with that of the growing commercializing landowner–urban bourgeoisie alliance. In those cases of non-democratic development, no similar revolutionary break from the past occurred. In the cases of the fascist path, such a break was averted by the exercise of hegemony over the emerging bourgeoisie by traditional landowners and the consequent consolidation of the established structure. In the Communist cases state and landowners had a perceived coincidence of interest in maintaining existing control structures largely intact.[40]

Thus, for Moore the crucial variable in the emergence of democracy is the absence of a conservative alliance against the lower classes which would be able to consolidate traditional power arrangements. The absence of such a structure was associated with the development of an independent, and powerful, bourgeoisie, which was itself the key to democracy: 'No bourgeois, no democracy.'[41]

There have been many criticisms of Moore's work[42] and not all of them will be canvassed here. What the following discussion aims to do is to highlight some of the main aspects of his discussion which are relevant to the question of the processes of democratization but which require some modification or amendment with a view to making them more pertinent to the question under review. Therefore, although Moore has been criticized, as all comparativists are, by specialist historians because he is deemed to have 'got wrong' some aspects of his case studies,[43] which may thereby call into question his explanatory principles, no attention will be given to the accuracy of his individual historical accounts. Rather, the emphasis will be upon those explanatory principles and how well they explain the emergence of democracy.

One area of Moore's work which bears further investigation is the role he attributes to the bourgeoisie. This is a crucial factor in Moore's analysis, the dominance of this class being deemed essential for the emergence of democracy. One problem with Moore's analysis is that it is not clear how the strength of this class is to be established,[44] and yet it is the existence of a powerful, independent bourgeoisie which is essential for the democratic path.[45] The danger in the way Moore proceeds is that in the absence of any clear criteria for establishing the strength of class groups, and in a context in which there is no close analysis of the workings of national politics (see below), the dominance or otherwise of a particular class may be judged by the primacy or otherwise of its putative interests. In England, America and France, where industrialization proceeded initially primarily on the basis of small and medium-sized entrepreneurs acting in substantial independence of the state, these people did define their interests in terms of principles which were consistent with democratization. The classic liberal arguments about individual freedom, limited state and the value of individual initiative were all relevant here as part of the struggle by these urban forces to create a society in which their interests would gain primacy. However, in other cases, the bourgeoisie may not have shared such values and instead have entered an alliance with conservative landowners and state less because of their weakness, and therefore need for support against a rising working class, than of their perceived interests. For example, in Germany the bourgeoisie was a very different sort of class to that in the countries noted above.[46] German industrialization was characterized by two factors greatly at variance with that of England in particular. First, the early development of large enterprises tended to crowd out the smaller 'traditional liberal entrepreneur'. Second, because of the late beginning of German industrialization, the state played a far larger role in shaping its contours and forcing its pace. Economic development was significantly shaped by considerations of national policy. In the context of these two factors, the interests of the German bourgeoisie were much more closely bound up with the state, and thereby with its landlord allies, than with a policy of opposing the state and rolling back its power. A powerful state constituted a powerful ally, and the German bourgeoisie therefore had no reason to seek to oppose it. Thus, if we argue that the bourgeoisie is characterized by liberal political predispositions, the failure of such views to achieve primacy in Germany might be taken as a sign of bourgeois weakness. However, if we accept the sketch of the German situation given above as accurate, the opposite conclusion could be drawn: the predominance of illiberal political sentiments and arrangements reflects the interests of the bourgeoisie and might therefore indicate that it was a more powerful force than Moore's thesis implies.

But this suggests not only the problem created by the absence of criteria whereby the strength of the bourgeoisie could be measured; it also implies that faith in the democratic consistency of this class may be misplaced. There appears to be little substantial evidence that the bourgeoisie universally has played a democratizing role. In Moore's own case studies, no evidence is provided to show that in Germany, Japan, Russia or China the bourgeoisie consistently pursued a democratizing path but were rebuffed by more powerful forces. Indeed, the argument that the bourgeoisie participated in a reactionary alliance with traditional landowners and state in a constellation which ultimately ushered in Fascism suggests precisely the reverse. Similarly, studies of some of the smaller European democracies allot a more ambiguous role to the bourgeoisie: there is no evidence that prior to the twentieth century the Dutch bourgeoisie were strongly committed to bourgeois values,[47] while in Sweden the main part in pushing for democracy was taken by the independent peasantry rather than the bourgeoisie.[48] Moore's 'No bourgeois, no democracy' clearly does not mean that the presence of a bourgeoisie ensures democracy.

The emphasis Moore places on the need for a revolutionary break has been called into question by students of Swedish history.[49] In Sweden, the passage to democracy occurred through a series of reform measures introduced through the national parliament. Electoral laws enabled sufficient farmer representation to prevent the passage of measures which would close down democratic options and to facilitate adoption of measures extending the franchise. Furthermore, the reliance of the industrialization effort overwhelmingly on foreign capital meant that agriculture did not have to be squeezed, with the consequent absence of sharp antagonisms between urban bourgeois and rural farmer groups; there was no need to destroy the peasantry in order to foster industrialization, 'no need for a revolutionary break with the past, of a bourgeois revolution to unleash the bonds by which the countryside held down the emergence of urban enterprise',[50] because the resources for industrialization came from elsewhere. Popular pressure exercised through the parliament and the streets, added to fears of revolution following the abortive German revolution, encouraged the conservatives to compromise, resulting in Swedish democracy via reform and without a revolutionary break from the past.

It is clear that reform through parliament was a major element in the Swedish path to democracy and that there was no violent conflagration to match that of the English or American civil war or the French revolution. But is it true to say that there was no revolutionary break from the past? Agricultural commercialization led to the dominance of family farms and the displacement of many peasants from their traditional agricultural pursuits. Many of these were taken up in industry, but also a very large number emigrated to America; Tilton even suggests that 'massive emigration may substitute (in large measure if not wholly) for the growth of commercial agriculture as a means of eliminating a financially unstable and politically dangerous peasantry'.[51] Even if the enclosure movement, which was a central component of commercialization, had been a peaceful process, the effects of it were revolutionary, with the traditional communal structures of rural life replaced by the individual family farm. This placed the farming sector on a much more stable economic basis and shaped the rural constituency which could exercise power in the parliament. This suggests that while the revolutionary break must in some cases take the form of widespread armed conflict, this is not essential. Moore's purpose behind the revolutionary break was to destroy existing social barriers to democratic progress, and if this could be achieved without armed conflict, it should be seen as no less revolutionary. Clearly, a decisive break occurred in Sweden, and such a break facilitated the democratic future.[52]

This argument reinforces the need for us to be clear about what Moore is offering. His study presents a series of historical generalizations stemming from a range of specific cases, not a set of formulae which can be abstractly applied without concern for context. Consequently, there must be some flexibility in how his principles are applied. However, if his principles are to give us any guidance in seeking to understand the course of democratization outside his core cases, a number of more serious reservations must be addressed.

One of the most important of these relates to what some have seen as a major weakness in Moore's explanation, the lack of attention to the role of the working class. This argument has been made forcefully by Goran Therborn.[53] Therborn notes that the shift to full democracy followed mobilization by the labour movement which was, in his view, the only consistent democratic force in the political arena. Full democracy was not won by the labour movement in the midst of political struggle, but tended to be conceded by the bourgeoisie following a period of successful resistance to popular pressure. However, argued Therborn, the labour movement was nowhere able to achieve bourgeois democracy on its own; it needed assistance from victorious foreign armies, powerful domestic allies, or splits among the ruling groups. This argument has been substantially elaborated, and given empirical backing, by others discussed below.

The role of the working class is clearly a gap in Moore's analysis, but how serious is it? To the extent that Moore's aim is to analyse the role of lord and peasant in the making of the modern world, the omission of the working class may not appear serious. However, if the intention is to explain how and why a democratic structure emerged, ignoring one of the major social actors would appear to be a serious deficiency. But in discussing this, it needs to be borne in mind that Moore's book is directed at laying out the *social origins* that made for a democratic or a non-democratic outcome. He was not intent on exploring the specific dynamics leading up to the democratic breakthrough, but rather on setting out the social configurations which made that breakthrough possible. If the working class did play a decisive role in bringing about a democratic outcome, Moore would argue that they acted within the constellation of class forces that he has explained. He is interested in the social preconditions in the rural areas that gave rise to democratic political structures, not the intricate political struggles that produced those structures.

Another way of looking at this is in terms of the termination point of Moore's analysis. His study stops broadly at the point when the class configurations either facilitating or preventing democratic development are in place in each of the countries he studies. However, it does create a difficulty with regard to Germany, Japan and Russia. In the case of the first two, both would now be classed as democracies and that democratic period has lasted longer than the Fascism which Moore seeks to explain. In Russia, the Communist system has fallen, and while it is not yet clear that it has been replaced by stable democracy, its reversion to Communism is unlikely. Why should these periods of Fascist rule in particular not be seen as temporary periods on the way to democracy, much as the post-French revolution reaction in England is seen by Moore,[54] or the Napoleonic military dictatorship in France? The argument that fascism was overthrown and democracy instituted in Germany and Japan as a result of external imposition following defeat in war is not a sufficient explanation because the same applied to Napoleonic France. Moore's end point does not seem to be explicable except in terms of explaining why those particular regimes emerged. But this is a different question to that of pathways to democracy.

The problem of Germany and Japan raises another difficulty in Moore's analysis, and one pointed to by Skocpol: his ignoring of the inter-societal dimension. The weight of Moore's explanation falls entirely on internal factors, with little consideration given to the effect of events outside the boundaries of the country with which he is concerned. Moore does recognize that international events can affect the course of domestic politics, as in his discussions of the English reaction to the French revolution and the Japanese reaction to foreign threats. But he does not build recognition of the international dimension into his explanation, even when that may be important for his analysis; for example, it has been claimed that pressures for commercialization in Prussia and Russia stemmed from the challenges to those states posed by the more rapidly developing and militarily powerful states of the West.[55] The effect of international events is regarded as unimportant or 'fortuituous'[56] rather than as having any intrinsic part to play in the explanatory process. But international events can be crucial in strengthening the move towards democracy, as discussed in the last chapter. War and the associated popular mobilization were instrumental in many countries in the extension of the suffrage,[57] while defeat in war led in some instances to the installation of democratic structures in the vanquished by the victors. The role of international models should not be ignored, as political actors seek to learn lessons from what has happened before and abroad and to structure their activity in the light of those lessons. Moore himself hints at this when he talks of his cases as having a 'determinate relation' to each other.[58] The location of the country in the international political economy can also be a significant factor in structuring the options of domestic development open to a particular society (see Chapter 2).

The final major criticism to be made of Moore concerns the nature of his explanation: political outcomes are explained overwhelmingly in social and economic terms. What is crucial for Moore is classes, the fate of classes and the relationship between classes. These are clearly important, but the problem is that Moore's analysis does not provide any means for translating the class configurations into political systems. There is no attempt to move from the level of broad class relations to the institutional details of democratic structures and procedures. What is missing is the political factor. What institutions translated the class relations Moore talks about into governmental relations? What role did political élites play in the working out of the outcomes Moore is interested in?[59] What of the role of central legislative institutions, so important in the case of Sweden noted above? So, the absence of a specifically political dimension to the explanation means that major political institutions and actors find no place. Once again, this may be justified by Moore's emphasis upon social origins, but it is a problem for any attempt to explain the emergence of democracy.

An attempt to deal with the problems noted above in Moore's analysis has been made in a very important book by Dietrich Rueschemeyer and Evelyne and John Stephens.[60] The central aim of this book is to examine the relationship between development and democracy, and in so doing the authors build on the work of Moore and provide a fuller analysis of the forces shaping the shift to a democratic political form. The time period of this work is different to that of Moore, stretching from the same origins into the contemporary world. It thereby seeks to link the forces which it sees as crucial to the emergence of democracy to the actual development of a democratic structure in a much more immediate way than Moore sought to do. Furthermore, the notion of what constitutes democracy is, in their view, different in a very important way from the position adopted by Moore. Rueschemeyer *et al.* argue[61] that for Moore the major features of democracy are 'public contestation of political issues and the institutions of mutual toleration', while in their view something which Moore considers only of secondary importance is the pivotal factor, 'inclusive political participation'. This combination of contemporaneity and inclusiveness compels Rueschemeyer *et al.* to include the working class in their analysis. It also sensitizes them to the effect of international factors.

Rueschemeyer *et al.* identify three clusters of power constellations which, in their relationships, structure the path to democratic or non-democratic rule. Those constellations are the balance of class power, the power and autonomy of the state, and the transnational configuration of power. But while these are the three main building blocks structuring the road to a democratic outcome, precise patterns of relationships and of multiple causations will differ, with the result that there will be various paths to a democratic outcome. Thus, patterns of interaction between these constellations will differ with the specific conditions of national histories. In seeking to elucidate these patterns, Rueschemeyer *et al.* analyse the road to democracy in three different settings: Europe and Britain's settler colonies, Latin America, and Central America and the Caribbean. The fate of, and prospects for, democracy in each of these areas is discussed in terms of the relationships between the different constellations of power. It is these constellations of power which are crucial.

In discussing the impact of class forces on the course of political development, Rueschemeyer *et al.* argue that classes have behaved in a systematic manner. The main classes have tended to behave as follows:

1. The chief opponent of democratization was the landed upper class which was reliant upon a cheap labour supply. This is a similar point to that made by Moore, except that Rueschemeyer *et al.* substitute Moore's notion of labour-repressive agriculture with that of a cheap labour supply, a change which extends the relevance of this class into a more fully marketized period. The landed upper class opposed democratization because it threatened to destroy this cheap labour supply.

2. The bourgeoisie supported constitutional and representative

government, but opposed the extension of political inclusion to the lower classes. This too was motivated by the fear that such an extension would increase the power of the workers and thereby adversely affect both their political and economic positions. Whenever the landed upper class and bourgeoisie felt their interests threatened by popular pressure, they opposed democracy; if a democratic system was already in place, they sought to undermine it.

3. The middle class played an ambiguous role. Like the bourgeoisie, the middle class sought its own political inclusion, but its attitude to the lower classes depended upon its need for and the possibilities of an alliance with the working class. If the landed upper class was intransigent and unwilling to be politically inclusive with regard to the middle class, and the latter did not feel threatened by the demands of the working class, it might ally with the latter to press democratic reform. However, if the middle class felt threatened by popular pressure, it was inclined to support an authoritarian alternative to democracy.

4. Peasants and rural workers played different roles, depending upon their capacity for autonomous organization and susceptibility to influence by the dominant classes. Those peasants who worked on large estates tended to remain largely unmobilized and therefore played no role in democratization. Rural wage workers did attempt to organize politically. Often they were repressed, but where they could avoid or overcome this, they tended to join other working class organizations in pressing for democratization. In smallholding countries, independent family farmers tended to be a force for democracy, but in countrysides still dominated by large landholding, smallholders tended to be more in favour of authoritarian outcomes.

5. The most consistently pro-democratic force was the working class. It was more insulated from the ideological hegemony of the upper classes than the rural lower classes, and generally had better organizational resources than the latter; concentration in urban areas facilitated organization. However, the working class could not bring about democratization unaided. To be successful, the working class needed cross-class alliances, but here the question of aims became important; if working class demands were too radical, they could destroy any possibility of creating the sort of alliance with the middle class that could bring democratic success.[62] Furthermore, although the working

class was the most consistently pro-democratic force, if the initial mobilization of the working class took place under the leadership of a charismatic authoritarian leader or a hegemonic party linked to the state apparatus, this class could become a force for authoritarian politics.

The picture of the role played by these classes is interesting. In contrast to Moore, the independent bourgeoisie is neither essentially democratic nor the main force pressing for democracy. While the bourgeoisie could certainly be significant in the initial widening of the political system, it was the working class, usually with middle class support, that was responsible for the achievement of full democracy. Furthermore, this view does not impute any fixed motives or positions to most classes. The landed upper class is the main exception. The position it took on political inclusion would dictate whether the bourgeoisie and/or middle class would seek alliances with other groups, which in turn had implications for the strategy and tactics of the working class. Similarly, the positions of the two seemingly most-pro-democratic forces, working class and family small-holders, were structured in part by circumstances of mobilization and dominant power in the countryside reflected in landholding patterns. Thus, while the class behaviour was predictable, its limits and contours were shaped by historical contingencies.

The second constellation is the power and autonomy of the state. The consolidation of state power, meaning that the state is largely unchallenged in the control it exercises over the territory it rules, is essential to democratization. The move to democracy is unlikely while the integrity of the state is under challenge. But also important is the autonomy of the state. Prospects for democratization are maximized when the state is autonomous from the upper classes (and they therefore cannot use the state to repress democratic forces) but is not autonomous from civil society as a whole. If the state is autonomous from the latter, and particularly if the means of coercion are dominant within the state apparatus, the capacity of organized forces from within civil society to press for democratic advances will be constrained and the prospects for democracy diminished. Civil society is important because this is the location of the development of working class organizational resources; it is the growing 'organizational density of civil society' which underpins the political organization of the subordinate classes and acts as a counterweight to the power of the state apparatus.

The third constellation is the transnational configuration of power.[63] What is meant by this is the relationship between the state and foreign politico-economic powers. One manifestation of this is direct intervention from abroad. This has often taken the form of military intervention to shore up authoritarian rule but economic involvement has also been common. This could be in the form of a one-off action, but the stronger argument relates to the structural location of the state in the international political economy. This argument is saying, at base, that the national economy is limited in what it can and what it cannot do by its relationship to larger and more powerful economic forces operating in the international system. This has a direct economic component (the type of economy possible is determined by these larger forces), but it also has a political aspect: the configuration of the domestic class structure, and thereby of political power, could be shaped by the operation of international economic forces. In particular, they argued, transnational economic dependence could shape class structure in an anti-democratic way: economic growth based upon agricultural exports strengthened the position of the large landowning class, while industrialization based upon imported capital-intensive technology kept the working class small and weak.

Of these three constellations of power, the crucial one was the first, the domestic class structure. The state and transnational configurations were important principally in terms of the way they related to and affected that class structure. What drives the Rueschemeyer *et al* theory is the assumption that democratization is promoted by those who will benefit from it and opposed by those who will lose from it. Capitalism is important in the rise of democracy because of the two principal structural effects it brings about: it strengthens the working class and other subordinate classes (but not the rural subordinate classes), and weakens the large landowners. It also strengthens the bourgeoisie, and where this becomes a counterbalance to the power of the old nobility, a liberal oligarchy results. In these conditions of approximate balance between bourgeoisie and large landowners, the state may become more autonomous from dominant interests and civil society can develop a greater sense of organizational density and thereby both counterbalance state power and strengthen democratic pressures. In contrast, an alliance could develop between bourgeoisie, landowners and state, a conservative oligarchic alliance which would create the conditions for further capitalist development without institutionalizing contestation or inclusion. The state would be subordinated to this alliance, its power unimpaired and the capacity for civil society to fuel democratic pressures restricted. Building on Moore, Rueschemeyer *et al.* elaborate six conditions which facilitate this sort of coalition:[64]

1. The landed upper class remain a politically dominant force into the modern era and retain significant power in the 'democratic interlude'.
2. Peasant agriculture is maintained under landowners oriented towards the market using labour repressive methods. These methods are the basis of alliance with the state.
3. The bourgeoisie remains politically significant, but is not more powerful than the landed classes.[65]
4. The bourgeoisie is kept politically dependent because of state direction of industrialization. Militarism and arms production seal the bourgeoisie to the state-landowner dominated coalition and its reactionary and imperialistic policies.
5. There is a revolutionary break with the past.
6. The state has sufficient capacity to repress worker and peasant protest.

If this sort of coalition develops, as in Moore's account, the prospects for democracy will be dimmed; according to Stephens,[66] whenever such a coalition was established, no alliance to overcome it was possible, with only changes in the balance of class forces brought about by war enabling democratic breakthrough, while Rueschemeyer *et al.* argue that in Europe there was a correlation between the maintenance of a strong landowning class and the failure of democracy.[67]

Regardless of the disposition of classes, the continued development of capitalism should strengthen the working class and thereby generate increased pressures for further democratization. The success or otherwise of such pressures was largely dependent upon the ability of the working class to establish alliances with other class groups and thereby to strengthen the pressure for widening democratic structures. This means that for Rueschemeyer *et al.*, the middle class remains an important actor, because it is from within this class that leadership of the working class will probably come.

In this analysis, political parties emerge as crucial institutions which mediate in the establishment and consolidation of democracy. They are major institutional mechanisms for mobilizing the pressures from subordinate classes for democratization, and along with labour unions constitute one of the principal organizational forms of both the working class and civil society. They are the bodies which provide organizational direction for the democratic struggle and which give voice to subordinate class demands. Their activity is therefore seen as crucial in determining the course of the struggle: if they are too radical, they may strengthen opposition to democracy by the dominant class. However, they can also be important in integrating the dominant classes into the new democratic structure once established. The party system is important in a working democracy for protecting the interests of the dominant classes, either directly and openly by championing those interests in the continuing public debate and contestation, or by providing an avenue into the state apparatus for that class. Parties may thus be the instrument both for subordinate and dominant classes in the path to democracy. In the analysis of Rueschemeyer *et al.*, political parties thus play the important institutional linking role between class and political structure that is absent from Moore's analysis. In this sense, class action and the structures of politics are more tightly bound together in the explanation, which is therefore much more satisfactory.

Ultimately Rueschemeyer *et al.* conclude that a number of factors will facilitate the development and consolidation of democracy. They may be summarized as follows:

1. The power of the landed upper class is destroyed. This presumably involves a revolutionary break with the past.
2. There is a degree of power balance within civil society such that none of the organizations of the working class, middle class or bourgeoisie dominate. The usual form of such organization is the political party.
3. Pressures from subordinate classes must be strong enough so that their demands for inclusion are credible, but not so as to increase the sense of threat on the part of dominating groups, thereby inducing them vigorously to oppose inclusion.
4. The state should be autonomous from dominant classes but not from civil society.
5. Transnational power structures should not support the strengthening of the coercive apparatus of the state nor the autonomy of the state from civil society. Nor should they generate the types of intervention which would undermine democratic governments.

These conditions should favour the conduct of political activity designed to bring about stable democratic rule.

These two examples of a comparative historical sociological approach demonstrate the value of this sort of analysis: it enables the identification of longer-term historical structures which both create and close off options in the search for viable courses of development, and which identify the principal forces acting to influence current developments. But the weakness in this sort of analysis is equally clear. Unless skilfully handled, it can leave no room for the operation of autonomous forces in the form of contemporary actors, of the sort focused upon by the transition to democracy school. Neither Moore nor Rueschemeyer *et al.* are wholly guilty of this: both were talking principally about possible class coalitions given certain sorts of structural constraints, so neither really addresses the role of contemporary actors satisfactorily. But it is this role within the context of the structural legacy from the past that does need to be addressed if democratization is adequately to be explained. How can this be done?

These comparative historical sociological studies have shown that a critical factor in shaping the disposition of social interests has been agricultural commercialization and industrialization and the corresponding changes to the social and economic structures these have involved. However, these analyses do not go far enough. They need to explore the nature and patterns of the social forces which emerge as a result of the longer-term socio-economic processes upon which they focus and the arenas within which they operate. The effect of these processes on society has not been uniform, either within individual societies or across societies. Nevertheless, one constant has been that the development of an industrial sector of the economy has introduced into the national power equation at least two new actors, an industrial bourgeoisie and a working class, and possibly a third in the form of international bourgeoisie if the country's industrialization has had substantial international involvement. The introduction of these new actors has not only complicated the nature of domestic politics, but also substantially shifted the balance of power away from traditional, landed interests.

In the societies which have undergone the transition to democracy, the pre-industrial power structure was one in which the government rested upon, and reflected the views of, traditional landed interests. The dominance of these interests reflected not only their primacy within the national economy, but their role as the source of national élites in most walks of life. Their interests have concerned protection of their dominance economically, socially and politically, and this has been pursued principally through support for governments of a clearly authoritarian hue or a sort of semi-parliamentarism in which representation was strictly limited. The success of this group is illustrated by the fact that democracy has not been stabilized where a strong land-owning élite has maintained a dominant position in the export economy and has relied upon labour-repressive agricultural methods.[68] This is consistent with the arguments given by Moore and by Rueschemeyer *et al.* discussed above. What is needed to increase the prospects for democratic development is the breaking of the power of this traditional land-owning group, and this cannot be achieved by the commercialization of agriculture alone but by the emergence of a new urban industrial bourgeoisie and working class. This is not to assume that such a bourgeoisie and working class will automatically be forces for democracy. Rather, it assumes that, given the disposition of forces that prevails, both bourgeoisie and working class will see it as being in their interests to displace the power of the traditional landowners by one which is more in accord with their interests and concerns.

The capacity of these two new social forces to play a significant role in the shift towards democratization is dependent upon a number of factors. While some of these are highly specific and relate to the precise circumstances of individual countries, there are also some more general concerns which have wide applicability. It is upon these that the discussion will focus.

The first factor is the nature of the industrialization experienced in the country. One element of this is the depth of industrialization, or the degree to which industrial development has transformed the economy. The greater the extent of industrial development, the more dominant its place in the economy, then the greater is the likelihood that the power of the bourgeoisie and working class will be extensive. As a corollary, the larger the profile industry has in the economy, the smaller will be that of agriculture and the traditional landed interests. But it is not only the extent of industrial development that is important; its pattern may also be significant. Where industrial development takes the form principally of manufacturing, and it is concentrated in the cities (and in particular the capital), the scope for bourgeois and working class influence increases. Location in the cities implies a degree of geographical concentration which can not only increase the capacity for organization and joint activity on the part of both groups, but can maximize the effect of disruptive activity on the citizenry and, indirectly, on the government. In contrast, if development takes the form principally of mining (and perhaps processing), then the areas of development, and therefore concentration, may be widely dispersed and situated at significant distances from major urban areas. The effect of this may be to dilute the organizational strength of the working class and to fragment the bourgeoisie, and make concerted political action logistically more difficult.

The social origins or affiliations of the bourgeoisie and working class may also be important. Turning first to the bourgeoisie, if this group emanates from or is closely affiliated with the traditional landowners, it may be that it will see its interests as continuing to be bound up with the interests of that group, as in Moore's iron and rye alliance which he sees as leading to German Fascism. The interests of traditional landowners and bourgeoisie are not necessarily in conflict; both could favour repressive labour laws, extensive state subsidies and economic policies designed to facilitate the import of consumption goods. Of course, those interests could also diverge, depending upon the forms industrialization takes and the perceived need on the part of the industrial bourgeoisie to establish an economic system operating on principles different to those which underpin the traditional landed agricultural economy. Similarly, if the bourgeoisie ties itself closely to the government, it is unlikely to be a force for democratization. In such cases, industrial development is often heavily dependent upon government support, not just in terms of appropriate policies, but of the provision of government contracts and the sorts of informal favours and backdoor deals which often characterized industrial development everywhere in its early stages. This sort of tying of the bourgeoisie to the government, and the consequent negation of that independence which Moore saw as crucial, is very important in shaping the way the bourgeoisie will act in circumstances of regime transformation.

The social origins of the working class may also be important here. If the working class is of recent rural origin, and especially if members of it return to assist with seasonal labour on the land, the capacity of workers to develop a sense of common class consciousness and outlook will be diluted. The more they see themselves as displaced rural workers as opposed to an industrial working class, the less likely they are to perceive a commonality of interests which can be pursued through joint political action. Or, put the other way, the higher the level of consciousness of themselves as members of a working class, the greater the likelihood that they will see the possibilities for common action in defence of perceived joint interests. Of course, the development of a sense of common identity is not simply a matter of time or of separation from the rural environment. Working conditions, the degree of concentration of workers, opportunities for communication and levels of organization can all be important for developing a sense of commonality. Clearly, such a sense of identity can be important in shaping the role the working class might play in a situation of regime transition.

The role of such broad social forces and class groups in structuring both the shape of civil society and the process of transition should not be underestimated. The interaction of classes and the shaping of that interaction by broader processes of economic development are central to the moulding of the map of interests in a society at any particular point in time, including the point of transition. And it is those interests which will in large part determine what sorts of élite are prominent at the time of the transition process. For example, the pattern of élites in a society in which traditional landed interests continue to predominate will differ from one in which private industrial interests are paramount, which in turn will differ from one in which social power rests with bureaucratic forces. Also important here is the way those interests are organized and the sorts of resources they possess, both elements which contribute to the capacity of these interests to shape the processes of regime transformation, principally through the activity of the élites which represent them, but sometimes also through mass action. This relates directly to the question of the arena within which social interests function, that of civil society.

Crucial to the capacity of these groups to play an influential part in transition is organization. Class groups like these must mobilize organizationally if they are to play a direct role in the structuring of transition. For the bourgeoisie, such organizations are usually professional bodies like the National Manufacturing Sector Congress in Brazil, or political parties. Through these sorts of organizations, industrialists and entrepreneurs can seek to exert influence on the course both of government policy and of political development. Similarly, workers can seek to influence these through such organizations as labour unions and political parties, with the former usually being in much closer touch with the shop floor sentiment than the latter. But for such organizational vehicles to be effective as conveyors of class sentiment, they must be/have been free to develop and to generate their own sense of institutional integrity and coherence. This depends not just upon their own internal capacities, but also upon the willingness of the state to allow them to exist and to pursue their concerns. Once again, this relates to structural considerations about the society–state relationship, and therefore to the strength of civil society forces.

Civil society is important here because of the way that it is the arena within which social forces and class groups in the society gain organizational form and potential opposition to authoritarian rule is based. When opposition élites engage the regime, or that part of the regime which seeks change, in negotiations about political change, the currency that they have is the support they possess in society more broadly. The stronger civil society is, the stronger are likely to be the organizational and institutional linkages which tie those élites to their constituencies. Fear of those constituencies often is a major element in persuading regime élites to contemplate political change. But as with the development of social interests noted above, the growth of civil society can only be seen in a perspective which is longer-term than that used by the transition literature. This does not mean that a particular case of transition cannot be understood unless the analysis encompasses a full scale study of the history of the society's development, but it does mean that the analysis must take into account the role of civil society forces in the transition. However, the shape and contours of the particular civil society (e.g. the strength of trade unions compared with worker groups, the role of non-employment-related organizations, the type and number of political parties) cannot be understood without the longer-term perspective, and it is that shape and those contours which are important for structuring the role played by civil society forces in the transition. This longer-term perspective is particularly important when we consider that most authoritarian regimes have sought to restrict civil society by placing curbs upon the activity of autonomous organizations. So what is important here is an assessment of the degree to which civil society forces have been able to grow and develop under the particular authoritarian regime. This will, in turn, be related to the question of whether civil society existed prior to the imposition of authoritarian rule, and if so, how powerful it was, and whether civil society has been penetrated (and thereby compromised) by the authoritarian regime. Only if we have a methodology which is sensitive to the need to explore the nature of civil society in the particular country can we hope to be able adequately to take into account the role it plays in the process of transition.

If we are to understand the nature and development of civil society in this way, we need to be clear about what we are studying. As argued above, civil society assumes three things: groups autonomous from the state through which people seek to organize and project their interests (including politically), a public sphere within which issues are discussed and those interests pressed, and acknowledgement by the state of the legitimacy of the activity of those organizations and of that sphere in which they are active. Both temporally and logically, the autonomous groups are primary; neither a public sphere nor state recognition makes any sense without the existence of such groups. But this also means that while a civil society cannot exist without state recognition, the development of these basic elements of civil society, the autonomous groups, is likely to proceed before that civil society comes into existence. As the populace, or sections of it, seek to pursue interests that transcend their more immediate private concerns and embrace matters that have a wider, collective, public provenance, the sorts of groups that form the kernel of civil society emerge. This sort of development is usually discussed in terms of the origins or emergence of civil society, and while there is a sense in which this may be true, it does prejudge the future course of development; it assumes that civil society as defined above will emerge. In many cases, as a result of state opposition, this development is choked off, and a real civil society does not eventuate. Consequently, it is better to see such developments in terms of the growth of civil society forces, of the sorts of organizations that will be the nucleus of civil society should it develop but, if it is prevented from doing so, may nevertheless be active within the society at large. Their capacity to do so will in significant measure be determined by the state's attitude to them.

These civil society forces emerge as a response to the need of people to pursue collective interests within the society more broadly. They arise out of the circumstances of people's lives, their associations with others and the challenges they face. An important element in the emergence of such groups has historically been the rise of new classes of the sort studied by Moore and Rueschemeyer *et al.* Organizations and associations designed to advance and defend the corporate interests of the class or sections of it are intrinsic to the growth of classes as distinct corporate entities. Ranging from private clubs through professional and trade associations to trade unions,

these groups emerge as important arenas for the collective organization of people with common interests. This commonality of interest
can also transcend class lines and unite people in pursuit of their
passions. Such organizations usually precede the formation of political parties, which are designed specifically to project these interests
into the political sphere, and in many ways may be seen as the
logical bases upon which parties rest. It is the organization and
development of such civil society forces which is fundamental to the
capacity of broader socio-economic classes and of segments within
and between them to play a part in the direct structuring of political
development, and to our understanding of the dynamics of democratic transition. The strength, organizational form and strategy of
these groups will crucially shape the course of regime change.
Consider the following questions: Why does the regime seek to deal
with opposition élites from outside the regime? Why are some
groups more important in this process than others? Why are the
élites of some groups more prominent than others at the time of
transition? What relevant resources do different groups possess, and
why do some have more of these than others? What relationship
exists between civil society force élites and regime élites? If no
groups are powerfully placed at the time of regime crisis, why is this
so? These are some of the sorts of questions which are central to the
understanding of any instance of democratic transition, and they can
only be answered through the longer-term comparative historical
sociological prism which gives a prominent place to the development of civil society forces.

Ultimately, democratization involves the reworking of the state
through the transformation of its institutions (either creating new
bodies or breathing substance into existing ones) and the opening of
it up to mass control through institutionalized means. In effect, it
means institutionalizing the sort of political society to which Linz
and Stepan refer, as the means for ensuring that civil society exercises control over the state. Indeed, democratization can be seen in
terms of the realization of a civil society in the terms outlined in
Chapter 1: the development of a new (or enlargement of an existing)
public sphere within which civil society forces may function is an
intrinsic part of democratization. Indeed, it is the classic case of liberalization. But, like liberalization, it alone is not enough. The consolidation of a civil society will not bring about real democracy
unless that civil society is the means for the popular exercise of
control over the rulers. Without popular control exercised through

civil society forces, substantive democracy is absent. What this means in terms of studying democratic transition is that it is not enough simply to look at political élites; civil society forces must be analysed as well. Only in this way can the dynamics of that process be understood.

Fundamentally then, the shape of transition is determined by the relationship between the regime on the one hand and oppositionist, popularly-based civil society, forces on the other. The nature of the regime internally and the strength of popular forces, and therefore the relationship between regime and society, is crucial. This structures the opportunities for and the processes of transition. These may be seen in terms of two axes, with the ends of each axis being ideal types:

1. *The nature of the regime.*
   (a) Unitary regime. A regime in which unity is highly developed and the mechanisms for restoring unity should it break down are rapid and effective.
   (b) Segmentary regime. A regime in which unity is weak, often characterized by substantial differences between different component parts of the regime.
   In this discussion, no distinction is made between regime and state,[69] although in principle these are separate entities. It is assumed that in unitary regimes, the state is subordinate to the regime and does not seek openly to pursue its own interests in conflict with those of the rulers. In a segmentary regime, the state (or parts of it) may follow a course independent of the regime élite. In the vast range of cases falling between these extremes, the role of the state is mixed.
2. *The nature of society.*
   (a) Atomized society. A society in which there is no public, independent organization which enables citizens to pursue their interests independent of and even against the regime. Regime organizations are primarily mobilizational in nature. There is no popular control of the rulers.
   (b) Civil society. There is a sector of society in which independent public organizations function to enable citizens to pursue their interests independent of and even against the regime. Their activity is recognized as being legitimate by the regime, and it is the means whereby popular control over political life is established and exercized.

These two axes can be represented diagramatically:

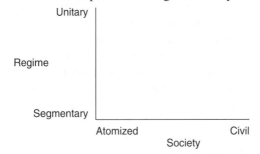

Where a particular country is located on these two axes will substantially shape both the prospects for transition and the contours that process is likely to take. This can be expressed in terms of a series of propositions and sub-propositions.

1. The more unitary the regime and the more atomized the society, the less likely is democratic transition.
    (a) The more unitary the regime, the less likely it is to split and break down when challenged, and therefore the better able it should be to meet that challenge.
    (b) The more atomized the society, the less able it is to generate an organized opposition to stimulate or participate in transition.
    (c) Pacted transition is impossible without a split regime and potential organizational partners from civil society.
    (d) The best prospects for a shift to democracy lie in the collapse of the unitary regime, either in terms of the disintegration of its unity mechanisms and its consequent shift in a segmentary direction, or its total collapse due perhaps to its own internal contradictions, defeat in war, or loss of support of an external hegemon. But democratization would be likely only if the atomistic society was quickly transformed in a civil society direction.
    (e) If transition does come onto the agenda and the regime remains united, it will play a major part in structuring the transition[70] and determining its terms (transaction); if social forces sweep it away, it will have little impact on the process.
2. The more segmentary the regime and the stronger the civil society, the better the prospects for democratic transition.

(a) The weaker the regime's unity mechanisms and the stronger the pressures from civil society, the less able the regime is to survive performance failures.

(b) The stronger civil society is, the greater the likelihood of the emergence of democratic opposition.

(c) The weaker the regime's unity mechanisms and the stronger the pressures from civil society, the more likely a segment of the regime is to seek out agreements with part of the opposition.

(d) A combination of segmentary regime and strong civil society is conducive to a pacted transition, unless:

(i) the regime fragments and different parts seek alliances with different groups in civil society. At the extreme, this could lead to civil war;

(ii) a segment of civil society is unable to establish and maintain a position of leadership over other forces in civil society for at least the early part of the transition.

(e) Where the forces of civil society are stronger than the capacity of the regime, replacement or extrication occurs; where the situation is reversed, transaction.

3. The more unitary the regime and the stronger the civil society, the greater the prospects for stand off and the escalation of violence.

(a) If the regime is committed to remaining in power and civil society forces press it to leave, it will either use force to blunt the opposition or be overthrown.

(b) Pacted transition is impossible, unless the regime splits and a significant part seeks civil allies.

(c) If the opposition has to fight for power, the differences in civil society may become submerged and therefore have to reappear if democracy is to be the outcome.

4. The more segmentary the regime and the more atomized the society, the weaker the prospects for transition to democracy.

(a) If a regime splits and there is no pressure for democracy from within society, the likelihood is the replacement of one authoritarian regime by another, possibly violently.

(b) Alternatively, there could be the collapse of both regime and state, leading to anarchy.

(c) If popular mobilization is not structured by groups and organizations which can exercise effective leadership, that mobilization is likely to contribute to increased chaos and the likelihood of the reassertion of authoritarian rule either by the old regime or by a new replacement.

This simplified schema[71] relating the nature of the regime to the nature of society and the strength within it of civil society forces, provides us with a means of explaining democratic transition that is more useful than the transition literature paradigm and simpler than that of Linz and Stepan. It acknowledges the importance of élite decisions and interests, but also makes provision for the crucial role played by non-regime élites. It also recognizes that the latter's power stems from their position in civil society. This type of explanation thereby overcomes the weakness stemming from the voluntarist nature of élite-focused explanations, and factors in the important structuring role played by broader social forces in the society without succumbing to the deterministic tone of many structural studies. In this way it recognizes the importance of both elitist and structural perspectives. Its value can be demonstrated by applying it to two sets of cases of regime change: first, the 'classic' cases at the heart of the transition literature, and second, those of the former Communist world which some have seen as being fundamentally different to the earlier 'classic' cases of transition.

5

Transition and Civil Society

In previous chapters the basic struts of a theory of democratization that brought together the élite focus of the transition school and the civil society emphasis which has been missing from that theory have been put in place. In Chapter 2 a number of considerations relating to regime breakdown were outlined. In Chapter 3 a typology of modes of transition was noted. In Chapter 4 a range of propositions concerning the relationship between state and society and the nature of both of these was suggested. It is time to bring these together into a more integrated treatment of democratic transition, using a number of the cases of such regime change which have been the foci of attention of the transition literature. These will be discussed in terms of the typology of modes of transition, with a view to showing how an understanding of the role of civil society and its relationship with the state is essential to satisfactory comprehension of the process of transition itself.

The most common mode of transition to democracy in the third wave according to Huntington[1] was transition through transaction, in which the leading role in bringing about regime change was played by regime élites. The key to this mode of transition is that the regime is stronger than the opposition, and therefore the ruling élite, or part of it, is able both to bring on the process of regime change and largely to define its parameters and course. The beginning of the process is the growth within some regime circles of the perceived need to bring about change in the prevailing political arrangements, principally in response to the onset of a crisis. The regime splits, although in the initial stages this may be neither public nor irrevocable. The reformers believe that some change is necessary if the regime is to surmount the crisis, while more conservative elements believe that change is unnecessary; what is needed is a tightening of control, perhaps with some minor adjustments to structure or policy.

In this dispute the reformers achieve the upper hand, and introduce a process of limited change, or liberalization. This fails, causing a hardening of divisions within the regime as some of the reformers interpret this as demonstrating the need for more extensive change, while other elements within the regime see it as proving the need for repression and the tightening of control. This tension comes to a resolution by the reformists moving against the conservatives, but in a way designed to avoid a conservative backlash, especially if conservative elements are well represented in the coercive arms of the state. The reformists turn to the leading elements of the opposition, coopt them into the process of managed change and, usually through negotiations and a pact, tie them to the peaceful transition of political rule in a democratic direction.

This view of transition through transaction, with the regime élite giving the process its overall guidance, is logical and can be seen in a range of instances of democratic change. But without more reference to forces outside the regime, the motor force and dynamism of this mode of transition cannot be understood. This is the mode in which the role of civil society forces is seen to be most limited, and yet those forces are crucial to the structuring of this process. This is the case both for the onset of crisis which brings on the transition, and for the course and contours of the transition itself.

When the regime runs into difficulty of some sort, be it economic, policy differences, the succession question, defeat in war, or some other issue, it is by no means inevitable that this will trigger a process of democratization. An important question here is how adequate the regime's means for maintaining unity and coordinating the interests within the regime élite are. The more developed and robust those mechanisms are, i.e. the more unitary the regime is in terms of the discussion in Chapter 4, the more likely the regime is to be able to resolve those differences internally and thus not become destabilized. But the operation of these mechanisms alone cannot explain the outcome of élite differences. Crucial, too, is the relationship with and the nature of the society. Where a society is placed towards the 'atomized' end of the 'atomized-civil society' continuum, where civil society forces are weak and underdeveloped, little organized pressure from society will be placed on the regime. In these circumstances, with little pressure from below that could push change in a democratic direction, the absence of mechanisms for resolving élite differences may not be fatal for the regime. Elite conflict may lead to changes in the composition of the ruling élite, and it may even lead to a change in regime, but this would be likely to be the replacement of one authoritarian regime by another. Without popular pressure, without the fear of the consequences of not responding to the perceived popular will, there is little incentive for élites to adopt a system of government which would render them regularly accountable to the populace at large. And unless there is some organized means for the expression and projection of the popular will, or at least what can plausibly be claimed to be the popular will, such pressure will not eventuate.

Where civil society forces have been able to develop, especially in the form of political parties underpinned by a broad network of public and private organizations, they are able to act as the means of the application of pressure to the regime. If those forces are particularly strong, possessing well-developed organizational structures, an identifiable mass base, and a clear means of aggregating the interests from their bases and articulating them in the political arena, their capacity to influence the course of developments within the regime will be heightened. With powerful civil society forces, even minor differences within the regime can have major political consequences. Indeed, it is the presence of such civil society forces, and fear of the consequences of ignoring them, that encourages most reformers to seek to bring about change which ultimately turns into democratization. Without such pressure, the incentive for élites to work out their differences without substantial change to the broader ruling structure would be almost irresistible.

Once the regime has split and a part of it looks to the civil society forces for support, the relationship between élite regime actors and the leaders of the civil society forces on the one hand, and between those civil society force leaders and their mass constituencies on the other, will be important. The relationship between élite regime actors and civil society force leaders will be a crucial factor in structuring the outcome of the pressures for regime change. Given that elements in the regime leadership feel they must respond to the popularly-based pressures, they must decide to whom to respond, and how. These decisions will be affected by the nature of opposition forces: are they united in a popular front organization of some sort which provides a single opposition leadership, or are they fragmented, and if so how much? The regime élite must also consider how much attention to pay to traditional supporters, often like the business community, whose views may be very different from those taken by oppositionist leaders. So, the decision to enter discussions with civil society forces is not always straightforward and is not something which can be defined in the abstract by regime élites. This is also related to the second point. The ability of the civil society force leaders to carry their constituencies with them will be crucial to the outcome of any negotiations they enter into with regime actors. If they can ensure the disciplined acceptance of any agreements they negotiate, their hand will be strengthened in those negotiations. In contrast, if they cannot ensure that their followers will accept agreements and commitments made on their behalf, if the linkages between civil society force leaders and putative followers are weak, their ability to exert focused pressure on the regime's negotiators will be limited. It is clear, then, that the nature of the discussions that occur between regime élites and civil society force leaders will be shaped fundamentally by the nature of those civil society forces, the relationship between them, and any relationship that any of them possess with the regime. The involvement of particular oppositionist figures in discussions with the regime occurs only because those figures are seen to have a leadership role in civil society forces. They are there not because of their personal qualities, but because of their positions in the broader civil society milieu.

Civil society forces thus play a crucial role in the course of transition through transaction. Even if at one level they are secondary to the role of regime élites, they are actually fundamental to the structuring of the actions of those regime élites and to explaining them. Civil society forces are even more crucial to the other two modes of transition, those by extrication and replacement. In both, the points made above relating to the role of civil society forces in the onset of crisis and the splitting of the regime in transition through transaction apply also. In transition through extrication, where negotiations occur between regime élite actors and oppositionist leaders, the case is the same as for transaction except that, in relative terms, civil society forces are stronger and the regime weaker. In transition through replacement, the relative power positions of the two sides becomes even more unbalanced, with oppositionist forces even stronger and the regime weaker. In this case, opposition activity is often not restricted to civil society forces, but can take on a more spontaneous mass form as well. But the crucial point is that in all modes of transition, the role of civil society forces is fundamental. This will be illustrated by a brief analysis of the transition experiences of some of those states that have been central to the transition school analysis.

Transition through Transaction

Spain

Spain is seen as the paradigmatic case of transition through transaction, 'a case in which those in power thought they could not stay in power without, given the Western European context, excessive repression, while those challenging the regime could not marshal, at least immediately, enough force to overthrow it, particularly in view of the loyalty of the Armed Forces to the regime.'[2]

In the 1960s and 1970s, as regime élites began to prepare for life after Franco, divisions within the regime began to manifest themselves. The regime under Franco had consisted of a congeries of groups and alliances which Franco had kept continually off-balance to sustain his own power and position,[3] and as the end of the Franco era approached, these rivalries intensified. The chief line of division was between the technocrats mainly associated with Opus Dei, who favoured further industrial development, opening up to outside forces and membership of the EC, and the corporatists and militarists based in the traditional institutions of the regime (especially the party, the *Movimiento*) who looked to a refinement of existing structures and a tightening of control.[4]

With the regime divided over longer-term survival strategy, the society it confronted had become much more complex, with civil society forces growing in number and strength in the post-war period.[5] The fostering of industrial development had transformed Spain from the rural society which had been the inspiration for Falangist ideology into an urban society in which education and social mobility had become much more prominent. An emergent industrial working class plus a growing university student population created two potential forces with which the regime formerly had not had to cope. Furthermore, their concentration in large numbers in specific locations meant that they were much more able to be mobilized for anti-regime political ends than the more dispersed rural inhabitants had been. Certainly the regime retained tight control, although the traditional channels were increasingly becoming less able to secure this. Independent political parties were still banned, but the memory of them from earlier times remained in the consciousness of much of the middle class and the intelligentsia; some parties also maintained an existence abroad, where party leaders continued to project their message back into Spain and thereby to provide an image of a future at odds with that of the regime. Regime control was never sufficiently extensive or penetrative as to lead to the atomization of the society, which retained an integrity and an ethos independent of the regime; civil society was not destroyed.[6] Workers had begun to organize to defend living standards, until such organizations were brutally suppressed in 1967.[7] Economic interests increasingly tended to see their concerns as best served through opening of the economy and entry to the EC, and direct negotiations with the workers rather than through the syndicalist structures provided by the regime. The end of the decade saw the emergence of clandestine trade unions, the politicization of strikes, the growth of university student demonstrations, and the beginning of ETA terrorist attacks on the Basque issue. In addition, the church began to edge away from the regime, finally withdrawing its support in the early 1970s.[8] Civil society forces were crystallizing more clearly, while at the same time divisions in the regime continued to open up.

The regime's response to this challenge from society was repression.[9] Under the leadership of Admiral Luis Carrero Blanco (with Franco stepping back from direct rule), from 1969 the regime embarked on a path of repression, using 'ultra-rightist terrorism'[10] against its opponents. However, this strategy of increased repression failed. It exacerbated the divisions within the regime without eliminating popular discontent. Labour unrest continued and the activities of ETA grew;[11] indeed the trial of Basque nationalists in December 1970 not only stimulated domestic opposition, but also generated foreign pressure on Spain for a moderation of its ways. The policy of repression was also instrumental in focusing opposition thinking on the strategy of the coming post-Franco transition. The regime's hard-line persuaded moderate oppositionists that the regime would not surrender power without a fight, and that any attempt to overturn it would lead to civil war. They thus began to look for ways to achieve transition without bloodshed, examining avenues through the constitution and through the newly-named monarch, Juan Carlos. For these moderate oppositionists, negotiation with moderate regime elements seemed to be a possible way forward.

On 20th December 1973 Carrero Blanco was assassinated by ETA. He was replaced by Carlos Arias Navarro, reputedly the 'hardest man' in Carrero's cabinet.[12] Arias was under pressure from both sides in the regime, with the hardliners, known as 'the bunker', pressing for a reassertion of the Carrero policy of repression and reformists pushing for measures of reform. Labour unrest continued, while the economic difficulties of the regime were exacerbated by the effects of the oil price rise in 1973. Confronted by severe economic difficulties, Arias followed a strategy of adopting some liberalizing measures designed to sustain the regime without substantially eroding its position, combined with attempts to divide the opposition through the application of selective repression, aimed specifically at marginalizing the left. He allowed scope for broader political participation within the regime's basic structure and a more tolerant attitude to the moderate elements in the opposition, and was less repressive toward the press. But this attempted opening failed to win much credit for the regime because of its limited nature and because of its association with the regime's continued repression; what one study has called a 'spiral of repression and concessions'.[13] The almost reflex response of repression was strengthened by the continuing pressure from the bunker, the shock of the collapse of the Portuguese regime in April 1974,[14] and the increasing isolation of the regime as relations with the church became strained and the numbers of businessmen looking towards the opposition increased.

The sense of isolation was reinforced with the crystallization of politically-oriented civil society forces. In July 1974 the Communist party established the *Junta Democratica*, which included people and groups from a wide range of leftist political positions. At the same time the Socialist party, PSOE, was undergoing a process of rejuvenation led by Felipe Gonzalez, and sought negotiation with regime moderates. In June 1975 PSOE organized the *Plataforma de Convergencia Democratica* (PCD), a combination of regional and political groups as a rival to *Junta Democratica*. On the right of the spectrum, meetings between prominent industrialists and financiers and moderate opposition leaders were instrumental in the creation of some moderate rightist parties. With the increasing organization of oppositionist forces, in July 1974 Franco fell ill and passed some of his power over to Juan Carlos. Although he soon retook control, this both encouraged the opposition and worried the bunker. In a context of continuing popular dissatisfaction, reflected in ferment in the Basque lands and universities, strike activity and even some expressions of unhappiness in the military, conservative forces in the government launched a wave of repression in early–mid 1975. This action only provoked further strike activity, alienated the remaining moderate elements (there had been a wave of resignations from the regime at the end of 1974) in the regime, even further disillusioned many commercial elements, and provoked an international outcry.

On 20th November 1975 Franco died. This accelerated the transition as both regime and opposition moderates stepped up their search for negotiations. Juan Carlos was convinced that the way forward lay in convincing the Franquistas of the need to proceed through reform of the existing institutions,[15] and he confirmed Arias in office, while the latter soon showed that his main aim was to ensure the continuation of the Franco regime. However, the king was sensitive to the need to reach out to the opposition, realizing that the only way the monarchy could gain legitimation was through popular approval, and that this required some form of reconciliation between regime and society.[16] Popular mobilization continued, with mass demonstrations and strike activity; in the year after Franco's death, there were ten times the number of strikes as in the last year of his life.[17] Arias responded with increased repression. Communist leader Carillo now realized the danger that the Communists would be totally bypassed if they continued to rely on working class militancy to bring about regime collapse. He fostered the unification of the *Junta Democratica* and the PDC in March 1976 to form the *Coordinacion Democratica* (called *Platajunta*). Despite regime harrying, the *Platajunta* expanded to include centre and centre-right groups, and thereby establish itself as the chief negotiating agent of the opposition. But in April 1976 Arias declared his refusal to negotiate with the opposition. It was clear that he could not satisfy either the bunker or the opposition, and in June the king sought his resignation.

The new prime minister was Adolfo Suarez. He was trusted by the bunker, at least initially, because of his impeccable Francoist credentials as a former leader of the *Movimiento*, but he moved quickly to reach out to the opposition. Suarez publicly announced his programme in July, declaring his support for the principle of popular sovereignty and committing his government to work for the 'establishment of a democratic political system'. He announced a limited political amnesty, accepted the principle of free trade unions, legalized political parties (except the PCE) and promised to submit to the people a referendum on political reform and a timetable for elections. The subsequent parliament would then pass a law on constitutional reform which would be approved by referendum. This strategy enabled Suarez to seize the initiative by promising something to both sides: to the conservatives, it offered a commitment to legal process and an affirmation of existing institutions and powers; to the opposition, it gave a commitment to the sort of change it favoured. In addition, Suarez reassured financial circles by guaranteeing that the changes would not call into question the capitalist system, and he sought to counter potential military hostility by guaranteeing the immunity of military and civilian authorities and respect for law in the implementation of the process. With the king's backing, Suarez opened private discussions with the opposition, including both Gonzalez and Carrillo. The latter gave a commitment to peaceful change,[18] but Suarez remained unable to publicly include the PCE in the process because of bunker opposition. However, Suarez was able to make a significant advance against the conservative opposition in August when he replaced the defence minister Santiago by the more moderate Gutierrez Mellado, who then proceeded to implement a policy of gradually replacing hardline military officers by those of more moderate disposition. This policy was conducted slowly, over a number of years, but did over time erode the basis of conservative opposition in the military. Suarez was also able to manoeuvre his programme[19] through the Francoist parliament, the Cortes, despite vigorous opposition from conservative elements, thereby giving it the imprimatur of the old regime's institutional processes and a certain legitimacy in the eyes of many conservatives.

But the opposition remained wary, uncertain of the strength of Suarez's reformist credentials. As a result, the newly-constituted opposition umbrella organization the *Plataforma de Organismos Democraticos* (POD – the *Platajunta* plus five regional fronts), on 4th November 1976 rejected Suarez's plan for the referendum on his political reforms and called for voters to abstain in the referendum. The opposition had also adopted a position of favouring a 'provisional government of democratic consensus' as the appropriate vehicle for managing the shift to democracy rather than the extension of the old regime under Suarez. November saw the strike wave reach its peak, including a general strike on 12th November, and some continuing ETA activity. But in December shifts began to occur in the opposition. The adherence of a number of liberal and Social Democratic groups to POD led to a moderation of its stance, including dropping the call for a provisional government, thereby recognizing that reform would proceed through the old regime. This recognition of Suarez as an authoritative negotiating partner was accompanied by a reversal of PSOE's position that it would not participate in the elections unless all political parties (principally the PCE) were legalized. This impetus within opposition ranks was stimulated by the result of the referendum on 15th December 1976; opposition calls for a boycott were ignored, as 77.4 per cent of the population voted, of whom 94.2 per cent supported the proposal.[20]

Buoyed by this result[21] and in response to a wave of terrorist violence by the extreme right, Suarez sought further to strengthen his position. In an endeavour to provide himself with an electoral base and to establish some independence from the old regime, in April 1977 he abolished the *Movimiento*. Many of the functionaries and Francoists from that organization moved into the new political organization Suarez now sponsored, the *Union del Centro Democratico* (UCD), a coalition of small centrist groups and *Movimiento* bureaucrats. But while this body may have marked a symbolic break with the past, the *Movimiento* flavour of much of its membership meant that it retained close links with business, industry and the banks, and ensured that power would stay in the hands of those who would guarantee the existing structure of economic and social power.[22] Against this background, and following a demonstration of the PCE's strength and discipline and commitments from Carillo that if legalized the party would support the monarchy and the monarchist flag for Spain and a future social contract to deal with the continuing economic problems, on 9th April 1977 Suarez announced the legalization of the PCE. In exchange, the opposition accepted that there would be no prosecution of Francoist officials, regional groups had to postpone pressure for regional devolution, while leftist parties had to forego more radical economic policies and accept the weighting of the electoral system in favour of the conservative parties. The legalization of the PCE, allied to continuing labour unrest and ETA activity, enraged the bunker and sections of the military; a surge of rightist propaganda swept through the military.

The election saw Suarez's UCD emerge as the most popular party; it received 34.3 per cent of the vote compared with 28.5 per cent for PSOE, 9.3 per cent for PCE and 8.4 per cent for the rightist *Alianza Popular*. The election was important in structuring the political situation in three ways.[23] First, it reduced the number of politically-active cleavages in the political arena compared with the pre-war period. Political competition at the national level was structured around 'an ideologically-polarized, class-based Left-Right division', with a less important 'center–periphery, nationalism–centralism line of conflict' in Catalonia and the Basque country.

Second, the extremes of left and right received little electoral support, thereby undercutting the position of those rightists who opposed the shift to democracy. Third, moderate elements on both left and right gained a clear predominance, thereby ensuring that an ideologically-driven constitution would not be imposed on Spain. The new Suarez government had to rely on support from either left or right on issues, and therefore had little alternative but to seek concessions and compromise. But its position among rightist military circles eroded, with some officers approaching the king in September 1977 to sack Suarez. The king refused, but the government did not discipline these officers.

Despite the weakening of his conservative support, Suarez, with the aid of the opposition, was able to introduce measures consolidating the course of change. Most important here was the Pact of Moncloa, signed by 31 representatives of virtually all parties following meetings on 8th–9th and 13th October 1977. The Pact was an attempt to meet the problems posed by terrorism from the left and right, and the continuing serious economic problems, most particularly inflation, unemployment and the growing trade deficit. In return for the government implementing a series of austerity measures in the economy, in particular the imposition of wage ceilings lower than inflation, measures designed to restrict credit and public spending and structural reform of agriculture and the tax system, the government promised a range of welfare, fiscal and political reforms. Greater autonomy was promised for the regions. Maravall and Santamaria[24] outlined the left-right compromise in the political sphere in the following terms:

> the rightist parties wanted a short constitution, institutionalizing the monarchy and protecting it against any threat of change by means of an extremely rigid procedure of constitutional amendment. They also insisted on explicit recognition of a free market economy and a strong, stable cabinet with clear supremacy over parliament. The leftist parties doubly conditioned their backing of the monarchy: (1) it should be a 'parliamentary' monarchy with limited, well-defined powers; and (2) the rigidity of the amendment procedure should be extended to cover all possible revisions of a progressive and detailed bill of rights that was to preface the constitution. They accepted the principle of a market economy in exchange for recognition of the state's powers of economic initiative and its right to intervene in the economy. They accepted the

principle of reinforced governmental stability within the framework of a greater equilibrium between government and parliament, in exchange for the insertion of proportionality within the constitution as the basis of any future electoral law.

The drafting of a new constitution in late 1977–early 1978 topped off this agreement. Worked out through a process of compromise and consensus, what Preston called a 'constitutional pact',[25] this provided further guarantees for the right. It affirmed the capitalist economy, gave the church a special position, and the armed forces, which were placed under the direct command of the king, were acknowledged as the defenders of the sovereignty, independence and territorial integrity of the state and constitutional order. The constitution was passed almost unanimously by the Cortes, and ratified by popular referendum held on 6th December 1978 in which 67.7 per cent of eligible voters participated and 87.8 per cent supported the constitution.

Despite these successes, the government remained under pressure as opposition built from the right, including an aborted coup in November 1978. In the lead up to the election of 1st March 1979, political terror again escalated, with attacks on higher ranking figures causing increased concern within the bunker. When the election was held, the UCD again won, increasing its number of seats from 165 to 168, while PSOE increased from 118 to 121 (although a smaller party, the Popular Socialist Party, holding six seats from the 1977 election, had merged with PSOE in 1978, so PSOE actually lost seats). However, the popular attitude may better have been reflected in the abstention rate of 33.6 per cent. Despite this electoral victory, the government's position remained somewhat uncertain. Increased strains were developing within the UCD, leading to Suarez's replacement by Leopold Calvo Sotelo in early 1981, there were continuing rumours of military action, and a coup attempt in February 1981. Gradually such military adventurism was weakened, but it was not until the election of a PSOE government in October 1982, and its acceptance by the military, that the Spanish transition was definitively ended.[26]

Thus the key to the Spanish transition[27] was the ability of the reformist leadership in the regime, principally Suarez and the king, to keep both conservative elements in the regime and, with the considerable involvement of moderate civil society oppositionist leadership,[28] more radical elements of the opposition within the boundaries of the unfolding procedure of regime transformation.

Brazil

The Brazilian hierarchically-controlled military regime[29] had come to power in March 1964. By 1969 there was an effective fusion between the military as government, military as institution and the security services, but with the security services strengthening their position as a result of the development of urban and rural guerrilla resistance in 1960–72, and the suppression of political rights after 1968; the Congress was closed, tight censorship imposed, and political rights narrowed. However, by the early 1970s, the fusion of these components of the regime was beginning to come apart, and it began its shift toward democracy following General Ernesto Geisel's assumption of the presidency in March 1974. Geisel and his principal political adviser General Golbery do Conto e Silva, embarked on a conscious process of seeking out allies in civil society in an attempt to bolster their position against a hardline element in the military and, in particular, in the security service which was opposed to any weakening of the regime's position. Geisel and Golbery accepted the original military line that military rule was an interim arrangement and should give way to a return to civilian control,[30] and were concerned about the way in which the security service (SNI) had been strengthening its position within the state at the partial expense of the military establishment.[31] They were also encouraged to move by the effects of the first oil shock, which suggested that the Brazilian economic miracle had ended and that more difficult times were in store,[32] and by the emergence of pressures on the part of commercial and industrial interests for a greater voice in economic decision-making.

The process of liberalization was initiated by the suspension of press censorship and the November 1974 election. In the period around the time of Geisel's inauguration as president in March 1974, extensive discussions were held with people in the media as Geisel's supporters tried to assure these opinion-makers of the bona fides of their reformist credentials and to sensitize them to the dangers posed by the continuing hardline position of elements of the military and the security service.[33] This danger was clearly reflected in the activity of the SNI; of all disappearances of political prisoners between 1964 and 1979, two-thirds occurred in 1973–74.[34] The election was the means for the consolidation of political opposition in a new political party, the *Movimento Democratico Brasileiro* (MDB), which was able to elect sixteen out of 22 senators and 34 per cent of federal deputies (a total of 160), and gained 37.8 per cent of the national vote.[35] This performance was a rebuff to the government, which now set about ensuring its control over the legislative process and preventing further advances by the opposition in the municipal elections scheduled for 1976. It sought to achieve the former through the maintenance of institutional controls over the legislature and by intimidation. Strict controls were placed over the dissemination of electoral material, criticism of the government and alternative programmes. The success of this strategy is reflected in the results of the municipal elections in 1976, in which the government party (ARENA) won 83.7 per cent of all mayorships. It was therefore guaranteed a majority in the electoral college which was to choose the next president in 1978.

However, the Geisel government was still not secure, and in 1977 it feared losing control over the process of liberalization to civil society forces. It sought to meet this challenge in two ways. There was an attempt to blunt popular mobilization by the waging of terrorist acts on individuals and groups prominent in the opposition. But, more importantly, the government again changed the rules whereby popular mobilization could be conducted. New measures, the *Pacote de Abril* of April 1977, included government appointment of one third of the senators, the indirect election of state governors, changing the criteria for membership of the electoral college to the disadvantage of the centres of opposition strength (the industrialized areas), and application of the same strict controls over electoral broadcasting as had applied for the municipal elections. In addition, the government introduced legislation on national security, strikes and the press, and a prohibition on the judicial review of any action undertaken by the regime since 1964 under the laws of exception. Geisel was also able, despite military disquiet, to impose his chosen successor as president, General Figueiredo. Thus, the initial liberalization of 1974 provoked the reconsolidation of control in 1976–77.

The new Figueiredo government promised to shift the country to democracy and continued the pattern of limited concessions begun by its predecessor. Some informal channels of communication were set up with the opposition, and the government did not adopt repressive tactics when labour disputes broke out (although it did attempt to break the union leadership after the strike had ended). It also announced a general political amnesty and allowed the return from exile of pre-1964 populist leaders, although this was in part intended to cause division within the opposition. The two-party system was abolished and procedures established to generate a new multi-party system, and thereby regulate and control the growth of politically-oriented civil society forces. Direct voting for state governors was re-established, but the Congress was prevented from regaining some of its lost powers and the planned municipal elections were postponed until 1982.

By the end of 1981, five parties had gained provisional registration. The two major parties were the *Partido Popular* (PP), a tame opposition party including some former members of the government party ARENA, and the *Partido do Movimento Democratico Brasileiro* (PMDB) formed from the former MDB. One of the most important consequences of the establishment of this new system was that the complex procedures required to obtain registration reactivated party life and competition throughout the country. The opposition was increasingly confident that a genuine shift to democratization was becoming possible, with the parties believing that a solid electoral performance would strengthen their hand in negotiating the course of transition with the regime. Despite confirmation in mid-1981 that terrorist attacks on the opposition were being sponsored by the government, this confidence did not evaporate; indeed, military acceptance of the idea that a civilian vice-president could exercise the functions of the president during Figueiredo's illness in the second half of that year reinforced such confidence. Emboldened, the opposition now rejected two government law projects, and sought to cement an electoral alliance between the PP and PMDB for the 1982 elections. Interpreting these as a threat to its continued control of the liberalization process, in November 1981 the government introduced new electoral rules (the *Pacote de Novembro*).

The new rules forbade electoral alliances among parties, forced parties to present consolidated lists of candidates for election at all levels (councillors, mayors, federal deputies, senators and governors) and invalidated any vote which did not apply to all candidates (e.g. a voter could not vote for a mayoral candidate from one party and senator from another). The principal effect of this was to force competition between the four opposition parties to the benefit of the sole government party. It also rendered the PP unviable, and this now merged with the PMDB. When the election was held in November 1982, the opposition made major electoral gains; ten governors came from opposition parties (nine from the PMDB and one from the *Partido Democratico Trabalhista* – PDT), while for the first time the opposition parties (PMDB, PDT, *Partido dos Trabalhadores* – PT – and *Partido Trabalhista Brasileiro* – PTB) gained a larger share of the popular vote (48 per cent) than the government party (36.6 per cent), the Partido Democratico Social (PDS). But despite losing its comfortable majority in the House, the PDS was able, through electoral tinkering, to maintain its majority in the electoral college that elected the president. In the Congress, the opposition lacked the numbers to introduce constitutional reform and thereby change the nature of the regime.

The result of the election greatly strengthened the position of the opposition. Its victory in the four most important southern states enhanced its political base. Its majority in the House forced the government to negotiate over controversial measures, while the election of governors by direct vote sensitized even some of the PDS governors to the need to be more attentive to their constituencies, with the result that some began to show signs of increasing independence from the regime. The regime's position was at this stage cast into further doubt by the onset of a severe financial and economic crisis which stemmed from the economic policies pursued by the Geisel and Figueiredo administrations. By mid-1982 the crisis was severe, and the regime appeared incompetent, indecisive and increasingly corrupt. This exacerbated the split in the regime between those who wanted military disengagement from politics and those afraid of the consequences of this. Uncertainty and factionalism were widespread: 'former *duros* [hardliners] were converted into *blandos* [softliners], and vice versa, according to their perception of the danger of social unrest, their place in the infighting between rival factions and cliques, their personal loyalty to Figueiredo, or their allegiance to one or another military candidate to succeed him.'[36] The result of this, plus Figueiredo's inability to exercise clear personal authority, resulted in a crisis of government and of regime.

This was exacerbated by the longer term erosion of the regime's position. The destruction of the guerrilla movement by 1972 and the acceptance of democratic rules of the game by more moderate opposition forces had effectively destroyed the credibility of claims that there was a serious leftist opposition movement threatening the country and its welfare. This was instrumental in the way in which entrepreneurial and business élites in the mid-1970s became increasingly critical of the government and the role it was playing in the economy.[37] This critical position was reinforced by many middle class groups, including lawyers and journalists, and working class organizations. By the early 1980s, the regime 'had lost its raison d'être in terms of credible threat, had a much narrower base of élite support, and faced a larger, more autonomous, but democratic opposition.'[38] The disarray of the government encouraged increasing levels of social unrest and political demands from outside the regime. For the first time since 1964 business leaders openly criticised the regime;[39] hunger riots and looting occurred in some of the towns, and levels of criminal activity rose; strike activity continued to increase during the first half of the 1980s.[40] But this did not automatically feed into the growing strength of the opposition, whose image was also tarnished by the actions of some oppositionist governors who took repressive and economic austerity measures in the face of these problems. But it was the government with the greatest problem. With the ending of economic prosperity, it could no longer provide those social infrastructure and welfare measures which underpinned popular support, or at least acquiescence, and the support of the business sector. When the economic benefits disappeared, so too did the political support.

In the first half of 1984, Brazil experienced a massive, broad-based popular mobilization in favour of direct elections to the presidency, with millions of people massing in the major Brazilian cities. This campaign was opposed by the regime because it would have taken selection of the president out of its control (exercised through its dominance of the electoral college) and placed it in the broader public arena. But at the same time, there was within the military a conviction that the next president should be a civilian. Reflecting recognition of the damage that remaining in office was doing to the prestige of the military institution (a damage not compensated for by large military budgets) and the different lessons of the Uruguayan military which was at that time extricating itself from power and the Galtieri regime which was doing immense damage to the Argentinian military by trying to remain in power after the Malvinas débâcle,[41] there was a strong sentiment favouring civilian rule. When the electoral college met to select the new president, the moderate opposition candidate Tancredo Neves was elected. Neves had been chosen through significant negotiation and compromise by the opposition parties, with a number of state governors also playing a role. Importantly, he not only united the opposition, but his moderation attracted some support from within the regime, thereby splitting the vote in the electoral college. However, Neves died before being inaugurated, and was replaced by the compromise vice-presidential candidate Jose Sarney.

Sarney remained in office until March 1990, when Ferdinand Collor de Mello was directly elected to the presidency. The military was therefore able to have a major influence on the identity of the president chosen in 1985, and it remained a major force in Sarney's government: the cabinet had six military ministers, the military often acted unilaterally to quell strikes, and major areas of policy including intelligence, the nuclear industry and agriculture remained under military oversight. The military was also able to engineer the rejection of most constitutional amendments that would have curtailed its room to move.[42] Nevertheless, this marked the return of power to civilian hands, a development pursued by the regime under pressure from civil society forces and popular mobilization.

Chile

The coup which overthrew the Allende regime in 1973 brought to power what was essentially a personalist regime resting on the military.[43] While Pinochet's support base was mainly in the army, the military as a whole underpinned his rule with little wavering until the late 1980s. Upon coming to power, Pinochet crushed democratic institutions and forces in the society. The left and much of the centre was driven underground, while the right suspended public political activity. But while civil society was restricted, it was not destroyed. The new regime could not destroy the legacy of a vibrant democratic political culture which had characterized recent Chilean history and the developed network of civil society forces which structured much public life. In part reflection of this, the regime sought to generate a sense of legitimation through formal institutionalization based upon a plebiscitarian mechanism.

In the midst of dramatic economic growth at the end of the 1970s, Pinochet held his first plebiscite in 1978. As a result of widespread manipulation, the regime gained an approval rating of 75 per cent.[44] A further plebiscite in 1980 was directed at establishing a firm institutional basis for his regime. This ratified a new constitution, according to the regime by a 67 per cent vote of approval,[45] and confirmed Pinochet in office until 1988. In that year there was to be another plebiscite in which the candidate nominated by the junta would present himself for popular approval and if supported by a majority of voters would rule as 'elected' president for a further eight years. This was clearly an attempt to give Pinochet's rule the sheen of popularly-based approval and legitimation. But this 1980 plebiscite and the constitution it introduced created conditions which stimulated the repoliticization of the party leaderships. Party activity still occurred in a semi-clandestine fashion, but gradually it pulled itself out of the state it was in at the start of the decade, described by one study as 'intimidated, fearful, fragmented and impotent'.[46] It was helped in this by the economic difficulties experienced in Chile in the early 1980s and by the general politicization that occurred as a result of this, while political support from abroad for many of the parties was also evident.[47] Economic crisis also produced some wavering in the regime's support base in the business community.[48]

The economic crisis of the early 1980s produced both an incoherence within the regime and increased openings for political mobilization from within society. Popular mobilization took three main forms: the formation of various political coalitions, the revival of trade unions, and the growth of popular protest. Many of the former political parties re-emerged, reflecting their ability to maintain their identity and autonomy regardless of regime pressure during the authoritarian period.[49] Three major political blocs emerged: the Democratic Alliance (DA) formed from among the political right, the Christian Democratic and Radical parties, and sections of the Socialist Party; the Popular Democratic Movement comprising the Communists and some from within the Socialist Party; and the Socialist Bloc formed from yet further factions of the Socialist Party. Leadership of the opposition was taken by the DA, which was the largest bloc and the only one with any likelihood of being able to exercise influence in the military. In negotiations with Pinochet during the second half of 1983, the DA sought to press for democratization. Initially it wanted legal recognition of political parties, the return of some political exiles, and a timetable for the shift to democracy. This was rejected by the president.

Independent unions had been vigorously suppressed by Pinochet, but the economic hardship provided fertile ground for their rebirth. A *Comando Nacional de Trabajadores* was formed, which sought both to give leadership to the protest movement and to provide an umbrella organization for all anti-Pinochet forces. However, the ability of this movement to have any major impact was limited. The workers did not have the capacity to sustain significant levels of strike activity (e.g. employers had the state-enforced right to hire other workers during a strike), and the government used repession and violence to combat union demands. Students also gained their voice at this time, but they too were unable to generate a sustained protest movement.

The popular protest movement, initially led by the *Comando Nacional de Trabajadores* and then by DA, comprised monthly demonstrations between March 1983 and March 1984 and September–November 1984. Despite the large scale of many of these demonstrations, they had little direct effect. They were met with both military force and the appointment of Sergio Onofre Jarpa as head of cabinet. Despite his brief to talk to the DA, Jarpa's appointment was not a concession; he did not commit the government to compromise or negotiation, and he mobilized troops against the protesters. A new anti-terrorist law was also introduced in 1984, which 'marked the beginning of a new period of legalized repression, since almost all forms of political actions and expressions fall within its definition of terrorism'.[50] In November 1984 a state of seige was reimposed and repressive measures vigorously implemented, but it was not until 1986 that the opposition was finally demobilized. The regime was able to restabilize itself. But this period of opposition was significant because it mobilized wide ranks into the opposition struggle; the church, students, labour movement, political parties, intellectuals, artists and cultural figures, and slum dwellers were all evident in the emerging opposition coalition. In addition, the unrest impressed upon opposition leaders the need for unity and gave them heart that the regime could actually be terminated. It also placed strains upon the unity of the regime.

Divisions now appeared at the top of the military, with some elements concerned about the political infection of the military as a result of their involvement in the suppression of the popular protests and Pinochet's intention to continue to rule beyond 1989; these favoured a managed transition to democracy. Furthermore, the use of terror was undermining the regime's support among the middle classes and the populace at large; in March 1988 50.5 per cent of people thought the military should return to its barracks, and by July–August this had risen to 67 per cent.[51] In this context, in August 1988 the commanders-in-chief of the four branches of the military named Pinochet effectively to run for the presidency in the plebiscite. However, he was not to have an easy time of it. In February most parties had agreed to come together in the 'Agreement of Parties for the "NO"', and four months later all parties agreed to adhere to the same strategy for confronting the government. The opposition's aim in participating in the plebiscite was to guarantee the regime that change would come about through its own institutions, to ensure Pinochet's withdrawal from power, and then to negotiate with the military to bring about constitutional reform and enable democratic elections in a short period of time.[52] While the unity of opposition forces was secured in considerable part by leaving many contentious issues ambiguous, it was strengthened by the establishment of an autonomous labour movement (CUT) and by the activity of other groups, including some from business. Despite the lack of formal negotiations, opposition pressure forced the government to concede measures guaranteeing the fairness of the plebiscite: the State of Exception was lifted, exiles were allowed to return home, a fair and reasonable system of registration was instituted, access to the media was guaranteed, and an independent system of monitoring was established.

The parties ran a conciliatory campaign while Pinochet tried to mount a scare campaign based on fear of a return to the past. This tactic failed and he lost 55 per cent to 43 per cent. This meant that he was to surrender power to a civilian president to be elected in 1989, with the actual transfer of power taking place in March 1990. In the lead up to the presidential election, the opposition pressed the military for reforms, which were granted: there was expanded civilian representation in the National Security Council (the body that was to exercise broad oversight of the government), restrictions against parties espousing 'totalitarian ideas' were weakened, the number of elected senators was increased from 26 to 38 out of 47, the suspension of habeas corpus under States of Exception was prohibited, the process of constitutional amendment was eased, and the presidential term was halved to four years. When the presidential election was held in December 1989, the candidate of the seventeen-party centre–left alliance (led by the Christian Democrats and the Socialists) Patricio Aylwin was elected with 55 per cent of the vote; the government and rightist candidate Buchi received only 29 per cent. Aylwin took over the presidency in March 1990, although because of the new government's commitment to honour the provisions of the 1980 constitution, the military remained in a very influential position;[53] indeed, Pinochet remained at its head.

The transition in Chile had clearly been managed by the regime, but it had been triggered by the successful pressure placed upon that regime by the opposition of civil society forces. The regime's quest for legitimacy and its consequent locking of itself into the commitment to abide by a popular plebiscite, meant that once the voters had made their views known, the regime had little more it could do. It had no legitimation, its support base had eroded, and it had little idea about where it might take the country in the future. In addition, concerns within the military establishment about the effects upon the integrity of the institution that remaining in power could have were also important in eroding its commitment to maintain itself in power.

Transition through Extrication

Bolivia

The 1964 coup which brought the military to power introduced a political system which was hostile to the interests of the left and the urban working class and rested upon an alliance with the peasantry. Although the essence of political power was the military, this was held in coalition with some civilian political forces, represented chiefly in the creation of a formal government party drawn mainly from among the Christian Democrats and the Falange. But the regime was not stable; there were frequent changes of personnel and of policy, especially after the death of the first military president Rene Barrientos Ortuno in 1969.[54] The military did not have a strong sense of professionalism and the officer corps was fragmented and unstable, and therefore subject to internal conflict;[55] between 1964 and 1982 fifteen military officers became president of Bolivia. Throughout this period, the military remained highly factionalized. One consequence of this is that the regime did not have a clear programme for societal transformation, with the result that existing civil society forces were left largely intact. Certainly, the powerful Federated Union of Mineworkers was dismantled and strike activity suppressed, but the labour movement was not destroyed. The private basis of the economy was maintained, with the result that many of the institutions of urban civil society were not eliminated. However, nor were these powerful. The overwhelmingly clientelistic nature of pre-1964 politics had severely inhibited the construction of effective institutions of civil society, and the generally oppressive atmosphere of military rule did not stimulate their development.

Following a series of short-term leaders after Barrientos' death, in August 1971, Colonel Hugo Banzer Suarez conducted a coup which brought to power a government initially supported by the two main civilian parties, the National Revolutionary Movement (MNR) and the Falange.[56] The Banzer regime was not a regime which was able to exercise close and continuing control over society, being 'little more oppressive than several earlier Bolivian dictatorships, and a great deal milder than the dictatorship established in July 1980.'[57] It lacked internal stability, with no established procedure for decision-making. Much effort had to be expended on maintaining the fragile coalition within the regime, especially in terms of the growth of opposition within the military to Banzer.[58] Corruption remained a problem both in the regime and specifically within the officer corps, and there was a confused notion of legitimacy surrounding the regime; the president acknowledged the constitutional convention of a six-year term (although he did change the starting date from when this was to be calculated) and promised to hold elections at the end of it, but also suppressed representative organs and political parties, and replaced elected union leaders by government appointees. Increased repression, violence and torture were the order of the day under Banzer. He also adopted what he saw to be the essence of the Brazilian model: the value of depoliticization and strong government, with longer-term military rule as an alternative to open politics.[59] He established an all-party non-military government based on technocrats and non-aligned ex-politicians, but real power remained in the hands of the military and himself. In November 1974 he overthrew this arrangement and took personal power himself, based upon the military and with the parties outlawed.

However, the exclusion of independent political forces could not be sustained. With the economy booming in the first half of the 1970s, new social pressures were unleashed. Strike activity grew, and by 1976 there were national strikes, the universities had been closed, and a two-month miners' strike had shown that the only way the government could hope to stop the growth of union activity was by force. Under pressure from this popular mobilization, economic decline in 1976, the inability to negotiate access to the sea with Chile, Andean Pact (and US) pressure over human rights, and the problems of terrorism, Banzer decided to opt for a process of electoral legitimation and in November 1977 removed many of the restrictions on political activity and announced that elections would be held in 1978. He believed that he would be able to use the electoral mechanism to stabilize his position in power. However, the strength of opposition to him within the military was growing, especially to the prospect that he might extend his tenure in power. Following significant factional manoeuvring in the military, General Juan Pereda Asbun was named presidential candidate. Banzer retained his position at the head of the military.

Given the disorganization of other political forces in Bolivia, the regime looked forward to a triumph in the polls when the voting was held on 9th July 1978. However, this expectation looked shaky from as early as January 1978. A government Christmas amnesty had had little positive effect; very few prisoners were released, troops remained in the mining areas, workers dismissed during earlier strikes remained out of work, many exiles were still not permitted to return, and the labour unions remained under government control. In protest, a limited hunger strike was begun in La Paz, which by 18th January had grown to embrace more than 1000 protesters throughout the country. This also stimulated the re-emergence of free trade unions (also in the countryside), as the official apparatus of labour control collapsed, and large-scale strike activity (the highest level since 1971) broke out.[60] The government could do little, and after an initial attempt at coercion, gave in to the strikers' demands. In the months following, political parties sought to organize themselves for the coming election. Business circles were increasingly distancing themselves from the regime as the economy experienced difficulties, while the clientelistic arrangements upon which the regime had substantially relied were also in tatters. In addition, the nomination of Pereda unleashed vigorous factional conflict in the military as different groups struggled to establish a position close to the future president.

The main opposition to the official candidate was former president (1956–60) Hernan Siles Zuazo, who sought to construct a coalition including workers, peasants, students, progressive churchmen and Communists. His campaign profited from the fact that the former clientelist relationship between peasants and military was eroding, with the result that officers in the country could no longer guarantee a malleable voting population. Electoral fraud and intimidation occurred on a wide scale as military officers sought to ensure that the vote in their regions was as the centre would hope. But the pressures such officers came under and the range of solutions they sought to deal with this undermined institutional consensus and military discipline. 'What began as a "controlled" liberalization slipped out of control, as long-repressed social demands surfaced, and the authoritarian regime split into warring factions.'[61] When the election was held and its results announced, Pereda received a suspicious 50 per cent of the votes and Siles 24.6 per cent. Amid wide recriminations and criticism from abroad (which the elections had in part been designed to blunt), on 21st July 1978 Pereda seized power and promised further elections following the introduction of new electoral and party laws.

The ensuing period saw continuing conflict between rival civilian factions and manoeuvring for power within the military. It saw massive government instability, with Bolivia experiencing seven military and two civilian governments between 1978 and 1982.[62] Civilian groups could not unite to bring about a united front and thereby tackle the military head on, while the military too were unable to settle their own differences sufficiently to reassert stable rule, particularly in the face of the tumult of demands coming from society at large. Popular mobilization, in the form of worker, peasant and student organizations, and demands by the church among others for retribution for human rights abuses, occurred on a wide scale. The expansion of organized crime, principally drug-related and in evidence during the earlier periods as well, occurred as the government was hamstrung. In this crisis situation, further elections were held in July 1979. However, the result of this ballot was deadlocked; no candidate gained a clear victory at the polls, and since no one had received more than 50 per cent of the vote, the election was cast into the Congress. But here, no candidate could muster the necessary 73 votes to be ratified as president, with the result that the president of the Senate (Guevara) took up the position on an interim basis for one year.

As Whitehead says, '(t)he failure of Bolivia's second presidential election to produce a broad-based civilian coalition or an indisputable victory for one party left the process of democratization in jeopardy.'[63] Following vigorous criticism of its actions and repeated demands by the Socialist Party, in November 1979 the army seized power and closed the Congress (with the support of some 50 Congressmen), but under popular pressure, it was forced to withdraw after a mere sixteen days; however, it still continued to exercise a sort of tutelage over the civilian government. Another attempt was to be made to establish democracy with an election in June 1980, but in the lead-up to it, stability could not be gained. The civilian government, under IMF pressure to impose more stringent economic policies, only succeeded in provoking a nationwide wave of peasant protest. Violent acts were conducted against various public figures, with widespread suspicion that they had their origin in the military. The civilian parties were still unable to bury their differences and come together in a broad coalition, differing temperamentally, in terms of strategy and tactics, and in terms of the sort of democracy that they wanted to see constructed.[64] In this sense, the civilian groups lacked the essential basis for agreement and unity either about the way in which democratization should proceed or what it should ultimately produce. When finally held, the election produced a clear but by no means overwhelming victory for Siles. However, this result was not sufficiently clear cut to provide unambiguous direction and momentum for the continuation of the democratization process. In the days following the election, it seemed that the two main civilian competitors, Siles and Paz Estenssoro were going to forget their differences and move into alliance, with the latter bringing his faction of the MNR back into unity with that part of the party led by Siles. This apparent reconciliation of the left provoked the military, who carried out another, and this time particularly violent, coup on 17th July 1980. This was motivated in part, according to Whitehead, by 'the prospect of large-scale illicit enrichment for the officer corps through a more unfettered development of the narcotics trade.'[65] This government remained in office for two years, a period characterized by high levels of criminality and corruption, and by the use of widespread repression and terror. The new government was opposed by all civilian parties and groups, and although these were declared illegal, they retained considerable popular support. The rule of the junta was marked by massive civil opposition, growing economic difficulties, foreign criticism and internal disagreement within the military. This eventually forced a form of unity on the major independent political parties and in mid-1982 power was passed into the hands of Siles.

The principal dynamic of the Bolivian transition therefore appears to have been the continuing disunity experienced by both civil society forces and the military. Unable to gain a stable disposition of forces within their respective arenas, neither side was able effectively to dominate the process of transition. Civil society forces could not construct the sort of stable coalition that could exert continuing pressure on the military, while the military could not unite ranks sufficiently to ensure either an orderly withdrawal from politics or the consolidation of military rule. Hence the erratic pattern of development, reflected most clearly in the succession of military governments and coups.

Uruguay

The Uruguayan transition, symbolized by the passing of power to a democratically-elected president in 1985, was led by a hierarchically-led military authoritarian regime and political parties rooted in a developed civil society milieu. The military-led regime had come to power in 1976, thereby interrupting an extensive period of democratic civilian rule; along with Chile, Uruguay had the strongest tradition of civilian democratic politics in South America.[66] While real power in the regime rested in the three-man *Junta de Commandantes en Jefe* (overseen by a *Junta de Oficiales Generales* consisting of the 21 top-ranking generals) and military figures headed major state enterprises and agencies, civilian technocrats filled many major policy-making roles and the cabinet remained largely civilian. Nevertheless, military figures intervened in government whenever they liked, with major policy decisions often coming from informal meetings between generals and technocrats.[67] Following the coup, many left-wing and moderate military officers were purged,[68] while traditional politicians had no part to play in the regime which preferred to rely upon technocrats to give it its civilian colouring.

The military regime did not seek to establish a coalition with civilians, initially preferring to rely upon repression to stabilize its rule. However, although the 'state penetrated further into the private lives of its citizens than did any neighboring regime'[69], there was no widespread terroristic activity and the mixed economy and political pluralism were not destroyed. Civil society, which had been well established in Uruguay, was repressed but not dismantled. Initially the trade unions and the left were severely repressed, with left wing presses confiscated and the leaders arrested. While the left became atomized and confused, the traditional political parties were found in a sort of 'suspended animation'.[70] Short of finance and weak and disorganized, with some of their leading figures abroad, the two main parties (the Colorados and Blancos) remained in existence only because the regime did not press to abolish them. Members of these parties were forbidden to stand for office, while members of leftist organizations who formerly had stood for office were not only prevented from engaging in political activity, but were even denied the vote.

But while these major institutions of democratic political life were suppressed, the strength of the democratic tradition was such that the military regime did not see itself as a long-term alternative to civilian rule. Nevertheless, it did recognize the need to stabilize its rule, and from the end of 1976 it sought to achieve this through a series of 'institutional acts' which introduced amendments to the Constitution. But these did not provide the military regime with a firmly-based sense of popular legitimation. In August 1977 President Mendez announced that a new constitution would be introduced in 1980, followed in 1981 by a presidential election in which there would be a single candidate agreed to by both traditional parties. This constituted an attempt by the regime to gain plebiscitarian legitimation, a popular vote which would generate a sense of legitimation consistent with the democratic political culture which had been so evident prior to the seizure of power. In the lead up to the plebiscite on the new constitution in 1980, the military saturated the media calling for a 'yes' vote. The traditional parties called for a 'no' vote, and appealed to broad sections of the populace which, by this time, were suffering as a result of the economic difficulties Uruguay experienced at the end of the 1970s. When the plebiscite was held, there was a turn-out of 85.2 per cent, with a 57.2 per cent voting 'no' and 42.8 per cent 'yes'.[71] This result destroyed any prospect that the military may have had of generating a sense of popular legitimacy.

Following the defeat in the plebiscite, the division within the military between those who wanted to press on toward democracy, and thereby to open negotiations with the parties, and those who wished to take this off the agenda remained unbridged. The military's position was ambiguous following the plebiscite; it remained in control and politically unchallenged, yet it had no way of justifying its continued tenure in power: the plebiscite showed its lack of democratic legitimacy, there were no meaningful internal or external enemies which might have provided a justification for continued military rule, it lacked a coherent economic programme to deal with the difficulties currently being experienced, and support among its main civilian support base, the business community, was slipping.[72] In September 1981 General Gregorio Alvarez became president, although he did not have full support from within the military. Under Alvarez, the regime moved to restore a limited degree of party activity, essentially in an attempt to fill the political void between regime and people that the plebiscite had made obvious to all. Initial contacts betweeen the parties and elements within the regime had taken place in July 1980,[73] and these had led to some lifting of restrictions on political activity. Further steps were taken following Alvarez's inauguration as the regime sought 'valid interlocutors' from within the traditional party structures. Following further negotiations, it was announced that new machinery for primary elections would be established so that the traditional parties could choose new leaders, but at the same time various publications (including that of the Christian Democrats) were closed down. Following further discussions, the parties were made subject to a new statute on parties in January 1982. This decreed, *inter alia*, that unless parties were democratically organized internally, opposed violence and lacked 'international links', they could not register to participate in elections. The mode of their selection of leaders was also restructured; leaders were to be chosen by conventions elected in open primaries in November, and those primary elections were structured in such a way as 'to disrupt the ability of leaders to form cohesive blocs, to reduce the clarity and public impact of the whole process, and (as a result) to increase the power of the smallest local clientelistic bosses and patrons.'[74] The parties were able to gain the restoration of the electoral system known as 'double simultaneous vote', and therefore multiple presidential candidacies, but the bans remained on the left and many leading Colorado and Blanco politicians. The parties felt they had little option but to accept this. As the primaries approached, the military increased harassment of the opposition press and arrested four Blanco candidates and one from the Colorado Party for attacking the honour of the military.

On the eve of the primaries, the government had to announce the floating of the peso, thereby acknowledging the failure of the economic policy it had followed since 1978. The turn-out of 60.5 per cent in the primary elections in 1982 was better than might have been expected, given the gagging of the media, confusion about the voting lists and therefore who the people were actually voting for, the abolition of absentee voting, and recent emigration levels. Although this was not a plebiscite on the regime, those members of the parties participating in the primary elections who supported the regime received far less support than the critics; within the Colorado Party pro-regime figures received only 27.8 per cent of the vote, while their counterparts in the Blanco Party got less than 20 per cent.[75] The military strategy in allowing these elections to be held had been to promote the emergence of a new generation of party leaders, hopefully more cooperative than the former generation, who were now mostly in exile, had been. But the leaders who emerged at the end of this process seemed to be as strongly committed to a democratic future without military tutelage as their predecessors had been. The Blancos had chosen the exiled Wilson Ferreira as their leader, a person strongly opposed by the military and whose choice symbolized the intransigent position the Blancos were adopting with regard to the military. The Colorados chose as their leader and presidential candidate Julio Maria Sanguinetti, a choice whose moderation clearly contrasted with that of the Blancos. Not only were these new leaders committed to an anti-military future, they had some claim to democratic legitimation.

As civilian political life began to resurface, divisions within the military continued, although they were for the most part kept behind closed doors. The army remained the mainstay of the regime while the navy had become disillusioned with the process of managing change and the air force was split. The junta remained more loyal to the military as an institution than to Alvarez, thereby opening up the military as institution vs military as government tension. Within the military there were differences over the issue of returning to democracy, but all opposed any investigation of human rights abuses and the return to political life of Ferreira and the left. In practice, this meant that the military had no clear strategy to deal with the impasse into which the political situation was drifting. By 1982 the traditional parties were beginning to doubt the military's commitment to continue the move to democracy, a doubt which only strengthened the more radical elements within the civilian political forces.

Following the breakdown of talks between the military and the political parties in July 1983, a decree temporarily 'suspended' all public political activity and its reporting, while a new institutional act allowed the arbitrary banning of politicians. Student demonstrations were suppressed, with hundreds arrested. But this did not halt the surge of popular mobilization which had begun in May 1983. On 27th November an organization consisting of all parties (both legal and illegal) and many social movements organized a large rally in central Montevideo (if attendance estimates are correct, almost one sixth of Uruguay's population participated[76]) calling for all parties to take part in elections. Public rallies occurred, followed on 18th

January 1984 by a general strike. The response to the strike was mild; the trade union federation was made illegal, but its leaders were not arrested. Opposition publications appeared once again in greater numbers, and the number of unofficial organizations expanded, but the levels of popular mobilization were lower than in Chile.[77] The ban on public political activity was clearly ineffective. The military's lack of a viable strategy was evident in the moderate repression with which it responded to this mass-based activity along with the re-establishment of secret contacts with the political parties. But it is clear that there were strengthening sentiments within the military in favour of extrication, although the terms upon which that could be achieved remained under debate. This shift in favour of extrication became clear following the ascension to power within the army of General Medina, who believed that the military should be apolitical and, supported by the junta of generals, favoured negotiations with the opposition.[78] This made Alvarez even more isolated within the regime.

In early 1984 the two main parties held their conventions to choose presidential candidates for the election scheduled in November. The Blancos chose Wilson Ferreira despite his remaining in exile, banned and under threat of arrest. The Colorados chose Sanguinetti. In March the leader of the Broad Front (a leftist federation of parties and groups) Liber Seregni was released and, in an effort to achieve the rehabilitation of the left, called for national rehabilitation and pacification. Under Seregni, the left adopted a moderate, conciliatory position toward the military, an attitude which led to a break with the Blancos. At this time, too, the Colorados accused the Blancos of conducting secret negotiations with the military, charges which were damaging to the Blancos despite their denials. Relations between the two parties deteriorated significantly. In May the military set out a series of proposals, the effect of which would have postponed any transfer of power to civilian hands until 1986, but this was rejected (more emphatically by the Blancos than the Colorados). When Wilson returned to Montevideo near the middle of the year, he was immediately arrested, thereby ending any chance of negotiations between the regime and the Blancos.

In late June, a multi-party alliance (the *Multipartidaria*) voted to authorize Colorado leader Sanguinetti to negotiate with the military commanders-in-chief. This caused the Blancos to withdraw from the alliance and highlights the fundamental division within civilian ranks. The Colorados and the Broad Left favoured negotiation with the military to bring an end to military rule while the Blancos placed their faith in popular pressure as a means of bringing the shift to democracy. The tactic of seeking negotiation stemmed from the strategy designed by Seregni: what was needed was a combination of mobilization, thereby ensuring a strong left presence in the streets, concerted action, meaning achievement of consensus with other parties and movements about the way forward, and negotiation, which was essential because of the monopoly of force held by the military. The negotiations proceeded, with the opposition figures always intent on extracting concessions from the military in order to defend themselves against attacks from the non-participating Blancos. In a series of measures encapsulated in the so-called Naval Club Pact, bans on individual party leaders were lifted, the ability to fire civil servants and ban further politicians was revoked, the Broad Front and most parties (except the Communists) that formed it were rehabilitated, political rights were restored to many former politicians and militants, and the right to vote was restored to the military. No formal document was signed at the end of the talks, but the participants all agreed with the Nineteenth Institutional Act published on 3rd August: the commander-in-chief would be chosen by the president from a list prepared by the military, the National Security Council would have a majority of government ministers and continue to provide advice to the president, parliament could vote a 'State of Insurrection' suspending individual guarantees, government decisions could be appealed to the courts, military trials would be held only for those arrested under a State of Insurrection, the National Assembly elected in 1984 would act as a Constituent Assembly, and if amended the text of the constitution would be submitted to plebiscite in November 1985. The Blancos attacked this pact as being regressive and prolonging military rule, but popular opinion was more positive, even though there were still large numbers of people, including Wilson and formally the Communists (although they were able to run lists within the Broad Front), who were unable to participate in political life. Nevertheless, politics again burst into the media and onto the streets.

The military's attempt to construct a new political situation had failed, although it had done much to structure the process; many of the old politicians had survived, and the new ones were strongly anti-regime. In the lead-up to the election in November 1984, the regime tried to manipulate the electoral process by permitting multiple candidates in each party and by fostering the development of a pro-military faction in the Blanco Party and further support in the Colorado Party. This strategy also involved the legalization of the left. The strategy was successful. The Blancos vote fell from 40 per cent to 35 per cent, the Colorados remained stable on 41 per cent and the Broad Front grew from 18 per cent to 21 per cent. With the inauguration of Sanguinetti as president in March 1985, power was returned to civilian hands.

The essence of the Uruguayan transition was negotiation between regime and opposition moderates, with the more radical elements (the Blancos) largely sidelined. Continuing pressure from civil society forces was crucial in the outcome, although so too was continuing military oversight; through the Naval Club Pact the military was able to ensure the continued exclusion of its main opponent Wilson Ferreira and to avoid the prosecution of officers for acts undertaken under military rule.[79]

South Korea

From the end of the Second World War until the election of Roh Tae Woo in December 1987, with the exception of nine months in 1960–61, South Korea was ruled by authoritarian regimes. The last of these, headed by Chun Doo Hwan, had come to power following the assassination of his predecessor as president, Park Chung Hee, in 1979. Like its predecessors, the Chun regime was based substantially on the military, with significant support from the security apparatus, the state bureaucracy and large capital in the form of the *chaebols*.[80] However, a clear attempt had been made to separate the military as institution from the military as government; serving officers usually left the military before taking up leading government positions. Control was exercised principally through a combination of patronage and clientelism within the ruling structures, reinforced by a web of surveillance exercised by the security apparatus. Like all such governments it was characterized by factionalism, reflected most importantly in the way in which the promotion of Chun (and also of his predecessor Park) had been brought about by a small group of officers rather than the institution as a whole.[81] While factions were clearly identifiable, they were not seen as being of sufficient importance to call into question the stability of the regime.

The Chun regime moved swiftly to consolidate its control. Martial law was declared, a range of political parties were banned and their leaders purged, many other politicians and activists were banned from engaging in political activity, and governmental control was extended over the press and labour movement. In October 1980 a new constitution was introduced, which provided for new presidential elections after the current incumbent (Chun) had been in office for seven years.[82] Popular discontent was vigorously suppressed, including the so-called Kwangju uprising. Chun's quick action to consolidate his power reflects not just the sort of uncertainty that a new leader might experience when he came to office following the assassination of his predecessor, but the circumstances which had surrounded all of the authoritarian regimes in Korea. Throughout the post-war period, the regime's rule had always left space not just for the functioning of a large range of civil society forces, but also for some quasi-political activity to be carried out. There was public debate on policy, but this could not question the nature of the system or of the rulers. Elections since 1963 had been competitive, but the regime had been able to ensure that the opposition was never able to topple it at the poll, despite possessing substantial popular support.[83] A wide variety of non-regime organizations and institutions were allowed to function, but within clearly defined parameters. Furthermore, there was a history of student activism: major demonstrations occurred in 1964, 1965, 1967, 1969, 1972, 1979 and 1980, and although the authorities did what they could to suppress these, their consistency generated a tradition that gave substance to the notion of a sphere of activity independent of regime control.

This notion had been strengthened as a result of the regime's own development policies. Much has been written about the economic performance of South Korea, in particular the role the state has played in bringing about the massive and rapid process of industrialization that catapulted the country to the top of the tree of economic performing states in the 1980s. This development transformed the Korean social structure, expanding the boundaries of the urban middle class, massively increasing and strengthening the working class, and creating a layer of influential private businessmen. In addition, this process expanded educational opportunities throughout the country, and thereby multiplied the ranks of the student body. At the time of Chun's accession, the students were already weary of authoritarian rule, as the history of demonstrations suggests, while many businessmen were beginning to chafe under government restrictions.[84] It was the success of the government's own development policies which substantially undermined its rationale for rule: authoritarian regimes had successfully industrialized the country, and in so doing created large constituencies which were increasingly inclined to question the need for the continuation of the sorts of restrictions with which authoritarian rule was associated.

During the first half of the 1980s, popular opinion hardened against the regime. For many, the replacement of the Park authoritarian regime by another similar regime was disappointing, given the recent apparent trend toward democratization in other parts of the world. The introduction of austerity measures in response to an economic downturn in the late 1970s, including high tax burdens on the less well off, soured the regime in many people's eyes, and reinforced the growing conviction among many businessmen that the state should play a lesser role in economic affairs.[85] This popular sense of disquiet about continued authoritarian rule was reflected in the transformation of the opposition into a genuine political force at the time of the 1985 election.[86] This transformation was shown less in the votes the opposition gained in the poll than in two other developments. First, the newly formed New Korea Democratic Party (NKDP) overwhelmingly outpolled the former major opposition party, the Democratic Korea Party, many of whose members now flocked to the NKDP. This effectively united opposition forces under one umbrella. Second, the fact that the pressure the NKDP brought to bear on the regime for changes in the constitution struck an obvious resonance among the populace at large. The NKDP was concerned that unless it could push the regime to change the constitution to replace election of the president by the legislature to direct election by the populace, the regime would utilize its powers to simply choose a replacement for Chun from the ranks of its own Democratic Justice Party (DJP). The party's pressure was bolstered by increased public activism in the streets on the part of students, church groups, intellectuals and sections of the middle class.

Under pressure from this popular mobilization,[87] and in particular a number of violent rallies in April–May, pushed by the US government and aware of the recent fall of the Marcos regime in the Philippines as an apparent result of 'people power', in February 1986 the Chun administration announced that the constitution would be revised before the election due at the end of 1987. However, this opening to the opposition proved abortive. Neither side would compromise on the issue of the mode of election of the president: for the regime, this was seen as the means of guaranteeing their continued hold on power, for the opposition, the long-standing competition between the two chief figures, Kim Dae Jung and Kim Young Sam, prevented either from agreeing to a compromise because of the fear that this would advantage their rival.[88] The deadlock could not be broken, and when in September the NKDP boycotted the talks, the regime's tactics hardened.[89] This created increased tensions within the opposition coalition, leading sections of it to propose that the opposition seriously consider the regime's constitutional proposal in return for concessions in other areas. The Kims were opposed to this, and in early April 1987 they left the NKDP with their followers to form the Reunification Democratic Party.

The split in the opposition encouraged the regime to try to increase the pressure on it. In April Chun suspended constitutional discussions. The result was widespread popular disapproval. The death of a student in police custody in January had already inflamed popular passions, and Chun's attempt to halt the liberalization he had begun further exacerbated this situation. Widespread protest activity, reaching a peak in June,[90] erupted in the cities, involving students, church groups and members of both the working and middle classes.[91] Against the background of this popular mobilization, the ruling DJP chose as Chun's successor Roh Tae Woo. This further enraged the demonstrators because it seemed to imply that the regime was intent on maintaining the existing rules for choice of the president. Chun tried to blunt this popular outburst by opening discussions with Kim Young Sam, but this failed. Chun's position was further undercut by a split within the regime itself. A moderate wing, worried about the effect on the military of continued involvement in political life and favouring an opening to the opposition, had taken form in the regime since 1985[92], but it had been kept under broad control by Chun's supporters. However, on 29th June 1987 his chosen successor, Roh, publicly announced an eight point plan for democratization which accepted the demands of the opposition, including constitutional revision to provide for the direct election of the president. Despite his presumed reservations,[93] Chun formally endorsed this package. These measures, which received wide support within business circles and the middle class, effectively blunted the more radical demands being made by many of the protesters. A new constitution was worked out in negotiations between Roh and the opposition and was formally adopted in October 1987.

In the lead up to the presidential election, the fragile unity of the opposition was destroyed as neither Kim would agree to stand aside for the other in the presidential poll. While this was a function of their long-standing competition, it reflects the fact that Roh had been able to write into the constitution a presidential position without a vice-president, thereby removing the possibility of some sort of compromise between the Kims based on a sharing of positions, and election by a simple plurality rather than a majority. As a result, the opposition vote was split and Roh won with a vote of 36.6 per cent to Kim Young Sam's 28 per cent and Kim Dae Jung's 27 per cent. During Roh's period of rule, parties were able to develop more substantially and a democratic structure was embedded, and in December 1992 Kim Young Sam was elected president.

It is clear that popular pressure was a major factor in bringing the regime to the negotiating table. Important, too, was pressure from outside, especially from the US and Japan, while the approach of the Olympic Games which were to be held in Seoul in 1988 was also significant; the regime feared the impact popular unrest would have upon their hosting of this event. But it was the pressure from within, spearheaded by the opposition leadership of the two Kims and resting on their moral authority as well as their party positions which applied the sort of pressure which split the regime and led to the democratic compromise.

Transition through Replacement

Portugal

The conservative Salazar regime rested principally upon the support of the smallholder rural peasantry of the north, the large landowners of the south, petty functionaries in the bureaucracy and its agencies, the interlocking financial and industrial interests in the economy, and the church. It was, in the words of one scholar, 'an extremely conservative structure permeated by corporatist, autocratic, and authoritarian components.'[94] It was a civilian regime resting upon close military support, although as the regime aged, and in particular when Caetano succeeded Salazar, relations with the military were not close. Within the military itself there was mounting dissent in the late 1960s–early 1970s. Unhappiness at the continued dragging on of inconclusive colonial wars, professional grievances over pay levels and poor conditions, blocked promotion opportunities, and the perception that the middle ranks of the officer corps were bearing the real military burden while many of their seniors spent their days in lucrative and easy civilian postings, stimulated the build up of frustration and opposition within the military establishment. It was reflected in the formation of the Armed Forces Movement (MFA), an organization of middle-ranking officers which sought to protect their interests.

In the civilian sphere too, the regime's basis was looking increasingly shaky. The economy was characterized by massive conglomerates which had close links with the state and were effectively run by the state. The workers were organized in state-run unions. In the 1960s and 1970s foreign investment had fuelled industrialization and had encouraged these conglomerates to internationalize their operations. As they increasingly looked to the EEC, they became more and more critical of the state's interference in the economy, its inward-looking orientation, and the cost of its attempt to maintain empire. The very foundation of Salazar's *Estado Novo*, corporatist autarchy, was therefore coming under questioning from within. Furthermore, the industrial development of the 1960s and 1970s had generated major social change. It had led to increased urbanization, and with it increased social problems in the cities. This provided fertile ground for non-government forces, especially the Portuguese Communist Party (PCP), which had been operating as an underground organization, and the Socialists who in 1973 had formally established the Portuguese Socialist Party (PSP). The regime had held periodic elections (the last in 1973) which had been the opportunity for political forces to organize and to participate in political debate; while various political parties were legal under the old regime, the PCP had to disguise itself in an umbrella alliance with the PSP, and it was thus linked at the time of the coup. Nevertheless, these parties did constitute a vehicle through which interested forces could play some part in the political process. Civil society forces were not destroyed under the Portuguese dictatorship, but were kept within strict bounds.

In April 1974 the MFA seized power. Its Programme provided for the establishment of a Junta of National Salvation to rule until a civilian provisional government consisting of 'members representing groups and different political ideologies and independents who identify with this present programme'[95] was established. The provisional government was to prepare for elections to a Constituent Assembly to be elected by direct and secret universal suffrage within a year, which was to draw up a new constitution. This would be followed by elections to the presidency and a new legislative assembly. In the interim, the former regime party, the secret police and Portuguese Legion were dissolved, the military and para-military arms of the state were to be purged and reorganized, and a range of freedoms announced, including the abolition of censorship and prior notification, and freedom of expression, assembly and association, including political parties and trade unions. As well as some vague measures in the economic and international spheres, the Programme also committed the new authorities to resolution of the colonial issue by frank discussion rather than military means; the original draft of the Programme had also acknowledged the right of self-determination of the colonies, but this had been dropped at the insistence of General Spinola.[96] The new regime was thus clearly committed to a programme of political reform, including the return of power to civilian hands within a relatively short space of time, but its position on economic policy remained unclear.

The seizure of power by the MFA caught most of society by surprise. The MFA had consciously remained aloof from opposition forces in society because of fears that the clandestine parties had been infiltrated by the regime, with the coup being motivated by professional military interests rather than broader pro-democratic sentiment. A series of parties soon emerged. Of these,[97] the Portuguese Communist Party (PCP) possessed the strongest organization and was therefore best placed to take advantage of the conditions that were to prevail until the formation of a new political structure. Led by Alvaro Cunhal, it adopted a moderate stance; chastened by the overthrow of Allende in Chile in 1973, the party sought to attract the support of the urban middle class and to take action against the large landowners and the oligarchic cartels in the economy. It sought to restrain labour disputes and to end strike activity. Spinola and the centrist Popular Democratic Party (PPD) sought to foster the economic development of Portugal, and therefore looked to those groups which the Communists targeted, the large industrialists and financial institutions in particular. Despite this contrast in perspectives, Spinola invited the Communists to participate in the first government, thereby in contrast to Spain, making them central institutional actors in the transition process. But this tension within the new regime was to have important consequences for the structure of future political developments; when the MFA split with Spinola over decolonization and economic policy, the basis existed for alliance with the PCP. Even so, the dynamics of élite politics was very different to Spain: the political forces of the old regime had no part to play in structuring the course of political development, which instead lay with young and politically inexperienced people.[98]

The coup also stimulated popular mobilization. Labour conflict erupted, with strikes and industrial disputes breaking out across the country. In the capital, people gathered on the streets in meetings and demonstrations, the size of which was soon swelled by official action cancelling entry to the universities and thereby releasing all school leavers for political activity. They strengthened the leftist trend of political events, which was the natural course given the right wing nature of the regime that had just fallen. This popular mobilization was therefore important in consolidating this trend of movement: it provided a buffer against possible counter-attack by remnants of the former regime and helped to radicalize the political agenda. Such a radicalization was also fostered by events within the regime.

Following the coup, the MFA expanded considerably, from 350–400 in April to about 2000 by September 1974.[99] This created greater diversity of views within the MFA and led to the crystallization of factions ranging from supporters of Spinola who were committed to a strict interpretation of the MFA Programme to those populist radicals who favoured a vague concept of 'people's power'. The most important group were the Democratic Socialists led by Melo Antunes who saw the military as an essential part of the revolutionary process, opposed the vanguardist role adopted by the (post-June) pro-Communist prime minister Vasco Goncalves, and believed that the MFA needed a broad social base and to collaborate with the political parties in order to bring about the transition to socialism. The MFA sought to strengthen its position in July by creating a military command structure, COPCON or the Operational Command for the Continent, a development which clearly bypassed the formal command structure of the armed forces. This was led by Otelo Saraiva de Carvalho, an adherent of the populist radical faction within the MFA.

There was always tension between the MFA and Spinola and his government, and this came to a head in June when Spinola tried to dissolve the MFA. This failure led to the collapse of the first provisional government and the resignation of prime minister, Palma Carlos, who was replaced by Goncalves. In September this tension reached its apogee, as Spinola tried to mobilize the populace in a show of support for his government, but this was frustrated by COPCON-supported roadblocks around the capital[100] which prevented the conservative sections of rural society from rallying to his support. At the end of the month he resigned, being replaced by General Costa Gomes, who brought in a new, more radical[101] third, provisional government headed by Goncalves and including members of the PSP, the PCP and the PPD. In March 1975 Spinola and his supporters staged a coup attempt, which failed utterly. This not only finally discredited the right, but it confirmed that the MFA was the leading political force in the country. The MFA had undergone some organizational restructuring in the last quarter of 1974, with the establishment of an official coordinating organ, the Committee of the Twenty, which was transformed into the Council of the Revolution following the March 1975 coup suppression. This became the key institution of state, and its creation was accompanied by the purging of moderate elements from the MFA.

This consolidation of the MFA and the primacy of more radical elements within it was accompanied by a rupture in relations among the civilian parties. There had long been tension between PSP and PCP, and disagreement over organization in the trade unions in early 1975 provoked a rupture. At the same time, the PCP's popular base of support was eroding in response to disenchantment at the party's ambivalence toward wage increases and labour militancy.[102] The difficult position the PCP found itself in in pursuing a moderate course was illustrated even further when, in mid-March, the Council of the Revolution decreed the nationalization of the banks, insurance companies and much of large industry, and promised expropriation of the large landed estates. These measures widened the divisions between the populist radicals and the Democratic Socialists in the MFA. The leading echelons of the Portuguese polity were splitting into moderate and radical camps, and the PCP was being pulled between the two.

With the Constituent Assembly elections approaching, on 11th April 1975 the MFA had all political parties sign a pact which effectively guaranteed military supremacy for three years.[103] This pact provided for the MFA Programme to be implemented regardless of the result of the promised legislative elections (thereby ensuring that those elections would not result in power-sharing between the parties and the MFA), and gave the MFA Assembly (a general assembly of 240 military men established in March with unclear functions) an equal voice with the yet to be elected National

Assembly in choosing the president. But this attempt to entrench military power was significantly undercut by the results of the election to the Constituent Assembly held on 25th April. This saw the PSP emerge clearly as the most popular party. The PSP gained 37.9 per cent of the vote, the centrist PPD 26.4 per cent and CDS 7.6 per cent, the PCP 12.5 per cent, the pro-Communist MDP/CDE 4.1 per cent, and the ultra left wing Popular Democratic Union 0.8 per cent. With a 91.7 per cent participation rate, the election gave democratic legitimation to the organized political forces outside the government, and thereby placed explicit limits upon any aspirations that the military may have had to consolidate their rule. But the election was also important in a number of other ways. The clear victory of the moderate parties[104] contrasted sharply with the March rise to supremacy of the radical pro-Communist military elements in the MFA. It also showed the sharp regional distribution of party support: communist support was concentrated in the south, PPD and CDS in the north, while the PSP gained good support from all areas of the country, especially the central region and major urban areas. It was clear that no coalition of forces could now ignore the Socialists.

This near coincidence of radical dominance in the MFA and support for moderate forces in the election created a kind of impasse in the politics of the élite, and it was into this opening that mass mobilization stimulated by the economic difficulties thrust the people as a new political force. Initially mobilization occurred among three groups: industrial workers, shantytown dwellers, and rural labourers. Industrial workers pressed for better pay and conditions, and ousted many managers, replacing them with workers' committees. Shantytown dwellers moved into vacant housing, refused to pay rent, and turned to radical military officers to support them. Rural labourers in the south seized control of the estates and established their own management committees. However, this radical mobilization depended for its success upon state, and especially COPCON, support. Furthermore, it evoked a popular reaction. The urban middle class became worried about narrowing wage differentials, security of property and the breakdown of law and order, while rural smallholders in the north of the country mobilized in defence of property and religion. They expelled the Communists from the region (in August at least 49 PCP offices in the centre and north were sacked), and the radical military elements who came to try to spread propaganda among them were sent back to the barracks.

By late summer 1975, the radical phase of the Portuguese transition was drawing to a close. The counter mobilization to the radical popular activity in the summer was successful in blunting the political effect of such action. Among the political parties, the PCP's position was being eroded by ultra-left radical groups which were more in tune with the mood of those sections of the population which had been involved in the radical mobilization, and given that its Socialist opponents were firmly ensconced in the centre–left of the political spectrum, it had nowhere to move. The party was becoming isolated, particularly as its relationship with the military radicals was becoming less potent, and disunity became increasingly important in its ranks. Within the military, factionalism had become so pervasive that the integrity of the entire institution had come into question.[105] In the MFA the Goncalves group had become increasingly isolated as the initiative shifted to those around Melo Antunes who believed in the need for a much broader-based support structure than that provided by the PCP. In July both the Socialists and the PPD withdrew from the government, an action which boosted the credibility of the opposition and severely dented that of the regime. The fifth provisional government, headed first by Goncalves and then by Pinheiro de Azevedo and dominated by the PCP and MDP/CDE was sworn in on 8th August. Pinheiro was viewed as a left winger and Goncalves was promised the position of chief of staff, but just over a week later his appointment was blocked from within the military. The sixth provisional government took up office on 19th September, headed by Pinheiro and including the PSP, PCP and PPD and many original members of the MFA who had opposed Goncalves over the summer. A purge of radical and Communist sympathizers in the military was instituted. This prompted an attempted left wing coup in late November 1975 which was put down by the 'Group of Nine', officers with impeccable anti-Fascist credentials around Antunes. COPCON was closed down and, under commander-in-chief Ramalho Eanes, the hierarchical principles of unity of command which had been disrupted by the April 1974 coup were restored within the military. Moderate control of the political process was now clearly established.

Work had been proceeding on the drafting of a new constitution. There was broad consensus among the drafters, but their room to manoeuvre was bounded by the 13th April 1975 agreement between the MFA and the parties and a further such agreement of 26th February 1976.[106] This latter agreement modified the earlier one by doing away with the MFA Assembly and providing for election of the president by universal suffrage and secret ballot, but it also set limits to the ability of future governments to change the Socialist aspirations given voice in the constitution. The new Constitution referred to the 'transition to Socialism' and collectivization of the means of production, and it retained the military-dominated Council of the Revolution as an advisory and constitutional review organ. Constitutional revision was also very difficult. The Constitution was proclaimed on 2nd April 1976, to come into effect with the presidential election in June.

In April, elections were held for the Legislative Assembly. The PSP won 35 per cent of the vote, the PCP 14.6 per cent, PDP 24 per cent and the DSC 15.9 per cent.[107] In the June presidential elections, Eanes was elected with almost two thirds of the popular vote. He called on Socialist leader Soares to form a government. Civilian rule was now established, although military oversight was not formally eliminated until 1982. Henceforth politics was structured by the dynamics of party interaction.

The Portuguese transition was thus initiated by middle level officers against a militarized civilian regime. But the coup leaders and the provisional government they established, had to rely for stability upon organizations with their roots in civil society, and yet those organizations had very different aims to the MFA. It was the split between the increasingly radical section of the military and the Communists on the one hand, and the more moderate officers and the socialists and centrist parties on the other which produced the tension and governmental instability. This was exacerbated by the radicalization caused by popular mobilization, until the attempted coup of November 1975 led to a counter coup by moderates, which reasserted traditional military discipline and brought to power a group intent on the early passing of power to the civilians. The division and disunity at the top of the state structure reflected in governmental instability ensured that for a time the authority of the state collapsed, but this does not mean that the bureaucratic apparatus of that state also collapsed. The instability of the political élites did not destroy the political infrastructure, and this enabled the building of a democratic structure without too much more disruption.

Greece

The Greek regime was based on a small section of the army with little support either from the traditional right (both inside and outside parliament) or the monarchy; conservative Greek society felt excluded from power and refused to support the colonels' regime. The air force and the army had simply gone along with the coup launched by the colonels in 1967, lacking deep commitment to it. Upon coming to power the regime had sought to consolidate its position by imposing martial law, suspending key sections of the constitution, freezing political activity, arresting many civilians and purging the military. A new constitution was introduced in 1968 with some democratic elements, but these were to remain suspended until Greek society was deemed to have returned to health.[108]

However, the military regime had difficulty coping with challenges in the economic sphere. Prior to the coup, the course of Greek industrialization had led to higher levels of urbanization and social mobility. Political consciousness had been raised, and the number of professional groups and associations had expanded. When economic difficulties were experienced in the early 1970s, there was therefore a broader-based network of knowledgeable civil society forces than had existed in the past. The regime's difficulties were highlighted by the way in which one of its original bastions of support, business circles, began to shift its support away from the regime. By 1972, the colonels' regime was at an impasse: the effort to restore Greek society to health had stalled with the economic difficulties at the time in a way that was obvious to all, and yet the regime had no viable plans for the future. The regime had little popular support, being widely seen as ineffective and illegitimate.[109] Internationally, it was seen as standing in the way of Greece's accession to the EC, something popularly seen in Greece as crucial given the scale of contemporary economic problems.[110]

The regime's problems exacerbated divisions within its leading ranks, including the highest decision-making organ, the 'revolutionary council'. Upon coming to power, the regime had consisted of three groups. The first advocated an early return to civilian rule, but was soon neutralized in leading circles. The second, led by George Papadopoulos, initially favoured extended military rule but later came to favour some form of partial civilianization of rule. The third favoured indefinite continuation of military rule. In 1970, Papadopoulos began to open contacts with some civilian politicians, and moved to weaken those who sought an indefinite continuation of military rule.[111] In mid-1973, following an abortive coup attempt from within the navy, Papadopoulos announced an opening to civilian politicians. He announced the abolition of the monarchy and himself as provisional president, both to be ratified by plebiscite on 29th July 1973, after which he (as president for eight years) would lift martial law, restore civil liberties, and appoint a cabinet with a mandate to hold elections for a new parliament in 1974. When the plebiscite was held, 78.4 per cent approved of the new constitutional arrangement and of Papadopoulos as president. Following the plebiscite, Papadopoulos gained the appointment of a civilian cabinet under Progressive Party leader Spiros Markezinis, lifted martial law and partially restored civil liberties.

Papadopoulos' opening to the civilian politicians failed. Most civilian political élites dismissed the results of the plebiscite and rejected Markezinis' efforts to encourage their participation in plans for an election. Popular mobilization mounted, exacerbating differences within the military as both pro-monarchists and those who favoured continuing military rule searched for a solution. In November 1973 a student uprising at the polytechnic was bloodily suppressed, hardliners in the regime led by Ionnides using this as an excuse to topple Papadopoulos and his government and cancel all of his liberalizing measures. But the new government had no better answer to Greece's problems than the earlier regime.

The Cyprus crisis of July 1974 radicalized the situation by portraying the regime as inept, stimulating popular demonstrations, and mobilizing reserve officers and civilians from the more radical cities into the countryside. It also exacerbated splits in the regime. The Joint Chiefs of Staff, supported by the president Lieutenant-General Ghizikis, began to search for a political solution to the crisis enveloping the regime, and, by reasserting the hierarchical lines of command within the armed forces (which as in Portugal had been challenged by the 1967 coup and its leadership by non-hierarchical military officers), neutralized the power base of Ionnides and his hardline supporters; the regime established by non-hierarchical military officers (the 'colonels') was thereby rejected by the hierarchical military establishment. The Joint Chiefs thus signalled their symbolic separation from the regime. This was made clear by their attempt to meet with selected civilian leaders to discuss the means of bringing about a transfer of power. Initially agreement was sought with the National Radical Union leader Panayotes Kanellopoulos and Centre Union leader George Mavros, whose two parties had won nearly 90 per cent of the popular vote in the last election before the 1967 coup. However, this agreement was soon replaced by a decision to look to the former leader of the Centre

Union and the person who had dominated Greek politics in the 1950s, Constantine Karamanlis, as the person best placed to guide the process of transition.

Karamanlis had gone into exile in Paris following his electoral defeat in 1963 and was therefore not tarnished by the events leading to the demise of democracy in 1967. Furthermore, he was acceptable to the military because of his anti-Communism, had the confidence of the non-royalist right and much of the traditional Centre, and was not totally rejected by the monarchists. When it was evident that a simple transfer of power was not possible without some restructuring of the system, Karamanlis appeared to be the better option than the Kanellopoulos–Mavros combination. Karamanlis seemed better able to present himself as a leader who stood above party politics and representative of the nation as a whole, and therefore more likely to be the uniting figure that was needed. On 24th July he was sworn into office, only subsequently appointing ministers to his government. His strategy was to shift the system in a democratic direction while marginalising extreme Left and Right and providing guarantees to the military to ensure it remained out of active politics.

Karamanlis' appointment through negotiation between the military hierarchy and civilian actors effectively constituted, in the words of one study, a 'transfer of power by a state institution to a caretaker government [that] precluded a revolutionary "interim government" as in Portugal.'[112] Karamanlis' initial cabinet was dominated by people associated with the right and centre-right in the post-war period, and although there were no representatives of the Centre-Left forces, it included a number of people (e.g. Mangakis) who symbolized the future break with the hard right. He introduced a series of measures restoring, at least temporarily, elements of the pre-junta political system. He retained the existing president as interim head of state, announced that a constituent assembly would prepare a new constitution, and legalized all political parties, thereby enabling the Communist Party to operate legally for the first time since the civil war. He postponed any action against officials of the colonels' regime until he had gained electoral legitimation, despite pressures for action, and he restored to their former positions many of those military leaders who had been purged by the colonels following their seizure of power in 1967.[113]

Karamanlis also acted to try to consolidate the position of the centre and centre-right forces, particularly by going to the polls early rather than later. The sooner he went to the election, the less time his opponents on the left, particularly the Communist Party and the newly-formed PASOK, had to organize. An early election also maximized his ability to run as a national leader, above party politics, and to give the election a plebiscitary sheen. This was aided by his attempt to restructure the system in such a way as to remove the legal and institutional nexus that had reserved the benefits of the system solely for the victors of the Civil War, thereby creating a sense of Greek society that was much more inclusive than before. The issue of the head of state was resolved in a December 1974 plebiscite which unambiguously declared Greece a republic. Thus Karamanlis was able, in the months before the November 1974 election, substantially to guide Greek development in the direction of democracy and, following his overwhelming victory in the election, that democracy was confirmed.

So, in Greece, a reassertion of control within the military by the established leadership over lower level ranks, associated with the cooptation of a civilian political leader who was able to mobilize, and control, civil society structures while retaining military support/neutrality, constituted the essential dynamic of the Greek transition.

Argentina

A hierarchically-led military regime ruled Argentina from 1976 to 1983, but its practice differed substantially from that of its neighbours. Its relationship with civil society forces was poisoned by the assault on society that was the so-called 'dirty war' of 1975–77 in which large numbers of people disappeared. The regime did not create tame parties or hold elections as in Brazil, did not construct a constitution and subject it to popular approval as in Uruguay and Chile and, at least in part because of the chronic internal disunity, had no coherent plan for ruling in the longer term. Indeed, the levels of disunity within the military were very high.[114]

Argentina had seen a pattern of political cycles since 1955 in which political mobilization had stimulated military coups and a tightening of control. This cycle was still in evidence at the end of the 1970s, when an attempted liberalization of the regime was brought to an end by the General Galtieri-led coup of December 1981; negotiations which had been under way with the coalition of five political parties called the *Multipartidaria*, were ended. Galtieri hoped to be able to consolidate his position of leadership by relying on the range of conservative provincial parties that had emerged, using them to build a new political force that would sustain his ambitions to continuing rule of Argentina. However, because of the deteriorating economic situation and the associated general strike and demonstrations throughout the country in March 1982, he knew that he could not hope to win an early election, so envisaged continuing military rule until the economic situation improved. To assist this, he signalled the adoption of neo-liberal economic policies.[115] However, this move was unable to end the economic crisis besetting Argentina, while the accompanying governmental crisis was exacerbated by the failure of the Falklands/Malvinas campaign in 1982. Following the military defeat, Galtieri was replaced as army commander-in-chief by General Cristino Nicolaides, who unilaterally appointed as president a retired army general Reynaldo Bignone. Bignone now formed a caretaker administration, promising 'an orderly, shared, and concerted transition to democracy',[116] despite the fact that the military junta was split over his appointment; both the navy and air force were opposed to his appointment, which had been made unilaterally by the army.

The military tried to sketch out the boundaries of this transition by issuing a fifteen point document in November 1982. This demanded, *inter alia*, military participation in the next government, no enquiry into the dirty war or military corruption, and no dismissal of military-appointed judges. It also contained a veiled threat that, should these conditions be refused by the parties, hardline officers might act to halt the whole process. The *Multipartidaria* rejected this document, mobilizing a huge public demonstration to repudiate the military regime. In April and October 1983 the military again sought to ensure that there were no recriminations against those involved in human rights abuses during military rule,[117] but both of these documents were also rejected. The military remained split, the economy continued to experience difficulty and popular activism and opposition increased,[118] with the result that the pressures for military withdrawal increased while the capacity of the military to shape the conditions under which it would withdraw weakened. In the words of one analysis, the weakness of the military meant that

the Argentine transition began with fewer agreed-upon restrictions by the political parties than in Brazil, Uruguay or Chile. The parties did not accept an indirect presidential election as Brazilian parties did in 1985. The parties did not accept the exclusion of a major presidential candidate as they did in Uruguay. And the parties did not have to agree to begin government with key parts of the authoritarian regime's constitution still in effect as they did in Chile. Argentina had the only unpacted and the most classically free transition [of these South American cases].[119]

In the period leading up to the October 1983 presidential election, it was widely assumed that the Peronists would win the election. With this in mind, the junta sought to negotiate the transition with the Peronist trade union leaders who were the principal powers in the Justicialist (Peronist) Party. Rumours of a deal whereby control over the unions under a government trusteeship was to be exchanged for immunity from prosecution for the military gave public substance to the suspicion that a pact had been reached between the junta and some union leaders. This was given some support by the declaration of the Peronist presidential candidate Italo Luder that if he was elected he would respect the amnesty the military had accorded to all who had committed crimes during the 'dirty war'. 'Had the Peronists won the elections, Argentina's transition would have been interpreted as a carefully staged, incumbent-controlled one on the Brazilian, Chilean, or Spanish model, not as a case of "regime collapse" as in Greece or Portugal.'[120] However, the military made no attempt to revise the constitution in an endeavour to secure their position, and although the new electoral law introduced in June 1983 made it easier for small parties (and therefore the conservative provincial parties to which Galtieri had looked) to gain seats in Congress, the major parties did not see this as an issue worthy of major conflict. Popular mobilization mounted in September 1983, with demonstrations in support of human rights and democracy, a tax revolt in the Buenos Aires metropolitan area, and a general strike. There was a significant increase in party membership, with nearly 25 per cent of eligible voters having joined/rejoined parties by March 1983. Finally, in the presidential election in October, the leader of the Radical Party Raul Alfonsin defeated Justicialist candidate Luder 52 per cent to 40 per cent.

Ultimately in Argentina, the hierarchically-led military regime sought to extricate itself from power in the face of mounting opposition from civil society forces and an incapacity to deal with the country's problems. It sought to negotiate aspects of this transition with one section of civil society, maintaining itself in power for a significant period after its humiliation in the Malvinas conflict while it sought to structure its withdrawal. However, in practice, its attempt to entrench defences for itself failed because those forces with whom it had mainly negotiated were defeated in the presidential election.

Two things are clear from the summaries of these cases of transition. First, how imprecise the distinction between the different modes of transition (transaction, extrication and replacement) is. While the essential difference between them is clear in principle, in practice this is not always easy to discern. The key to this is who takes the lead (regime or opposition) in the process of transition, and, where the opposition plays the leading role, the capacity of the regime to play a positive part in this process. This involves judgements about both the strength of the respective sides and who played an initiating and who a reactive role at various stages of the unrolling of the transition. Sometimes this latter judgement is easy to make, but at other times it is very difficult, at least in part because the process of change is an unbroken one in which successive developments are linked together by a long chain of causation in which primacy is not clear. Ascertaining the relative strengths of the two sides is also not always easy. This is something which can change over time, both in terms of an overall judgement about the relative strength of each party, and the changing relative importance of the component elements of what constitutes that strength. A number of different elements can contribute to the strength of the respective actors: unity, organization, popular support, possession of a clear programme, and leadership all contribute to this, but at any one time the state of each of these may be different. It is not clear, for example, what the effect would be if an opposition had high levels of unity and popular support but was deficient in the other three areas, while the regime had little unity or support but high levels of organization, effective leadership and a clear programme. It is difficult to generalize about such judgements; they must be analysed on a case by case basis, but this remains a very difficult matter.

This relates to the second thing that is clear from these case studies: transition cannot be understood without full recognition of the role played in structuring that process by civil society forces.

These remain central to an understanding of that process, but they do need to be seen in the context of the state of the regime. The process of transition is an interactive one, with regime and opposition both playing a key part in shaping how that process unrolls. The part played by civil society forces in the above case studies illustrates the ways in which transition is structured by such forces.

In looking at the role played by civil society forces, five distinct contributions to the process of transition are evident. First is the sense of threat perceived by sections of the regime which then encourages that regime to embark on a process of liberalization. When a regime runs into difficulties, usually as a result of the sorts of performance failures discussed in Chapter 2, it could respond by tightening control and trying to ride out any political consequences of those difficulties. But in those instances when transition occurs, the regime, or a section of it, has decided that this is not a viable option and that there needs to be some sort of opening to the society as a whole in an attempt to bolster the regime's stability and better enable it to handle the putative crisis. The focal issue here is what causes a regime to adopt one strategy rather than another. Many factors may be relevant here, including the internal state of the regime itself, the personality of individual leaders, and the depth of the crisis. But also important will be the state of the society. If the society is atomized and there are few or no organized groups with the capacity (even if only potential) to be politically active and to mobilize popular support onto the streets to put pressure on the regime, the rejection of liberalization and the tightening of control may be a viable option for a regime under pressure from performance failures. However, if civil society forces have been able to develop, and particularly if this has included a political dimension through autonomous political organization having taken root, the situation will not be so apparently straightforward for the regime. Autonomous political organization implies the ability to act independently in the political arena and to thereby mount pressure upon the authorities, and if this is combined with a perceived capacity to mobilize large numbers of citizens onto the streets, the case for granting concessions by the regime becomes more compelling. In this sense, the presence of strong civil society forces can be a key element in persuading regime élites of the need to embark upon a course of liberalization, while the absence of such forces can confirm such élites in the belief that compromise is not necessary (although it need not; an élite may believe that liberalization is the only way the regime can escape from its difficulties eg. Gorbachev in the USSR).

Spain provides a good instance of the operation of this factor. There was no single precipitating crisis for the regime which brought on the shift in a democratic direction. Although the imminence of Franco's death did raise the issue of succession, there is no evidence that this could not have been handled in a regularized fashion by the regime. But what had changed is that, over time and as a result of official development policies, the society had become more complex, autonomous organization had multiplied and become stronger through the increasing density of civil society networks, and the citizenry had become more demanding and critical of the government. Consequently (although admittedly after the use of force had failed) the regime responded to such pressure, even before it could be said to have been in crisis, by opening to the society and embarking on the course of transition. Similarly, in Chile and Uruguay, the strength of democratic and civil society traditions and forces encouraged the respective regimes to seek a plebiscitarian form of legitimacy. The strategy backfired in both cases, but its genesis lay in the belief in the efficacy of such legitimation on the part of both regimes, a belief that had its roots in the strength of civil society tradition in both societies. These three cases are merely particularly clear instances of this general point: the presence of civil society forces embodies a real sense of threat to the regime when it suffers setbacks because those forces imply the possibility of popular mobilization and the consequent unseating of the regime. Under such circumstances, regime élites will often see cooperation and compromise with those forces as the option with the best prospects of ensuring their longer-term survival.

The threat posed by civil society forces is related to the second function performed by civil society forces, the giving of a democratic orientation to regime change. In historical terms, the overwhelming majority of cases of regime change have involved the replacement of one type of authoritarian regime by another. Even when this regime change has been motivated by performance failure, rarely historically has it resulted in a change in basic regime type. The states which experienced transition to democracy have therefore been unusual in this respect, and it has been the presence and strength of civil society forces which generally have been crucial in this regard. In principle, there is little reason for regime élites to choose democratization as a response to regime difficulty.

Democratization introduces new, non-regime élite players into the political game, it increases the level of élite uncertainty, and it takes control of that élite game out of élite hands. From the perspective purely of élite self interest, it would seem to be more advisable to opt for some sort of reconfiguring of élite relations within an authoritarian structure than to overthrow that structure and replace it with one characterized by the uncertainties of democracy. But this option was rendered more difficult by the presence of civil society forces. At the philosophical level, civil society can be realized only through the strengthening of democracy and the conduct of public affairs with the openness and wide involvement that goes with a democratic structure. In this sense, then, the functioning of civil society forces posed a philosophical challenge to authoritarian rule and thereby stood in the way of the replacement of one authoritarian set of arrangements by another. But at the more practical level, many of the civil society groups were less advocates of democracy in principle, than people who saw democracy in an instrumental way: support for democracy was seen as the means of them gaining entry to political life. In this sense, they would support democracy in order to gain such access for themselves, but sometimes would then seek to close off such access to other groups. The attitude of business groups is illustrative of this tendency. When they deserted the regime in Brazil and took up the call for democracy, they were seeking to entrench themselves in a position of influence with the new regime, but they were not in favour of the sort of democracy which would admit the masses into political life in a major way. A similar attitude was evident in Korea. But in practice, this sort of position rarely can be sustained. Where civil society forces cover the spectrum, one section usually cannot monopolize political life to the exclusion of the others, with the result that even when their real aim is limited to their own involvement, simply by mounting the principled argument, the way is opened for others. Thus, even when civil society forces struggle for their own narrow interests, providing there is a spread of such interests and groups, the democratic cause should be advanced. The simple presence of civil society forces thus embodies a form of political arrangement at odds with the authoritarian structure of the regime, and thereby pushes change in a democratic direction. The failure of the attempts to reassert the control of military elements in Portugal (the MFA), Greece (the toppling of Papadopoulos) and Argentina (the Galtieri coup of 1981) illustrates the importance of civil society forces in narrowing the authoritarian options and promoting those of democratization; in none of these cases was the rehabilitation of authoritarian rule possible.

This is related to the third function performed by civil society forces, the maintenance of the course of change on track towards democratization. One form this takes is through negotiation with regime élites, and this is discussed below. But another has been through the continuing exercise of pressure in an endeavour to support reformist elements in the regime and to prevent any backsliding on the regime's behalf. A number of forms of such pressure have been evident. One has been through the generation of a high level of public discourse and disclosure. Those civil society forces which are active in the political realm seek to generate and participate in public political debate and discussion. They use the press and the media to advance their points of view, to criticize their opponents, and generally to promote the cause of change. By doing so they are not only educating a wider public and thereby building up momentum behind the course of change, but they are also making it more difficult for an authoritarian backdown on the question of political change. By cultivating the public sphere in this way, they not only assist in the transition, but are helping to build an essential pillar of post-authoritarian democratic life. They are often aided in this by the holding of elections. When the regime holds elections, even when it tries to limit their impact by restricting involvement or competition, this provides a boost for non-regime civil society forces. It provides them with a platform, it focuses public attention upon them, and it legitimates their criticism of the regime. Furthermore, if anti-regime forces do very well in the polls, as for example in Brazil, Uruguay and Portugal, it boosts their standing, gives them the status of viable political actors, and diminishes the regime.

Another way in which civil society forces can exert pressure on the regime is through the mobilization of supporters. Electoral success is one form of this, but another is the organization of direct popular activity – principally strikes and demonstrations. The development of this sort of activity is of particular concern to authoritarian rulers because mass activity threatens a loss of control both of the process of change and of society more generally, which in turn could mean unrestrained reprisals against those rulers. The organization of direct popular activity can be a potent symbol of opposition strength, as for example in late 1983–early 1984 in Uruguay, highlighting the isolation of the regime and tingeing the message with a vague sense of threat of 'the mob'. The organization of such activity can be a potent symbol of the strength of civil society forces, although in practice it could also represent the weakness of those forces. If popular activity is spontaneous and weakly guided by civil society forces as in Bolivia, if for example the trade union structure is weak and workers embark on uncontrolled strike activity, this may both highlight the organizational weakness of civil society forces and in itself constitute a powerful argument for a strengthening of those forces. In this sense such activity may encourage the regime to try to boost the role and importance of civil society forces in order to blunt the possibility of popular upsurge. Such a course of action would also be supported by many of the civil society forces themselves, which would see the danger posed to their own future by a radicalization of the process of change through popular direct action. The exclusion of the Communists from the process in Spain and of the Blancos in Uruguay reflects this concern to blunt radicalization and consolidate moderate control over the process. Thus, the conduct of direct popular action can be a potent means of exerting pressure on the regime as well as of boosting the position of civil society forces. The role civil society forces can play in blunting the drive to radicalization that may be embodied in direct action is also related to the next function.

The fourth function performed by civil society forces is provision of a negotiating partner for the regime. Central to successful transition is the working out of agreements between the regime and other political actors. The issue here is the basis upon which regime élites choose with whom to negotiate. They need to negotiate with people who have a broad base of support and who can carry their constituencies with them. It is no use negotiating with someone who is likely to carry little authority within opposition ranks more broadly because they will not be able to give the sorts of guarantees or make the sorts of commitments which regime élites require. As a result, those with whom regime élites seek to negotiate will be people who exercise authority within the civil society milieu; the turn to Karamanlis in Greece and Kim Young Sam in Korea are examples of this. Often these are leading figures in political parties or trade unions, people whose prominence and authority stems in part from their institutional positions. It is essential if negotiations are to be successful that major players among the civil society forces are involved. The danger for the regime in failing to involve the relevant forces in such negotiations is evident in the Argentinian experience, where the negotiations with the Justicialists were overrun by the latter's defeat at the polls and the rise of Alfonsin. In this case the agreements worked out came to nothing, and the impact on regime élites was to prove significant. Thus it is the civil society forces which in large part shape the identity of the negotiators with the regime, and it is their interests, concerns and perspectives which help to shape the course of those negotiations; what they will accept and what they will not defines the options for the regime élites.

Fifth, civil society forces constitute the basis upon which any stable democratic regime which issues from a process of transition must rest. In this sense civil society forces provide the basic social and political infrastructure which is necessary to sustain an emergent democratic system. Once the shift from authoritarian rule has been set in train, the unleashing of civil society forces (even if some like the Communists are either excluded from participation or kept under restraint) provides not only an important stimulus to that process as noted above, but also a crucial constituent part of the construction of the new order. The development of a vigorous civil society characterized by public contestation of issues and autonomous organization of interests provides the basis for a well-founded political system based on democratic principles. Without it, politics will remain an élite activity and the achievement of a democratic system will be compromised. During the transition, the development of a vigorous civil society can give confidence to those seeking democracy because it promises to facilitate the consolidation of democratic government. This is discussed in the Conclusion.

The capacity of civil society forces to play the sorts of roles outlined above depends in part upon the state of those forces themselves. The more developed and powerful civil society forces are, the greater the role they should be able to play during the course of transition. But what do we mean by 'developed and powerful' civil society forces? The principal component in this is organization, defined broadly. If the essence of civil society is autonomous groups, one of the keys to group success is effective organization. This refers to the existence of an organizational structure which enables the group both to conduct its activities and to do those things necessary to maintain the group's coherence and integrity, to the capacity for the articulation of interests and views from the membership to the leadership and vice versa, and to the capacity of the leadership to ensure that its decisions are accepted by the membership. When these characteristics exist, effective organization is present, and the group should be able to function effectively as a unit. To the extent that individual civil society forces (parties, trade unions, interest associations, etc.) possess these characteristics, they can act in a coherent and disciplined way in pursuit of the interests they represent. To the extent that such groups dominate the civil society milieu, then civil society forces generally are well developed.

The capacity of groups to develop such organization will depend upon a range of issues, including the nature of the interest which unites people, the ease of contact and communication between members, and the personalities of the individuals involved. But also crucial is the attitude of the regime to the development of groups. If a regime takes a conscious decision to break up such groups and it has the capacity to penetrate society to its lowest levels, the development of such groups characterized by effective organization will be very difficult. It could only occur in a clandestine fashion and both its activities and support would be likely to be highly circumscribed. Regimes which seek to penetrate society to this level and thereby atomize its citizenry are usually called totalitarian. None has achieved complete atomization. Most authoritarian regimes have not sought the degree of control that goes with atomization, instead ceding to civil society forces an arena of activity within which, as long as they do not threaten the regime, they can function with some independence. Sometimes a pseudo civil society can emerge, but it is pseudo because it lacks the political components which are essential to any genuine civil society; a real network of groups and organizations can grow up representing a diversity of interests, and sometimes even acting as intermediaries with the state on behalf of those interests, but unless there is the capacity to act politically, this does not constitute a civil society. Nevertheless, the very existence of these civil society forces and the way in which they can embody a public culture so at odds with that demanded by the regime, constitutes a basis from which political activism can emerge should the controls of the state be weakened or removed.

Under most authoritarian regimes, then, civil society forces can exist even if there is no fully developed civil society. These forces knit together public life and provide the non-regime structures through which much of that life is pursued. These organizations also underpin political activity, although they do not normally participate in it themselves. Political activity is conducted by organizations whose principal *raison d'être* is such activity, principally political parties. Sometimes other types of organization can play a significant political role, such as trade unions and employers groups, but this is usually a by-product of their primary concerns. In any event, it is these politically-oriented civil society forces which usually are repressed even when scope is given by the regime for other civil society forces to function. It is the capacity of these politically-oriented forces to take advantage of the weakness of the regime to assert (or if they were suppressed under the regime but had a pre-authoritarian presence in the society, to re-assert) their positions, to develop their organization and mobilize their support, which will go a long way toward shaping the course of the transition. The ability of such groups to come to the fore, to cobble together some common positions among leading oppositionist forces, and to mobilize civil society more broadly will have profound implications for how the course of regime change is played out, as the case of Bolivia compared with Spain shows in sharp contrast.

As this makes clear, the other side of the coin is the regime. The Linz/Stepan emphasis on the nature of the regime discussed earlier is relevant here. The type of regime and its particular institutional contours can have implications for the course of transition as they argue and as the comparison of the Argentinian with the Greek and Portuguese cases discussed above illustrates very clearly. But what may be more important, at least in the current context, is the capacity within the regime for the leaders to demand and obtain unity, or at least prevent obstruction and disruption. Given that, as argued in Chapter 2, regime change involves at an early stage a split within the regime élite which the regime lacks the institutional means for resolving, if the transition is to proceed peacefully, reformers must ensure that this split does not derail or poison this process. Depending upon the strength of the conservative elements (and often these are associated with the military, so their perceived strength may be out of proportion to their numbers in élite councils), reformers may have to compromise on their plans and persuade their civil society-based partner negotiators to accept less than their optimum demands. The role played by the so-called 'bunker' in the Spanish case is a good instance of this. They may have to negotiate exit guarantees, including promises of immunity, in order to head off conservative opposition. In any event, what is important is that those favouring change are able to ensure that those within the regime opposed to that course of developments do not interfere with the process. Where they cannot ensure that, as for example in

Bolivia, the process will either be aborted or rendered that much more difficult to achieve.

So it is the interaction of civil society forces and regime élites which is central to the course of transition. The case studies illustrate this interrelationship.

In Spain divisions developed in a long-lived regime, principally as a result of the imminent demise of the leader, the emergence of new generations of regime functionaries, and the growth of social pressure stemming from the major socio-economic changes the society had undergone in preceding decades. The interest on the part of sections of the regime in opening dialogue with the society was therefore not prompted by any single development, but rather by a gradual shifting both of the composition of the élite and of the ground under the regime. When reformist regime elements sought negotiating partners within society, they benefited from the strength of civil society forces, particularly in terms of the ability of political leaders to build parties quickly and to meld them into united alliances. Furthermore, although there were periods of mass mobilization, the opposition leaders were able to keep their mass supporters in line, thereby preventing the excessive (in the eyes of their regime partners) radicalization of the process while keeping pressure on for that process to continue. This ability was related to the developed nature of Spanish civil society forces and in particular to the linkages that existed between electorate and parties. With regime reformists holding the upper hand within the regime and moderate opposition leaders heading organizations with their roots firmly embedded in a developed civil society, the conditions were perfect for a negotiated transition.

In Brazil the regime was under greater pressure than it had been in Spain. Divisions had developed within the regime, the harsh policies of repression it had been associated with had alienated wide sections of society from it, and it was buffeted by the consequences of economic downturn. Civil society forces were not as strong in Brazil as they were in Spain, but there was still sufficient basis for the development of opposition parties, which were able to gain significant sustenance and strength through successive elections. Pressure from the parties, bolstered by significant popular mobilization and the loss of regime support from the business community, plus the growing realization within the regime that continued tenure of office threatened considerable damage to the military as an institution, persuaded regime figures to reach agreement with the opposition on the terms of the military's return to the barracks. The greater potential strength of the regime (in particular its capacity to wield coercive force) relative to the opposition civil society forces explains the protracted nature of the transition and the way the regime was able to determine its terms.

In Chile, a vibrant democratic culture rooted in a strong civil society had not been destroyed by the regime and when, in its search for plebiscitary legitimation, that regime provided the opening for political activity on the part of opposition forces, they were well set to take advantage of it. Although there were periods of popular mobilization, the parties were able effectively to head and guide the opposition, enabling them to keep the process on track and not become so radicalized as to tempt regime conservatives into precipitate and decisive action. The parties, bolstered by the obvious strength of popular support, were able to pressurize the regime, wring concessions from it, and finally defeat it at the 1988 plebiscite. Under pressure both from within the regime and the society more generally, Pinochet was left with little option but to negotiate the terms under which power would be returned to civilian hands. But his position remained sufficiently powerful that he was able largely to dictate those terms.

Bolivia marked a clear contrast with the more orderly process in the three countries already discussed. The principal factor shaping the course of the transition in Bolivia was the lack of unity on the part of both sides. The regime was constantly split and factionalized, and the mechanisms for keeping this within bounds were clearly deficient, as shown by the succession of coups between 1978 and 1982. But on the side of civil society forces, too, there was little effective organization and activity until the eve of the transfer of power in 1982. While the civil society had not been destroyed by the regime, the development of civil society forces had been weak, reflecting in part the historical legacy, but also the inability of potential opposition forces to come together in a united front. Despite the evident instability of the regime, the weakness of civil society forces meant that it was able to remain in power longer than might have been expected. Neither side was able clearly to dominate the process of transition, thereby rendering it messy and extended.

In Uruguay, where like Chile there was a history of vibrant civil society and of democracy expressed through party activity, the regime's attempt to open up links and dialogue with society by reviving the parties which had been suppressed only provided the opportunity for these bodies to press for democratic change. Using their still strong links with the mass electorate and sponsoring various forms of popular mobilization, the parties were able to use the opening provided by the regime to restore their positions and increase pressure upon that regime. Despite subsequent setbacks as a result of regime crackdowns, part of the opposition (the Blancos boycotted talks) was able to use its mass support to persuade the regime to enter into negotiations with it. As a result of these negotiations, the path was laid down for the change in regime. The discipline of both regime and that section of the opposition which took the lead in negotiating with the regime were crucial in reaching this outcome.

In Korea, civil society forces had developed principally as a result of the course of Korean industrialization, and they were able to achieve a degree of unity around the moral leadership of the two Kims. The regime's strategy of limited liberalization through constitutional talks did cause a split in opposition ranks, but the attempt to wind back liberalization was met with increased levels of popular mobilization. This provoked the split within the regime and subsequent negotiation of the principles of the shift to a more democratic system.

The old regime élite played no part in the shift to democracy in Portugal, having been removed from office by a coup at the outset. But the new rulers stemming from the middle reaches of the military did not have effective mechanisms to ensure continuing unity among the factions which developed, and this was exacerbated when policy was radicalized in late 1974. This radicalization caused a breach with the political parties, which had emerged in the wake of the overthrow of the old regime. Resting on a legacy of a developed civil society, something which had actually grown and become more complex under the Salazar regime largely as a result of its economic development policies (although independent political organization was weak), moderate parties established their leadership over a significant part of the opposition. However, outside their control mass mobilization occurred on a large scale, both in the cities and in parts of the countryside. It was this which provoked a conservative coup from within the military against the radical officers in November 1975, a reassertion of traditional military discipline, and a commitment to pass power to the civilian parties. Negotiations with the moderate parties then ensued, leading to the peaceful transfer of power by means of elections.

The Greek regime was a narrowly-based military regime with little substantial social base in the society. As a result of the development policies of successive Greek governments, the conditions for the development of civil society had been present, and such a society had emerged. It was not crushed by the military regime, although its political elements were substantially constrained. However, when the regime suffered a number of setbacks, including the failure of an attempted opening to the civilian politicians and the radicalization of popular opinion, those at the top of the military hierarchy jettisoned the colonels who constituted the government and opened negotiations with oppositionist forces. Ultimately those negotiations occurred with a leader whose stature and position enabled him to exert leadership over civil society forces, to agree a course of transition, and get most of the opposition to support it. In effect the military leadership coopted a civilian leader who could deliver broad public support, and used him to extricate the military from power, bypassing those within the regime who had reservations about this course. But civilian involvement was clearly crucial.

In Argentina there was a legacy of a developed civil society and a competitive political system and these were not destroyed by the military regime. The regime was itself divided, but following military defeat and the onset of economic problems, a new leadership sought to find a way for the military to withdraw from power. Attempts to place significant restrictions on the post-military regime and on political life were rejected by civil society forces, which, resting on clear popular support, were strong enough to resist regime pressures. The regime entered negotiations with one section of the civil society in an attempt to gain favourable conditions for its withdrawal, but these plans were thwarted by the election result and the defeat of the regime's negotiating partner, the Justicialists. The regime's position had thus been so weakened that it was unable to structure the transition, which was taken out of its hands.

The experiences of these countries suggest the outlines of an explanation of democratization that acknowledges both regime élites and civil society forces as essential to this process. What is crucial to this is the relative strength of both of these sides: where the regime is stronger and decides to seek to institute regime change, it is likely to be able to manage that process to its own benefit; where oppositionist or civil society forces are stronger, the capacity of the regime élite to control the process is reduced significantly. It is clear that both sides are crucial. It is unlikely that regime élites would opt for democratization in the absence of forces based in society pressing for such an outcome. In this sense, the actual presence of democratization is usually inexplicable in the absence of civil society forces. But those forces do more than just place democratization on the political agenda. They help to structure the process whereby that is achieved. They provide the pressure which can keep regime élites on the path to political change. They provide the negotiating partners for regime élites to engage with. They can be the means for preventing the radicalization of the process as a result of uncontrolled (or controlled by the extreme left) mass mobilization and thereby avoid the possibility of inciting a conservative backlash which could halt the process of change. If civil society forces are sufficiently strong to be able to be involved in the process of negotiation with regime élites in a major way, it is likely that the initial restrictions upon democracy will be fewer. If those forces are less involved or are significantly weaker than the regime, as in Chile, the likelihood is greater that the outcome will be one in which democracy is more constrained, at least in its initial stages.

But it is not only the relationship between regime and opposition that is important here. The internal dynamics of both is also central. While it is important initially for democratization that the regime should split, with one section of it committing themselves to political change, once that split has been established how it plays out in practice will directly affect the course of transition. If the split leads to fragmentation within the regime and no section of it able to clearly establish its control and deal with the others (either by imposing unity on them or by expelling and disarming them), the regime's ability to play a positive part in structuring the new political arrangements will be greatly reduced. If there is a strong and united opposition rooted in civil society, it is likely that it will be able to take over and simply expel the regime. However, where there is a situation as in Bolivia where the civil society was weak and not united, an unstable and divided regime will not necessarily hasten the shift to democracy. If the split in the regime leads not to fragmentation but to the continued existence of factions, it creates serious problems of management for the process of political change. Those in the regime favouring change must ensure that those who oppose it or who are more wary of it are not able to disrupt the course of change. There must be a means within the regime to ensure that the differences do not become disruptive, that those who disagree with the prevailing policy will go along with it, or at least not act to derail it; or if they do, they can be quickly pulled into line. Only if this happens will the regime be able to participate as a positive partner in the process of democratization.

Similarly, the state of civil society forces is also important in this way. If those forces are able to come together in a bloc to negotiate with the regime with one voice, their position will be strengthened and the likely impact of their views increased. In contrast, if they remain divided and fractious, their capacity to impose their stamp on the course of change must be reduced, particularly if they confront a regime in which the divisions have been kept under control. This question relates to the type of civil society legacy that has been inherited (was there a tradition of civilized competition, compromise and cooperation, or has it been one of all-out competition?) and that has survived throughout the authoritarian period, but it is not determined by this. The contingencies of the moment and the personalities of the individuals involved will be important in shaping the contours of the civil society forces and the role they can play.

But what is clear is that democratization can only be understood through appreciating this interaction between regime and civil society forces. This dynamic is also evident in those cases of political change which some have suggested should be seen as completely different to the cases discussed above, the former Communist countries.

6

Transition and the Collapse of Communism

The literature on transition to and consolidation of democracy emerged as an attempt to explain developments in Latin America and Southern Europe in the 1970s and 1980s. Most of the case studies come from these two regions, and most exponents of this literature, if they had a regional specialism, were specialists in one or a number of countries of these regions. However, the most spectacular, because of its range, unexpectedness and geopolitical power of the subjects, instance of democratization occurred in neither of these two regions, but in the former Communist world of Eastern Europe and the former Soviet Union. The issue this raised was whether the sorts of explanations that had come out of the transition literature could usefully be applied to the Communist–post-Communist situation. Some sought to use this literature in their analyses of communist transitions[1] while others believed that the Southern European and Latin American experiences were so different that they could not spawn a useful explanatory literature for these other cases.

The chief basis upon which arguments about the inapplicability of this literature rested was the view that the nature of the regime changes differed so much that a single methodology was not able to embrace this diversity. The sorts of differences to which critics pointed were as follows:[2]

1. The nature of Communist rule was distinctly different from that of the authoritarian regimes in Latin America and Southern Europe. Even though the totalitarian label was not appropriate for the communist regimes in the late 1980s (if it had ever been appropriate), there was a significant difference between the Communist regimes as a group and those of the

other regions. This lay in the much greater penetration of the society by the control apparatus of the state, and thereby the level of continuing control, characteristic of the Communist states. While there had clearly been some loosening of that control in many countries during the 1970s and 1980s, it still seems to have been of considerably greater magnitude than was evident in the other cases of transition.

2. Communist political economy. Under the Communist regimes, there was a fusion of the political and the economic, with the latter lacking the degree of autonomy evident in the other cases of transition. Simply put, this was the difference between a state-run and organized economy and an economy based upon private ownership and market principles. The growth of an informal, privately-based sector of the economy in the last couple of decades of communist rule does not offset this point: the economy was centrally bound up with the state in a way that differed considerably from the situation in Latin America and Southern Europe.

3. Level of economic development. All of the former Communist states which experienced regime change, with the exception of Albania (and Mongolia), were highly industrialized. Even if they had significant agricultural sectors, it was industry which drove the economy and was the principal source of wealth creation. Furthermore, the profile of industrialization meant that in many of the countries economic development required de-industrialization, whereas in the less developed states of Latin America and Southern Europe, economic development was seen principally in terms of building up industry.

4. The Communist societies had a flattened, less differentiated social structure than those of Latin America and Southern Europe. There were fewer independent bases upon which class differentiation could develop and class groupings could rest. This had implications for the capacity of the society to throw up autonomous political actors who could influence the course of regime change.

5. Civil society elements were far stronger in the countries of Latin America and Southern Europe than in those of the Communist world. In the latter, the pre-Communist societies had at best only weak manifestations of civil society, and under the communist regimes, these were crushed.

6. The collapse of Communism had an explicit identity aspect

that was missing in the other cases of transition. There were two sides to this. First, for all of the former Communist states except Russia, the collapse of Communism was also a struggle for national liberation, for the casting off of the domination perceived to be exercised by a foreign ruler: for the former republics of the USSR this ruler was Russia, for the states of Eastern Europe it was the Soviet Union.[3] Second, and the reverse side of this, was the question of the creation of their own independent state. This involved the creation of an almost entire apparatus of independent statehood for the former Soviet, Yugoslav and Slovak republics, and of breathing life into all aspects of that apparatus in the case of the other states (with the exception of the GDR, where the reverse process applied). It also involved issues of borders and national minorities.

7. Ethnic diversity. This was a major issue in the case of the Soviet Union and Yugoslavia, where levels of ethnic differentiation, and therefore political sensitivity and potential conflict, were significantly higher than anywhere in the other regions covered by the transition literature.

8. International influences. Some (e.g. Bunce) argue that international forces, principally in the form of Gorbachev and the change in Soviet line towards Eastern Europe but also the less hospitable international economic climate, were much more significant in structuring the post-Communist transition than they were in the earlier cases of the shift towards democracy. Certainly, the infection effect was much stronger in Eastern Europe than in either of the other two regions, even if it did operate to some degree, and the removal of an external constraint on change more public and dramatic.

9. Role of the masses. Some (e.g. Bunce) claim that the masses played a much more significant part in the post-Communist transitions than in the other areas.

10. The agenda of transition. In Latin America and Southern Europe, the agenda was focused almost overwhelmingly upon regime change, although in some cases the issue of structural adjustment of the economy was also present. In most post-Communist transitions, regime change was ineluctably associated with economic transformation (not merely structural adjustment in an economy that was privately-based, but a change in the basis upon which the economy as a whole

rested), state building, the restructuring of society and the creation of a new sense of national identity. The multiple nature
of these tasks was seen to complicate the process of transition,
especially when the different tasks were believed to be incon-
sistent, e.g. the creation of a market economy and a political
democracy.[4]

This is an impressive list of apparent differences, but what are we
to make of it? It is clear that, while there is much of substance in
these differences, there is also some exaggeration and blurring of
differences within the categories. As will become evident below, in
particular the degree of state penetration of society and the role of
non-élites in the transition differed considerably from one country to
the next. To the extent that the former Communist countries can be
ranged along a spectrum on these sorts of issues, the distinctiveness
of them as a group compared with the earlier cases of transition is
diminished. Nevertheless, the post-Communist transitions were different: their starting points and the resultant combination of problems with which they had to deal was very different from the other
cases of transition. So can they be treated as similar?

The catalogue of perceived differences noted above for the most
part involves aspects of political change which are absent from the
primarily élite-focused analyses of the transition school. If the
analysis in the last chapters is accurate, it may be that some of these
differences would either evaporate or narrow considerably were the
focus of the transition analysis to be broadened by inclusion of a
comparative historical sociological perspective. Indeed, an adequate
understanding of the post-Communist transition could not be obtained
if we used only the élite focus of the transition literature. This must be
supplemented by an analysis grounded in the comparative historical
sociological approach that recognizes the importance of civil society
forces. If this sort of approach was applied to both the communist and
the earlier transitions, three conclusions would follow:

1. the earlier cases of transition would appear more similar to
    those of post-Communism;
2. the differences to which scholars point between the Communist
    and non-Communist transitions would be explicable in terms of
    the contexts within which the respective transitions occurred
    rather than as a result of seeing these transitions as essentially
    different processes;

3. we would gain a better understanding of both the individual
    instances of transition and of that process itself.

Substantial support for these conclusions comes from analysis of the
Communist transitions that encompasses both the immediate élite
focus and the historical sociological civil society forces focus. To
demonstrate this, we must now examine the patterns of post-
Communist transition.

Post-Communist Transition

One of the most singular features of the post-Communist transition
was the way in which it occurred almost simultaneously in all the
European countries ruled by Communist regimes. Although opinions may differ over the starting point in the respective countries, it
is clear that between 1989 and 1991 all nine countries had undergone the process of transition, albeit experiencing different patterns
and different outcomes. This simultaneity suggests a commonality
of forces propelling change, and to a degree this is accurate. But it is
also important to recognize that there were particular factors within
each country which shaped the course of the transition and which
explain the different national experiences. While the impetus came
from within the countries, the opportunity (except for the USSR)
came from without, and it is this combination which explains part of
the different patterns within the simultaneous process.

    In retrospect, it is clear that by the mid-1980s all of the
Communist regimes faced a legitimation problem. Significant sections of the respective populaces were, if not alienated from their
current rulers, willing to contemplate a change in regime. The levels
and strength of popular alienation cannot be measured, but the
rapidity with which sections of the populace moved to oppose the
Communist authorities suggests that both of these were considerable. This continuing problem of popular commitment, always much
more evident in Eastern Europe than in most of the Soviet Union,
was sharpened in the 1980s by the economic difficulties faced by
these regimes at that time. Indeed, in many of the countries of the
region, the initial opening made by the regime was prompted by the
need to respond to economic difficulties. But what created the
opportunity for the ultimate change in regime for the states of
Eastern Europe was the shift in Soviet policy under Mikhail

Gorbachev. Gorbachev was important for two reasons. First, he instituted reform policies within the Soviet Union and encouraged Eastern European leaderships to follow suit in their own countries. Second, he made it clear that the Eastern European states were free to follow whatever course they desired and the Soviet Union would not interfere. The prospect of a repeat of Hungary in 1956 and Czechoslovakia in 1968 when reformist (or, in the case of Hungary, revolutionary) leaderships were removed from power by Soviet force was thereby ruled out, leaving the way clear for domestic induced change to take its course. Significant also was the infection effect, as developments in one country stimulated developments in neighbours. The subsequent discussion of individual cases will be in general chronological order.

Poland

Popular alienation from the Communist regime was both acute and obvious in Poland by the late 1980s. The earlier attempts by sections of society to wring change from the regime had been rebuffed, with the suppression and effective legal dissolution of Solidarity in 1981–82 and the imposition of martial law from December 1981 to July 1983. However, this action did not destroy Solidarity, which continued as an underground organization, nor did it alleviate the basic economic problems besetting the Polish economy. In an attempt to generate a popular basis for action, in November 1987 the government staged a referendum seeking to gain popular support by offering limited political liberalization and decentralization in exchange for a programme of economic austerity. The referendum failed. However, it did show that there was a recognition within the regime that change was needed in the way the country was being run if the economic problems were to be overcome; it reflected a recognition of the need to engage society more fully in questions of governance. However, this was not universally accepted within the regime, and was a cause of major division.

Towards mid-1988 Poland was wracked by widespread strike activity over price rises. Industrial unrest escalated in August–September, with the relegalization of Solidarity as one of the chief demands of the strikers. In response, the government made unofficial overtures to Solidarity leader Lech Walesa, proposing Round Table talks[5] involving the government, the still-outlawed Solidarity, and a range of other social forces with a view, *inter alia*, to gaining a consensus approach to the economic problem and relegalizing Solidarity. Although this proposal met strong opposition within the leading ranks of the authorities, as the January plenum of the Central Committee of the ruling Polish United Workers Party (PUWP) demonstrated, General Jaruzelski (who was both state president and party leader) was able to gain official approval of it in January. The Round Table talks opened in February and were brought to a conclusion in early April. They resulted in the signature of a series of complex agreements which were designed to provide a framework for Solidarity to gain a share of power under Communist rule, but which in fact effectively laid down a timetable for the phased change of regime.[6] Multi-party elections were to be held in June, although the Communists and their allies were to be guaranteed 60 per cent of the seats in the Sejm, or lower house (the church was guaranteed a further 5 per cent); completely free elections were to be held four years later. Solidarity was legalized, and a package of economic reforms was agreed. In May, the legal position of the Catholic Church was bolstered, gaining independence from state supervision, the right to operate its own media, the right to proselytize and run schools, and the return of property confiscated in the 1950s. The Round Table negotiations between authorities and oppositionists was clearly an agreement between ruling élites on the one hand and oppositionist élites on the other on the ultimate dismantling of the Communist power monopoly.

When the election was held in June, the Communists were humiliated. They and their allies won only the seats set aside for them in the Sejm, while the Solidarity Citizens' Committee won all 161 Sejm seats in which it was allowed to compete and 99 of the 100 seats in the upper house, or Senate. The election result was followed by some months of political manoeuvring as both the PUWP and Solidarity tried to gain a leading place in the new government. Solidarity did not push vigorously to take over the government and supported Jaruzelski's election to the presidency. In mid-August, worried that it could be excluded from the government altogether (Solidarity had been negotiating to form a coalition government with the Democratic Party and the United Peasants' Party, two nominally independent parties which had always supported the Communists during communist rule), the PUWP agreed to enter as a junior partner in a coalition government led by Solidarity. This government, led by Tadeusz Mazowiecki, was sworn in on 12th September 1989, with four members from the PUWP. This was the first non-Communist dominated government in Eastern Europe, although the country did not gain a new president until Walesa was elected to that post at the end of 1990. A programme of economic 'shock therapy' was announced in October, marking the beginning of the deconstruction of the Communist command economy, while in January 1990 the PUWP dissolved itself, and then re-established itself as a new party, Social Democracy of the Polish Republic. Although new parliamentary elections were not held until October 1991, effectively the transfer of power was completed with the accession of the Mazowiecki government.

The major dynamic of the Polish transition was therefore agreement between regime élite and oppositionist élites, with the latter, chiefly in the person of the Solidarity leadership, gaining its privileged position in the process through its leadership of an organization whose chief currency of power was its levels of mass support. The mass of the population was important not only in terms of its support for Solidarity; it was crucial also at the outset of the process through its strike activity and through the casting of its electoral choice in June 1989.

Hungary

By the late 1980s, with the Hungarian economy experiencing difficulties, a reform wing had emerged within the leadership of the Hungarian Socialist Workers' Party (HSWP). This had gained a more solid form at a September 1987 meeting of party and non-party reformers where Imre Pozsgay established his leadership of the reformers, calling among other things for genuine freedom of expression in Hungary and the introduction of a more liberal set of political arrangements. A crucial shift in power occurred in the party in May 1988 when long-time party leader Janos Kadar was replaced as leader by prime minister Karoly Grosz, who immediately formed a new Politburo including reformers Poszgay, Nyers and Nemeth.

The impetus for change continued to gather strength, as the already liberal Hungarian society responded positively to the lead given by this new leadership. Unofficial organizations emerged in increasing numbers, the most important being the Hungarian Democratic Forum (HDF) in September 1988, which was a lineal descendant of the group at the meeting attended by Poszgay twelve months earlier; in November another of these unofficial organizations constituted itself as the first independent political party, the

Alliance of Free Democrats. In November, the party leadership announced that it would legislate to provide for the legalization of independent political parties, and this was done in January 1989. Henceforth, independent political organization was legal within Hungary and such bodies proliferated. However, there was little unity within the opposition, which remained weak and fragmented. This radicalization of reform had as its consequence increased political conflict within the party, leading to a reshuffling of the leadership in April resulting in a strengthening of the position of the reformers at the expense of more conservative elements.

The crucial breakthrough came in September–October. Round Table talks between the HSWP, opposition groups and Communist-led social organizations ended on 18th September with an agreement for the introduction of a genuine multi-party democracy.[7] This agreement involved acceptance by the Democratic Forum of the HSWP proposal to hold direct presidential elections before an election for the parliament, but this was opposed by other opposition elements. In October the HSWP dissolved itself and reconstituted itself as the Hungarian Socialist Party (HSP). The following month, a popular referendum supported the view of the more radical oppositionist elements that the president should not be elected directly as agreed at the Round Table talks, but should be chosen by a democratically-elected parliament. Parliamentary elections were held in March–April 1990, with the HSP gaining only 33 seats and the HDF 164 of a total of 394 seats. A coalition government was formed in May under HDF leader Jozsef Antall. The following month a programme of radical economic reform was announced, while in August the parliament elected as president Arpad Goncz, the leader of the Free Democrats, who had been acting president since May.

The transition in Hungary was thus driven initially from within the ruling élite, where reformist forces headed by Poszgay were able to shift the agenda in a radical direction despite conservative reservations. They were assisted in this by the growth of independent political forces in society, recognized in the holding of the Round Table in September 1989. However, the agreement between the regime élites and some of the oppositionist élites at the Round Table was overturned at the urging of other oppositionist élites by the mass of the populace in the November referendum. So, although élites were the prime movers and the main forces structuring the transition, the mass of the populace also played an important part.

Czechoslovakia

In Czechoslovakia, as in Poland, popular alienation from the regime was substantial, reflecting the fact that in the mid-1980s the rulers were basically the same people who had been put into power by Soviet arms following the crushing of the 'Prague Spring' of 1968. The economic crisis was aggravated in Czechoslovakia, and this did not improve following the replacement of party leader Gustav Husak by Milos Jakes in December 1987. Jakes did introduce some limited reform measures, but in essence the regime remained highly repressive and reluctant to change, despite the presence in its ranks of people who were convinced that some change was necessary. The most important of these was Ladislav Adamec, appointed prime minister in October 1988. The pressure for change mounted in 1989, chiefly through the unrolling of mass protest.

In January 1989, on the twentieth anniversary of the self immola-tion of Jan Palach, a demonstration had been held to protest human rights abuses. This was broken up by the authorities, with some 800 dissidents, including the playwright Vaclav Havel, arrested. Although shortly after this Adamec expressed the desire for dia-logue, nothing substantive followed. In July a petition calling for political reform signed by some 10,000 people was presented, and condemned by the authorities, while the following month a large demonstration marked the twenty-first anniversary of the invasion which ended the 'Prague Spring'. Further demonstrations occurred in late October, and on one occasion riot police attacked demonstra-tors with clubs. The momentum for change became irresistible in November when a pro-democracy rally and demonstration was bru-tally broken up, with 140 being injured and one student reported to have been killed. This evoked widespread popular outrage, and now opposition began to take a more organized public form. On 18th November, the day following the demonstration, an umbrella orga-nization of opposition groups was formed in Prague, Civic Forum, with Havel as one of its leaders and Charter 77 its nucleus; a parallel body was established in the Slovak capital Bratislava, Public Against Violence. These organizations gave a focused voice to the welling popular protest; demonstrations continued on most days, and on 27th November workers came out in a two-hour nationwide general strike in support of the opposition. The day before the strike, the regime, through the person of Adamec, opened negotiations with Civic Forum. This resulted in Adamec agreeing to form a new government and the party agreeing to the revocation of its formal 'leading role'.

In early December huge demonstrations and protests occurred again when Adamec proposed a new government which had a Communist majority. The regime seems to have now realized that its capacity to control developments was at an end. On 7th December Adamec resigned as prime minister and on 10th December Husak resigned as president; a new government led by Marian Calfa with a non-Communist majority was put into office. At the end of the month Havel was elected president by the Federal Assembly. In January–February 1990 the political parties and movements con- vened Round Table talks to organize competitive elections and to reduce Communist representation in the legislature. Free multi-party elections were held in June, and they returned a majority in both chambers for Civic Forum and Public Against Violence. Although the Communists won the second largest number of seats (but only about 13 per cent of the votes), the new government formed by Calfa excluded them from its ranks.

The main impetus for transition in Czechoslovakia thus came from below, in particular from students, intellectuals and the middle class; workers were important, but not as significant as in Poland. Organized opposition forces emerged in the wake of popular protest. This is starkly reflected in the fact that Round Table talks were not initiated until after the regime had been replaced in power. The ruling élite was little disposed to venture down the reform path, even those like Adamec who recognized the need for change lagging behind the impulses coming from below.

German Democratic Republic

In the GDR the regime's legitimation problems were even more serious than elsewhere in Eastern Europe as a result of its ambiguous relationship with West Germany. What precipitated the regime's crisis was a massive increase in the flow of its citizens out of the country and into West Germany. Facilitated by the opening of the Hungarian border with the West on 11th September 1989 (an unprecedented breach of bloc solidarity), during that year more than 300,000 left the GDR, compared with some 40,000 in 1988. Increasingly people were voting with their feet, especially with the breaching of the Berlin Wall on 9th November.

But it was not only the bleeding of the populace out of the

country that propelled the regime towards crisis; it was also the growth of open opposition within the GDR itself. In May 1989 the local elections were observed by church-based pro-democracy groups who publicly denounced as fraudulent the official result of near unanimous support for the official list of candidates. Although the demonstrations launched by these groups were suppressed, the nucleus of their activity, the Catholic Church of St Nicholas in Leipzig, became the focus of weekly meetings of groups pressing for democracy and defence of civil rights. These became the kernel of the massive demonstrations that emerged in Leipzig and spread elsewhere in October. They were also a rallying point for the newly-emergent organizations which sought to press for change in the country. Groups like New Forum, Democracy Now and the Peace and Human Rights Initiative were soon joined in their criticism of the regime by political parties which had either disappeared under regime suppression or had survived as part of the official national front. Parties like the Social Democrats, Liberal Democrats and Christian Democrats added their organizational resources to the growing protest movement.

The main impetus came from the growing size of public demonstrations, especially in Leipzig; these grew from about 2,500 people in mid-September to 500,000 in early November.[8] A crucial turning point came on 9th–10th–11th October. On the 9th the largest protest demonstration yet occurred in Leipzig, and for the first time the local security forces did not attack the demonstrators. The local authorities had realized that discussion had to be opened with the demonstrators, and although this view was shared by some in the national leadership, it was vigorously opposed by others. The Communist élite was split. The replacement of Erich Honecker as president by Egon Krenz in October did nothing to stop the unrolling of protest, even though Krenz did make some significant concessions. But as a former head of the Stasi (the secret police) he was not convincing as a reformer. Demonstrations increased in size and in geographical coverage. In November the government and party leadership resigned. The former was replaced by a new government with a Communist majority led by a reform-minded local party leader from Dresden, Hans Modrow. In December the new party leadership resigned, as did Krenz as head of state. In the same month a Round Table involving the new organizations and those associated with the old regime agreed on the ground rules for democratic elections. Between this agreement and the holding of the elections in March 1990, increasing numbers of parties and groups emerged onto the political stage, and ultimately it was one of these, the conservative Alliance for Germany, which was victorious. The main issue in the election was the question of reunification with West Germany, and the dominance and speed of this process overran autonomous East German pressures for the structuring of its own political system.

The German is a clear case of transition propelled from below. Although the regime was divided, the reformers were unable to gain a clear upper hand, with the result that they could do little to shape the course of developments from October on. That course of developments was moulded by the unrolling of popular protest and by the way in which popularly-based bodies were able to give some guidance and direction to it.

Romania

Since coming to power in 1965 the Ceausescu regime had pursued a strongly nationalist line in both foreign and domestic affairs. By the late 1980s, two aspects of this were a cause of major popular resentment. First, in an attempt to render Romania self-sufficient, in 1982 Ceausescu had launched a major drive to eliminate the country's foreign debt. This involved the introduction of a wide range of harsh austerity measures, leading to food rationing, power shortages and extended working hours. The living standards of the populace dropped significantly, and for the first time in November 1987 there were major riots in protest. These were vigorously suppressed, but the cause of popular resentment was not eliminated. Second, the drive to transform the national minorities within Romania into Romanians. The chief object here was the substantial Hungarian population of the Transylvanian region, a group which had bitterly resisted all efforts at Romanization since the incorporation of the region into the country following the war. This was given an added dimension with the policy of forcible 'systematization' announced in 1988, which involved eliminating the villages and resettling the people into larger towns. This was seen by both the Hungarians in Romania and by the Hungarian government as a measure aimed directly at the Transylvanian region.

Although there was widespread resentment at what was going on, there appeared to be little evidence of opposition within the regime itself. Certainly a critical letter had been written by six prominent figures, all party members, in March 1989, but this appears to have had little resonance within the regime's ranks; at the party congress in November Ceausescu was unanimously re-elected as party leader, while giving voice to criticism of many of the changes that had occurred elsewhere in the region.

The transition was precipitated by a popular demonstration in the Transylvanian town of Timisoara against the removal of an ethnic Hungarian priest. The demonstration was suppressed, but when the demonstrators returned two days later on 17th December, the troops opened fire, killing some one hundred people. Rumours of a 'massacre' in Timisoara provoked widespread protest demonstrations in Bucharest which the security forces (the *Securitate*) tried to suppress by force. As the protests continued, the army changed sides to support the demonstrators. Ceausescu and his wife fled from the capital, as former Communists allied with the military leaders and opposition protesters came together to form the National Salvation Front (NSF), which on 23rd December declared itself to be in charge of Romania. Opposition on the part of the *Securitate* was then put down by the military, while the Ceausescus, once captured, were given a summary trial and executed.

The NSF initially presented itself as a provisional government with Ion Iliescu as president and Petre Roman as premier, and as such introduced a range of liberalizing measures, including the announcement of elections. There were some popular demonstrations against the NSF because it was seen by many to be simply a new vehicle through which the Communists could continue to rule, but these were put down by miners especially bussed in to the capital by the government. When elections were held in May, the NSF won an overwhelming majority in both houses with some two-thirds of the votes, while Iliescu was elected president with some 85 per cent of the vote. When further popular demonstrations met this result (there was fraud and intimidation in the election), the government again bussed miners in from the provinces to break up the demonstrations.

The transition in Romania was clearly one initiated by popular unrest, but the crucial factor was the split in the regime, with the military supporting the opposition. Without this, it is possible that the regime could have maintained itself in power. Instead the military, in unison with the popular opposition, formed the body which replaced the rule of the Communist party, and then used the electoral process to legitimate its position of dominance.

Bulgaria

The economic difficulties in Bulgaria and the course of developments in the Soviet Union prompted Bulgarian leader Zhivkov to announce a reform programme involving liberalization and some decentralization in July 1987, but this programme went little further than rhetoric. Although putting the issue of reform on the agenda, Zhivkov was reluctant to give it any substance. Instead, he cracked down on signs of public dissent and, by 1989, had begun a fresh campaign of assimilation of the Turkish minority in Bulgaria. However, this policy of reformist rhetoric and conservative action was instrumental in two significant developments, the beginning of the public organization of opposition movements, and a change in regime leadership.

During 1988 a number of organizations for the defence of human rights emerged, as well as a Club for the Defence of *Glasnost* and *Preustroistvo* (the name of Zhivkov's reformist programme). In February 1989 an independent trade union organization was created, and in March *Ecoglasnost*, an organization concerned about environmental issues, was established. In December, opposition groups came together to form an umbrella organization, the United Democratic Front (UDF). These organizations were to be important, but the chief precipitating factor which brought on the beginnings of regime change was public protest. Strikes and protest activity unrolled among the Turkish population in the middle of 1989, while in October–November a series of large public demonstrations occurred in Sofia; most important was one which coincided with an international environmental conference in the capital and turned into a call for regime change. The combination of the popular pressure and the regime's temporizing provoked a split within the regime, leading to the replacement of Zhivkov by Politburo member and foreign minister Petur Mladenov on 9th November 1989. This was followed by a large-scale purge of conservative elements from the leading ranks of the party. The new leadership in December proposed free elections, and therefore an end to the party's monopoly on power, to take place in June 1990.

The new, seemingly more reformist, party leadership entered Round Table talks with the opposition in January 1990. At the same time, the party held a conference at which it elected a new leadership and announced that, although it would remain a Marxist-oriented party, it would support a reformist course; in April it changed its name to the Bulgarian Socialist Party. The Round Table talks lasted into April, with the UDF refusing to enter a coalition government proposed by the authorities, with the result that when a new government was formed in February, it consisted only of members of the still extant BCP. The talks finished with agreement that the election would be held as scheduled in June, even though the UDF felt that this short time horizon advantaged the BSP.

When the election was held in June, the BSP was the clear winner, with some 47 per cent of the vote and 211 of the 400 seats in the National Assembly. Against a background of charges of intimidation and fraud in the conduct of the election, the BSP was unable to persuade elements of the opposition to join a coalition government. When the government was finally announced, it consisted overwhelmingly of BSP members (there were only two independents), with no representatives of the UDF. While these negotiations were continuing, Mladenov (who had been chosen by the parliament as interim president in April) was forced to resign, and following repeated ballots, the UDF leader Zheliu Zhelev was elected president in August. These political manoeuvres were a result principally of the UDF's refusal to compromise in the belief that it had been unfairly treated in the arrangements for the election, and it was therefore unwilling to share power with the former Communists. Their supporters were of the same view, and when it became apparent that no satisfactory outcome was likely to emerge, popular discontent rose. Popular demonstrations in November, an opposition boycott of parliament from 23rd November and trade union support through a general strike, all hastened the resignation of the BSP government and its replacement in December by a provisional coalition government led by the non-party Dimitur Popov. This was followed by agreements between the parties and between employers and unions on a period of peace which would allow the planning of new elections, constitutional reform and the implementation of economic reform measures. When new elections were finally held in October 1991, the UDF won the largest number of seats (110 out of 240; BSP gained 106) and then formed a minority government.

The transition in Bulgaria was prolonged compared with most other countries of the region. Its main dynamic was interaction between the populace, both in terms of strategic demonstrations and the involvement of the leadership of the mass organization representing them (UDF), and the established élite. At different times the opposition élite was the principal force for change, especially through its refusal to share power in a BSP-led government, at others the stimulus came from its mass supporters. The change was peaceful, with the established élite largely able to help define the circumstances under which it left power.

Yugoslavia

In Yugoslavia the national issue became the chief focal point around which the transition from Communism revolved. Like the other countries of the region, Yugoslavia suffered economic difficulties during the 1980s, but in addition, the country also experienced a crisis of political rule. From midway through the decade, it was clear that the political arrangements bequeathed to Yugoslavia by Tito in 1980 were coming under strain. This was principally because the different republics had governments which not only had different views about how the federation should function, but which interpreted the implications of the developments in the USSR and Eastern Europe differently.[9] In Slovenia, for example, greater scope was given to opposition and dissent, with the emergence of the opposition Democratic Alliance in January 1990.[10] A proliferation of dissident organizations followed throughout the republic. However, the leadership of the Serbian republic, and in particular its president Slobodan Milosevic, believed that the Yugoslav federation should be held together (and Serb dominance of it ensured), including the use of force if necessary to achieve this; the repression of rioting in the ethnic Albanian Kosovo region in early 1989 reflected this.

In September 1989, the Slovenian parliament approved constitutional changes, including the republic's right to secede from Yugoslavia. In December the Serb–Slovenian border was closed following the Slovenian government's refusal to allow an ethnic Serb rally and the Serb government's retaliation by imposing an economic blockade. The Yugoslav federal government was powerless to do anything about this. A similar inability was evident in the Yugoslav League of Communists (the Communist party), which held a congress in January at which an attempt by Milosevic to bring a reassertion of central control was rejected by the Slovenes, who walked out. The federal party was effectively destroyed. In April and May 1990 competitive multi-party elections were held in Slovenia and Croatia, bringing to power centre-right and rightwing nationalist governments (although in Slovenia the leader of the former republican Communist party, now renamed Party of Democratic Renewal, Milan Kucan was elected president). Similar elections were held in the other four republics at the end of the year, with Bosnia-Hercegovina and Macedonia returning centre-right nationalist governments while Serbia and Montenegro returned their former Communist rulers.

It was essentially the interactions of these republican governments, supported by their ethnic populations and at times opposed by ethnic minorities within their borders, that drove the Yugoslav experience. Both Slovenia and Croatia pressed on towards independence; declarations of sovereignty were made by the governments of Slovenia (July 1990), Croatia (December 1990), Macedonia (January 1991) and Bosnia-Hercegovina (October 1991), followed by declarations of independence – Slovenia and Croatia (June 1991) and Macedonia (September 1991). This process was not undisputed. In Croatia, in particular, the ethnic Serb community opposed this and sought, ultimately, reunification with Serbia. In Serbia, Milosevic sought to tighten his control, especially over the Kosovo region and in sidelining opposition elements within the republic. At the federal level, the government was hamstrung as the republican governments used their constitutional machinery to drive towards independence. It was the Serbian government, with the active involvement of Serbian ethnic communities in some of these other republics and of the national army which sought to prevent this process, which ultimately led to the wars of the Yugoslav succession.

So the course of transition from Communist rule in Yugoslavia is essentially the story of the break up of the country. Reacting in considerable part to the Serbian drive to reassert central (and therefore Serbian) control in the federation, republican governments rode popular nationalist sentiment towards independence. In this sense, the main impetus for regime change was the relationship between various regime élites, principally those at the republican (as opposed to national/federal) level, and although the mass of the populace did play a part, this was mainly at the instigation of those élites.

Albania

Although some demonstrations occurred in the north of the country in late 1989, the transition in Albania, the most hard-line regime in Eastern Europe, did not begin until 1990. In January of that year the party leader and president Ramiz Alia announced a series of liberal-izing reform measures, despite rhetorically dismissing the relevance for Albania of what had happened elsewhere in the region. During the year changes to the leadership seemed to strengthen reformist elements within it. Continuing pressure for change was evident throughout the year in the form of popular rallies, demonstrations and strike activity. In an endeavour to short-circuit some of this, in July the government allowed thousands of asylum seekers who had taken refuge in foreign embassies to leave Albania, but this only acted as a spur to increasing numbers seeking to leave. The German prospect, whereby thousands voted with their feet by leaving for the West, looked like recurring in Albania.

In December, Alia announced that opposition parties would be permitted, and on the following day the formation of the Democratic Party was announced. This was followed by other groups. In early 1991, with popular protest spreading and increasing numbers trying to leave the country for the West, and under pressure from opposition groups which threatened a boycott, the government postponed the scheduled elections from early February until the end of March. When the election was held, the Communist Party of Labour of Albania won a crushing victory; it won 169 of the 250 seats, with the Democratic Party winning only 75, mainly in the cities. The new parliament adopted an interim constitution in April, elected Alia as president, and brought in a new PLA government under Fatos Nano. However, under pressure from continuing popular protest, this government was replaced in June by a coalition led by Ylli Bufo of the PLA but including representatives of the opposition parties. Despite the government introducing a range of economic reform measures, the coalition collapsed when the opposition withdrew in December to the accompaniment of continuing anti-Communist popular protest. Alia then announced new elections for March 1992. When those elections were held, the Democratic Party won 92 of the 140 seats, with the Socialist Party (until June 1991 the PLA) winning 38.

The main impetus for the transition in Albania thus came from popular protest, with an important part played by the leadership of the Democratic Party. Its unwillingness to share power in any mean-ingful sense was the crucial catalyst leading to the collapse of the Albanian regime, even though the mass discontent had effectively robbed it of control of the streets before then.

USSR

The Soviet transition is dealt with last, even though it is the most important transition of all in the sense that change in the Soviet Union was a necessary, but not sufficient, condition for change elsewhere in Communist Europe. It is also the most important because of its international geopolitical ramifications, and because it generated the greatest number of new independent states (fifteen) of any of the political changes in the region.

A succession of elderly and sick leaders, combined with recognition of impending economic crisis and the existence of a range of other social problems, prompted the election of a reformist leader, Mikhail Gorbachev, in March 1985. The new leadership embarked on a programme of moderate reform which had very little effect upon the situation, leading to a radicalization of the reform programme in late 1986. Particularly important in this regard was the radicalization of the political agenda in January 1987 and the economic agenda in the middle of that year. The result was that the tensions that had been present within the élite for some time now became exacerbated as more conservative elements became worried about where this trend might lead. Late in 1987 one of the more radical members of the élite, Boris Yeltsin, was sacked from the Politburo and his position as party boss in Moscow, moves designed in part to mollify conservative elements in the élite.

In 1988, driven by Gorbachev and his immediate circle of personal advisers and confidants, the reform programme was further radicalized, with the introduction at the XIX Conference of the party in June–July of a comprehensive programme to reconfigure the Soviet political infrastructure. This involved the establishment of new legislative bodies, and thereby gave the opportunity for the representation of social interests in forms which had been impossible earlier. As a result of this opening, and of the policy of *glasnost* designed to encourage freer expression of opinion, small social movements began to crystallize, chiefly in the major cities. These acted initially as small discussion groups rather than significant vehicles for the mobilization of popular opinion, but as the election to the new legislature approached in March 1989, these groups did expand their activities and become more publicly prominent. However, they remained essentially on the sidelines of political life; the chief impetus for the radicalization of reform continued to come from Gorbachev and those immediately around him.

The situation changed markedly in 1989. The new style of parliament that was elected in March was one in which dissident voices were prominent, not in terms of their numerical representation but of their ability to shape the agenda; Gorbachev clearly tried to ensure that the critics of Soviet policy were well able to get their point of view across both within the chamber and to the community at large. As a result, the public debate escaped from the control of the reformist leadership around Gorbachev. In addition, in a number of the republics of the Soviet Union, and particularly in the Baltics, national front organizations came to the fore and, on the basis of widespread popular support, began to press initially for greater republican autonomy and then for independence. This radicalization of the agenda and the escape of that agenda from the control of the Soviet élite increased tensions within that group.

In 1990 the reformist part of the leadership continued to press the cause of reform while the conservatives dragged their feet. But a new element entered into the equation during that year. New republican governments were elected throughout the union, with most gaining office through elections in February–March. They brought to power in a number of republics élites who were closely allied with the national front organizations and who therefore used their new-found governmental positions to press the cause of reform and in some cases of independence. The most important of these new governments was in Russia, the largest republic. Here Boris Yeltsin emerged as government leader and, motivated in part by personal animus against Gorbachev as well as commitment to Russian sovereignty, he became the chief actor pushing for further reform, which he saw as coterminous with a reduction in the power of the central Soviet government and an expansion in that of the republics and Russia in particular. Most of the emergent political organizations, which in overall terms remained weak, switched their attention from the Soviet scene to press their concerns at the republican level, chiefly in the form of supporting reformist elements in the more democratically elected republican parliaments. Democratic sentiment thereby became joined with national concerns.

During 1990, conservative concerns mounted as increasing pressure was brought to bear for a revision of the Soviet federal structure; not all republics were pressing for independence, but the pressure coming from the Russian republic was sufficient to convince many that a real threat was being posed to the continued existence of the Soviet Union. In addition, Gorbachev had been able to get through a measure removing the party's leading role in the society (thereby opening the way for a multi-party system) and had been toying with the idea of full transition to a market economy. Conservative pressures mounted on Gorbachev, with the result that in the autumn he seems to have publicly swung away from the reformists and towards the conservatives. This manoeuvre lasted until April 1991, when he seemed to move back to the reformist side, supporting a fundamental revision of the union along the lines demanded by the republics, and a marketizing reform. The result was an attempted conservative coup against him, which was put down in part through popular opposition, in part through the personal stances taken by Gorbachev and Yeltsin, and mostly through the incompetence of the coup plotters. The coup destroyed the power of the centre and led the republics to increase their demands, leading ultimately to the dissolution of the USSR in December 1991 and the emergence of fifteen independent republics.

The key force in the Soviet transition was the élites. Initially it was the reformist elements around Gorbachev who drove the course of reform, despite opposition from within élite circles. There was very little substantial input from society at large in the early stages. This became more significant after the opening made by the élite in 1989, principally in the form of national front movements and some strategic popular rallies. However, when the main impetus for change passed from the Soviet élite, it went not to forces emerging out of society, but to those second echelon élites in the republics. The weak popular movements fell in behind leading republican figures to give their weight to the pressure for change. In this sense, the mass of the population played a part in the transition, but it was not as central to the process as the part played by élites.

It is clear from the above skeletal outlines of the course of regime change in the different countries that there was no single pattern of post-Communist transition;[11] there were a number of distinct patterns evident throughout the region. Those patterns were constituted by different relationships between three major actors: regime élites, opposition élites, and the mass of the populace. Regime élites refers to all of those those holding high office in a branch of the state structure, usually but not exclusively within the national political arena. Opposition élites are the leaders of independent organizations which emerged to challenge the ruling élite, civil society forces usually having their roots in society at large, reflected in mass support. The mass of the populace is important to the extent that it (or more realistically part of it) was involved in supporting opposition élites, in public protest and demonstrations in favour of change, and in some cases also through the ballot box. Demonstrations, rallies and meetings may be called by opposition élites or they may be spontaneous. The differences between the patterns are a matter principally of balance between the influence and role of these actors; in no transition was any of these actors wholly absent, but the role and importance they played differed substantially. What were these patterns?[12]

Regime Elite Initiated

1. Reforms implemented by the central regime élite open the way for opposition élites to enter the political system and radicalize the agenda. A split occurs between central and republican regime élites, with opposition élites supporting the latter, as do significant sections of the republican populations. Under this pressure, the centre collapses leaving republican regime élites in control. Cases of this pattern are the Soviet Union and Yugoslavia.
2. Reforms implemented by the central regime élite open the way for opposition élites to enter the political system and radicalize the agenda. They gain support for this from within the population. Discussions ensue, leading to a negotiated settlement which is, in effect, popularly ratified. Hungary is the only instance of this pattern.

Opposition Elite Initiated

Opposition élites make use of their mass support to pressure the regime élite for reform. Negotiations are joined, leading to a settlement. This pattern applies to Poland.

Mass Initiated

1. Mass pressures help to provoke splits within the regime élite and to open the regime up for the emergence of opposition élites. Negotiations ensue, under the shadow of popular pressure, leading to a negotiated withdrawal by the ruling élite, which is subsequently ratified by popular election. Two cases here are Czechoslovakia and the GDR. In Albania and Bulgaria

the pattern is similar, but the final settlement is not reached without a more prolonged period of pressure on the part of both populace and opposition élite.

2. Mass pressure provokes a split within the regime élite (and the state more generally), with one part of that élite (the military) going over to the mass opposition. An opposition élite is created from this, which takes power as the regime élite withdraws. This pattern applies to Romania.

Despite many common elements, these are definably different paths of transition. The issue is how they are to be explained, and it is this comparative question which highlights better than anything else the limitations of the approach of the transition to democracy literature. While this literature, with its focus on the élites, may be able to explain what happened in each case, it cannot explain why it happened and why the individual cases differed. The only way this can be explained is by going outside the basic paradigm with which élite study is infused. If the focus is overwhelmingly upon the élites, the involvement of the masses can be explained only in terms of either the disposition of the ruling élites (i.e. they were content to see the masses enter the arena) or the weakness of those élites (i.e. they could not prevent them from doing so). Nor can the élite focus really explain why opposition élites were able to play the role they did. Again, the only answers possible are the disposition of the ruling élite or the relative power of ruling and opposition élites. But this sort of explanation does not approach the issue of capacity. Even if we accept that the ability of an opposition élite to substantially affect the process of transition depends in part upon the willingness of the ruling élite to see it do so, we are still left with the issue of why some opposition élites are able to take advantage of such opportunities (as in Poland and Hungary) while others were not (as in the Soviet Union). To explain the differences in the way in which the various actors acted in the different patterns, we need to understand the sources of the capacity of those actors. Put more simply, why were opposition élites and mass publics able to play the parts they played in the various countries? The answer lies in the capacity for action and influence which they possessed, which in turn is dependent upon the historically-defined location which they occupied in society.

The capacity of these independent socio-political forces to play a major role in regime transition is determined by the nature of the regime and the degree of independent organization possible in the society. The latter is linked to the degree of penetration of the society by the regime. It is this complex of nature of regime, nature of society and relationship between the two which is therefore crucial and which will be used to explain the different patterns of regime change in former Communist Europe.

Although the regimes of this region were all labelled generically as Communist, in practice they differed in quite important ways. The most important way in which they differed for our purposes was the extent to which they had been characterized by a relaxation of central control. In the face of the growing complexity of their societies with the consequent increasing difficulty in exercising the sort of all-encompassing control which analysts in the West have labelled totalitarian, and stimulated by the liberating force of the policy of destalinization launched by Khrushchev in 1956, the regimes of the region experienced both pressure for and some opportunity to liberalize their internal arrangements. Different regimes did this to different degrees at different times. The regimes in the 1980s can be loosely characterized in terms of the extent of relaxation of control, as follows:

1. Tightest control, least relaxation: Romania, Albania, GDR, Czechoslovakia.
2. Weakest control, most relaxation: Hungary, Yugoslavia.
3. Median situation: Soviet Union, Bulgaria, Poland.

These divisions are a matter of judgement and may be disputed; the allocation of Czechoslovakia to (1) rather than (3) in particular may be queried, but the policy of 'normalization' and the suppression of dissent in the late 1970s pushes it over the edge into category (1). But clearly it is marginal. It is important to realize that we are talking about degrees here. None of these states even approached democracy as we understand the term. They all remained authoritarian, some more harshly so than others. Romania was close to a police state characterized by the use of terror as a principal instrument of control, while Albania had experienced some relaxation following the death of Hoxha in 1985 and his replacement by Alia, but control remained oppressive and intrusive. In Germany and 'normalized' Czechoslovakia, overt terror was not used, but in Germany the security apparatus was both very active and extensive, while in Czechoslovakia under Husak, the regime established by Warsaw

Pact troops in 1968 worked hard to ensure that its control was not eroded. In the Soviet Union and Bulgaria, the regime's control had effectively loosened somewhat, partly as a result of the longevity of the leadership. In the USSR, the Brezhnev regime had run out of steam by the early 1970s and as a consequence had let things drift, with the result that central control became in practice much looser than it had been. In Bulgaria, Todor Zhivkov had ruled since 1954, and although it would be exaggerating to label his rule benignly authoritarian, by the 1980s it was not characterized by the vigorous enforcement of control that had been evident during earlier periods (pressure against the Turkish segment of the population notwithstanding). Poland is a difficult case. The regime attempted to reassert strong central control with the imposition of martial law in 1981, but following its lifting in 1983, regime and society coexisted. Nevertheless, the regime did attempt to keep secure control over society and sought to restrict the activities of any groups which had some independence from its rule. The final two countries, Hungary and Yugoslavia, were characterized by much lower levels of regime intervention in society than the other countries. In Hungary, this reflected the attempt by the regime following its imposition in the wake of the 1956 revolution to reach a *modus vivendi* with the populace. As a result of reform measures taken by the regime, space was created for the emergence of some autonomous social groups and a sense of dialogue between regime and populace prevailed. In Yugoslavia, the model of Communism which was adopted by Tito had within it a tension between the assertion of strict central control and the encouragement of autonomous organization. This tension helped to ameliorate both tendencies, while the federal arrangement of the country helped to create further filters through which the exertion of central power and control was mediated.

While the relationship between regime and society was important, so too was the nature of the domestic structure of the regime itself. What is significant here is the scope within the regime for the development of substantial reformist forces which, when crisis approached, could play a constructive role in advancing the process of change.[13] The bases of reformism in the regime were particularly weak in four countries: Romania, Czechoslovakia, the GDR and Albania. In Romania the consolidation of personal control by Ceausescu and his family[14] and the elimination of all who opposed him created an environment within which the growth of reformist or dissident sentiment was stifled. The threat of terror remained to dissuade potential opponents even into the 1980s. In Czechoslovakia[15] there was a historical strand of reformism reflected most emphatically in official sponsorship of the Prague Spring, but the 'normalizing' regime of Husak[16] vigorously suppressed this, with the result that reformist elements were quite weak in the regime leadership. The GDR[17] always suffered a crisis of confidence because of its proximity to and the comparison with West Germany. As a result, orthodox elements dominated the upper reaches of the regime which, with the exception of some economic experimentation, showed little propensity to take up reformist views. In Albania[18] the history also was one of personalized rule, and although that ruler (Hoxha) died in 1985, any aspirations his successor Ramiz Alia may have had to adopt a more flexible policy were blunted by conservative elements in the leadership.[19] Albania's place as an outcast in Communist Europe for most of its life also acted as a force promoting unity and orthodoxy within regime ranks.

The prospects were somewhat brighter for the emergence of reformist elements in the leading ranks of the other countries. The prospects were brightest in Hungary and Yugoslavia, where both regimes were characterized by a degree of innovativeness in policy and a desire to distance themselves from the Soviet model. For the Hungarian regime,[20] this was a case of seeking a *modus vivendi*, and basis of legitimation, with the population following its installation by Soviet bayonets, while the Yugoslav model of socialism stemmed from the break with the USSR in 1948.[21] In addition, in Yugoslavia the federal system created spaces for liberal and reformist forces to operate distinct from the central authorities. In Poland,[22] too, there was a history of some flexibility, albeit interlaced with episodes of the vigorous repression of pressures for change. As in Hungary, the regime sought to reach a *modus vivendi* with the population and to generate a sense of legitimation to sustain itself following the events of 1956. Moreover, the strength of civil society forces (see below) sustained the view in the regime's leading ranks that a degree of flexibility was necessary. In the USSR[23] there was a tendency toward reformism in the party, illustrated most clearly (before 1985) by the Khrushchev experience. Paradoxically, the long period of conservatism under Brezhnev may have strengthened the conviction of the reformist forces within the ranks of the regime of the need for them to gain the leading position within regime councils. And, finally, Bulgaria[24] was the most orthodox of Moscow's followers and did not provide fertile soil within which reformists could prosper. However the long tenure of Todor Zhivkov (1954–89) did help to generate a sentiment within the regime sympathetic to change. So, although all the countries had regimes ruled by Communist parties, reformist sentiments were tolerated in leading circles to different degrees in different cases.

An important counterpoint to regime control over society is the extent to which within each society civil society forces formed and were able to eke out an existence. The issue is whether first-order groupings as discussed in Chapter 1 are able to give rise to second-order groupings.[25] In this regard, the countries can be divided into two categories during the Communist period: those in which a degree of autonomous social activity kept springing up (usually in the form of the creation of autonomous organizations pressing political demands) perhaps despite its suppression by the regime, and those where such activity was negligible or very limited:

1. Some autonomous group activity: Hungary, Poland, Czechoslovakia, GDR, Yugoslavia.
2. Limited autonomous group activity: Romania, Albania, Bulgaria, Soviet Union.

Again this is a mattter of judgement and may be subject to dispute, but the basis upon which the allocation of countries to categories rests is explained below.

An important factor in the propensity of the societies to generate autonomous social organization is the legacy that society carried into the Communist period. One element of this is political, but in this regard it is clear that the pre-Communist legacy seemed unpropitious. In the inter-war period, only Czechoslovakia was able to maintain a democratic system,[26] even if most countries maintained a facade of democracy by retaining parliaments and parties. In Hungary, reaction to the Soviet revolution of Bela Kun in 1919 led to the conservative dictatorship of Admiral Horthy. Military coups brought dictatorships to power in Bulgaria in 1924 and Poland in 1926, while in Albania Ahmed Zogu consolidated dictatorial rule after 1925, transforming himself into King Zog in 1928 and Albania thereby into a kingdom. In Romania a pseudo-democracy drifted gradually in a more authoritarian direction until a royal dictatorship was effectively established in 1930. A year before, a similar dictatorship had been established in Yugoslavia, bringing to an end a period of dysfunctional party competition. Germany experienced the democracy of the Weimar period, only to be superseded by the rise of the Nazis. In the Soviet Union, Soviet power had ruled since 1917 (although only from 1940 in the Baltic republics), and before that hesitant steps in a democratic direction had been choked off by the war. Throughout the region generally there was therefore no strong democratic tradition prior to the imposition of Communist rule and, where there was such a tradition in Czechoslovakia, the Communists had used it to gain power.

But while a political tradition of democracy can facilitate the development of autonomous social activity, it is rarely at the roots of such activity. These are to be found within the social structure of the society, in the first-order groups discussed above. Historically in the modern period the capacity of this substructure of civil society to generate a vibrant pattern of autonomous social activity through second-order civil society forces has depended upon the development of a bourgeois middle class with the resources, commonality of interests, and opportunities to unite in defence of those interests. The bourgeois middle class has been crucial because it has been this group which has sought to pursue its economic interests by carving out a space autonomous from state control, and thereby creating a shell within which autonomous social organization could blossom. The countries of Eastern Europe had different experiences in this regard.

The region was one of economic backwardness and late development, with the result that the state, principally in the form of its bureaucracy, was pre-eminent,[27] while society, and particularly autonomous elements of it, was generally weak.[28] The role of the state reflected the weakness of the indigenous bourgeoisie and the attractiveness of state service for those who left the land possessing the education and contacts to be able to enter this structure, principally from among the gentry and larger landowners. The statist orientation of these groups, and the early domination of commerce by foreigners,[29] resulted in the prevalence of an anti-entrepreneurial ethos throughout much of the region.[30] Serfdom had been eliminated and land reform introduced only in the nineteenth century but, except in Bulgaria and Serbia, this did not destroy large-scale land holding; large estates owned by traditional landowners coexisted with a myriad of small and inefficient family farms. Substantial industrial development had hardly penetrated most areas; at the end of the First World War, Bulgaria, Yugoslavia and Albania had almost no modern industry, Romania had only the oil complex on the coast, in Hungary there were some pockets of industry around Budapest, and Poland had concentrations of industry in various parts of the country (chiefly Warsaw, Lodz and Dombrowa-Silesia). During the inter-war period there was some industrial development in Romania, Serbia and Croatia in Yugoslavia, and in Bulgaria, although much of this was in foreign or state hands because of the shortage of capital among the native bourgeoisie. By the outbreak of the Second World War, only the Czech lands and Germany had a diversified industrial base. The development pattern in the region is reflected in the distribution of people across the industrial and agricultural sectors in about 1930 in the following table: [31]

	% of population dependent on agriculture	% of gainfully employed males in manufacturing
Albania	80%	n.a.
Yugoslavia	76%	14%
Bulgaria	75%	13%
Romania	72%	11%
Poland	60%	22%
Hungary	51%	26%
Czechoslovakia	33%	41%
Germany	c 20%	

With the exception of Czechoslovakia, the middle class was small, relatively powerless as a group, and tended to be closely aligned with the state through employment in government bureaucracies.[32] Although an indigenous bourgeoisie was developing during the inter-war period, it saw itself in competition with the existing domestic 'foreign' bourgeoisie, with the result that little sense of a single bourgeois society or an inclusive national public opinion could develop.[33] But within these general patterns, there were country differences.

In Poland in the inter-war period, the traditional gentry retained great prestige despite its impoverishment during the nineteenth century. This encouraged many to escape to the towns where they entered state service, the professions, or the army.[34] The gentry was a major source of the intelligentsia (although Jews were also important) which had emerged to symbolize Polish nationhood when the state had ceased to exist, with the result that that intelligentsia was strongly imbued with gentry norms. Even when members entered it from other classes, it was those gentry-inspired norms which were assimilated.[35] Such norms were by and large hostile to commerce and trade, with the result that the intelligentsia turned in large part to the state and to government administration as a means of earning a living. It was this group which was most important in ruling the new state once independence was gained in 1918, and as the demands of state administration increased and provision of education expanded, the size of this group grew. There was a small bourgeois middle class, Jewish and German in origin, but it remained weak and heavily dependent on the state for its economic well-being; by the end of the inter-war period, there were very close links between big business and the state. The main basis of middle class development was the state, with the result that the intelligentsia/middle class expanded as the state expanded; in the words of one analysis, 'there is clear evidence that an official class was developing within the state which provided a more substantial base for the middle class than did industry or commerce.'[36] This means that the middle class lacked any independence from the state. Poland had a small but skilled working class, and a union movement which was able to survive until the outbreak of the war. One further characteristic of Polish society should be mentioned, the position of the Catholic Church. For reasons that cannot be gone into here, the church occupied a position of influence unparalleled anywhere else in Eastern Europe. Its moral authority was unchallenged within Polish society.

In Hungary, significant sections of the landowning aristocracy also sold off their land during the nineteenth century, moving to the cities and entering government employment[37] and the liberal professions. Some also entered the urban intelligentsia (which had a significant Jewish component), which had close links with the state. Although there was a small emergent bourgeoisie, initially Jewish in origin but especially in the inter-war period becoming more Magyarized (although this involved as much acculturation of the Jews as it did an influx of ethnic Hungarians into commerce), the principal basis for middle class development remained state service. A small, but skilled working class had emerged, and its unions too remained in existence until the outbreak of war, despite the Horthy regime. There was very little change in Hungarian social structure over the inter-war period. The traditional ruling classes had been able to sustain their position from before the collapse of the Hapsburg Empire at the end of the First World War. In the words of one acute observer of the scene, the

> timeless, traditional, rural culture gave Hungary's historic ruling classes the impressive political cohesion and moral self-assurance that allowed them to retain their power so long, so stubbornly, and so effectively. They, in turn, guarded it by so structuring Hungarian society that each social class came to lead its own form of life, guided by its own codes of behavior and honor, its own set of eligible occupations, its own fetishes concerning titles, rank-orders, styles of address and modes of conduct.'[38]

Hungary remained a state with a traditional social structure, but with a large urban population and a vigorous intellectual life.

In Czechoslovakia there was a clear difference between the industrialized Czech lands and Slovakia. The latter remained overwhelmingly agricultural, traditionally having been more closely linked into the economic patterns of the Hungarian plain than the more dynamic Bohemia and Moravia. In the Czech lands, the gentry had been decimated in war (the Thirty Years War of 1618–48 saw the final breaking of this class), with the result that when the new state emerged following the end of the First World War (when most surviving large landowners lost most of their land), it was dominated by a native bourgeoisie and intelligentsia. The experience of industrial development[39] had produced a strong commercial bourgeoisie, which was closely allied to other commercial, intellectual and bureaucratic (state service) components of the middle class; there was also a developed professional sector. The strength and confidence of this group was reinforced by the scope provided for their participation in local administration,[40] something rare for this region. There was also a strong industrial working class, with its own substantial trade union structure; in the 1930s more than half of all industrial workers were members of trade unions.[41] In the view of one observer, the Czech class structure was 'a well articulated and modern one.'[42]

Germany also had a developed middle class which, despite the historic dependence of German industrialization on the state, had considerable independence by the inter-war period. Its prominence was facilitated by the destruction of the traditional landowning class as a result of the war. There were also in Germany significant professional and bureaucratic components of the middle class, as well as a powerful and organized working class, although rural workers remained unorganized.

In Yugoslavia there were significant regional differences, reflecting the different historical experiences of the various republics.[43] Nevertheless, Yugoslavia as a whole remained a country in which both traditional landowner[44] and middle class forces were quite weak, the working class very underdeveloped, and a massive peasantry mired in very backward agricultural techniques. In Croatia there was a small but developing middle class and a state administration dominated by the former gentry, while in Serbia, alongside a large class of independent smallholding peasants, the middle class that emerged comprised principally military officers, small town shopkeepers, artisans and rich peasants. This was not, therefore, a middle class which was concentrated in a large city and which could develop the sorts of interrelations and organizations that would be likely to generate autonomous organized public activity. In Serbia, state employees were the dominant social group. In Slovenia, where urban and industrial development was stronger than in Serbia, an indigenous bourgeois middle class had emerged to displace the dominance of ethnic Germans, and had been the source of pressures for a separate Slovene national existence in the period prior to the war's end.

In Romania, many of the traditional landed class had left the land in the nineteenth century and entered state service, the professions and the army, while of those who retained their landed holdings, many operated them on an absentee basis. A weak commercial middle class had developed in Romania, initially overwhelmingly Jewish in its ethnic identification but with an increasing ethnic Romanian component in the late nineteenth–early twentieth century. The Jewish nature of this group was principally a function of the fact that, in the independent Romanian state in the last part of the nineteenth century, the native intelligentsia preferred to occupy themselves with state service, politics and the free professions rather than economic activity.[45] The Jews remained viewed as foreigners despite the predominant position they occupied in the economy and their prominence in the professions; in Rothschild's words, '(t)he 'alien' middle class was economically essential but politically resented and socially unassimilated…'.[46] The remaining large landowners had lost much of their land in the reforms at the end of the First World War, but they had been generously compensated and

were able to move into bureaucratic, political or commercial positions with relative ease. The state remained the main basis of the
Romanian middle class, while peasant poverty continued to be a
major source of rural alienation from the regime.

Bulgaria had the most egalitarian society in inter-war Eastern
Europe, with no nobility[47], and an accessible education system
which facilitated social mobility.[48] The political, bureaucratic and
military élites were indigenous, recruited from among the peasant
and artisan groups in the population, and were dominant in
Bulgarian society and politics. Like Serbia, Bulgaria developed a
middle class consisting of military men, small town shopkeepers,
artisans and rich peasants, which, in part because of its dispersed
nature, was quite weak. The countryside was dominated by independent smallholding peasants.

Albania was the least developed of any of the countries of Eastern
Europe. It had no industry to speak of, and was divided into two
regions in which the social structures were quite different. The north
was inhabited by a group called the Ghegs, whose society remained
clan-based and was ruled over by patriarchal tribal chieftains. Their
economy was pastoral, supplemented by brigandage. In the south
the Tosks had an agriculturally-based society in which distinctions
were defined principally in terms of land ownership and tenancy,
with a strong class of large landowners. There was very little urban
development; only 15 per cent of the population lived in localities
with more than 5,000 people.[49] The ruling establishment consisted,
in Rothschild's words, of an 'interlocking network of politicians,
bureaucrats, latifundists, merchants, and clan chieftains...'[50] There
was no bourgeois middle class and little in the way of economic
development which could sustain such a group. Indeed, the clan-
based social and political life of Albania was completely antithetical
to the development of the sort of class structure evident in the most
advanced parts of the region.

Russia prior to Soviet rule differed from the countries of Eastern
Europe in that its traditional ruling class had not yet been overthrown and, although it was increasingly finding that it was being
pressed to share power with an emergent commercial and industrial
bourgeoisie, remained substantially in control. The half century
before the outbreak of the First World War had seen the slipping of
the position of the traditional landowners and an increase in the role
and importance of both the industrial/commercial bourgeoisie and a
growing professional class. The latter comprised state civil servants

as well as a burgeoning group of professions. This economic bourgeoisie and the professional groups therefore did constitute an increasingly important middle class, concentrated mainly in the big cities and becoming more aware of its interests both in a corporate sense and on a more individual basis. From 1906 they also had a parliamentary body in which they could seek to further their interests. Russia also had a growing industrial working class, and although this was geographically concentrated in a number of regions, those regions were a long way apart, making any sort of coordination difficult to achieve, although their capacity for organization is reflected in the emergence of the soviets in 1905 and 1917. The vast majority of the population remained on the land.

The above discussion of the social structures of the countries of the region has focused principally upon the patterns of class development in the pre-Communist period, and in particular on the presence or absence of a middle class.[51] The intention has been to establish whether in each society the conditions have been created which should foster the development and growth of consistent and solidly-based patterns of organized social activity. Such activity refers to the creation and functioning of organizations to press interests, the widespread discussion of issues, and the generation of a sense of civic responsibility; in other words, a civil society. The development of this sort of an arena has historically been associated with the emergence of a middle class, and in particular with a middle class which has the economic resources to make itself independent of the state. This means that such an arena is likely to be more solidly based when the middle class has a substantial bourgeois, economic, component. It is also more likely when that middle class is based in one or a few major cities. Urban environments make large-scale communication easier because of the concentration of people and the more developed technical infrastructure facilitating the sorts of personal and organizational interactions essential to the growth of civil society. The discussion above suggests that prior to the advent of the Communist regimes, the countries where the conditions were most favourable for the development of civil society in a developed form were Poland,[52] Czechoslovakia (or at least the Czech lands), Hungary, Germany and Russia.

The sketches of the social structures of the various countries given above assumes that once patterns of relationships and interactions are established in a society, those patterns are likely to be self-sustaining and self-replicating unless something intervenes to interrupt them. The more established and deeply embedded in the society the patterns are, the more extensive (and possibly violent) the interruption must be to destroy them. A change to authoritarian rule or in the type of authoritarian rule has often brought this sort of interruption to established patterns, including the patterns giving rise to civil society; indeed civil society can hardly be said to exist unless its right to both exist and function is accepted by the state. However, authoritarian rule is not always sufficiently interventionist in the society to be able either to change those patterns substantially or to eliminate them altogether. There is an important difference between destroying those patterns and simply suppressing them, or pushing them underground. If the patterns are simply suppressed by authoritarian power, it may be that once that power is lifted, those patterns may reassert themselves.[53] The issue is, in which of these Communist countries were the patterns sustaining autonomous social activity evident in the pre-Communist period able to reassert themselves under communism?[54]

Unlike most authoritarian regimes, Communist regimes came to power with a commitment to transform the society in which they were located. Their whole *raison d'être* was to build a Communist society, and this of necessity involved significant social and economic restructuring. The central element of this was the destruction of the private economy and its replacement by an economic system organized along collectivist lines. Associated with this was to be a cultural revolution in which the so-called bourgeois culture of capitalism was replaced by one more appropriate to a collectivist, communist society. The extent to which these aims were achieved was variable, but nevertheless all societies which came under communist rule experienced regime-initiated assault designed to wipe out the vestiges of the past and create a new order.

All Communist states experienced instances of dissent and opposition, including the organization of clandestine groups, strike activity and even popular riots. Furthermore, especially in the 1970s and 1980s, they all experienced pressures for the growth of informal associative activity, principally in the form of religion, youth subcultures and a critical intellectual discourse.[55] In only five of the states can it be said that opposition/dissent developed in a structured fashion which reflected the legacy of civil society.[56] The most dramatic instance of this was Poland. Following the abortive revolt of 1956, the Polish regime pursued a path of accommodation with the society, including the decollectivization of agriculture. Although autonomous organization was not officially sanctioned, a variety of types of such organization did emerge and for a time seem to have been tolerated. One important type of organization was discussion clubs among intellectuals[57] which provided a vehicle for the discussion and dissemination of unofficial literature and opinions; the so-called 'flying university' was a good instance of this type of organization. Important in this was the development of what Vaclav Benda in Czechoslovakia called the 'parallel polis',[58] the generation and circulation by intellectuals of a morality based on values autonomous from (and critical of) the official values adumbrated by the regime. Some attempts were made to link this 'parallel polis' with society more broadly. Following the crushing of the strikes in June 1976, the Workers' Defence Committee (KOR) emerged specifically to defend those the state sought to repress in the wake of the strikes. Its actions in defining a public profile for itself meant that KOR stimulated the development of a range of other groups in Polish society.[59] But politically more important was the continuing pressure on the part of workers to form independent worker organizations, in particular workers' councils, factory committees and trade unions. This strand of development reached its apogee with the formation of Solidarity in 1980.[60] Although the regime outlawed Solidarity in 1981, as the crisis approached towards the end of the decade it found that it had to deal with Solidarity as an equal negotiating partner. It is clear that this was an organization based in the working class but which was able to reach out to other groups, including intellectuals, and thereby come to represent a broad front of the Polish population. The other manifestation of civil society-type pressures was the Catholic Church.[61] With a history of close association with the idea of the Polish nation and strong commitment to it as an institution on the part of believers, the church was a constant (if not always vociferous) source of independent criticism of the regime's record on human rights. Intent on both defending its institutional position and prerogatives against regime incursion, it also spoke out from 1970 in support of human rights and against abuses of them. This became especially important following the banning of Solidarity in 1981.

In Czechoslovakia the strength of the civil society impulse is clearly reflected in the 'Prague Spring' of 1968.[62] When the regime relaxed its control and encouraged the development of autonomous social organization, this sprang up on a massive scale; groups of all sorts, espousing a vast array of different causes and involved in all aspects of life, emerged on the public scene. They so radicalized the political agenda, that they provoked armed intervention by Warsaw Pact forces. The important thing about this is that despite twenty years of Communist rule, once the pressure was lifted, civil society re-emerged. It had been suppressed, not destroyed. Similarly, despite 'normalization', the name of the policy designed to restore firm party control, the emergence of Charter 77 and the associated Committee for the Defence of the Unjustly Prosecuted (VONS) in the late 1970s and their survival into the 1980s shows the continuing strength of the civil society impulse.[63] Although mainly concerned with human rights issues and restricted largely to the intelligentsia, Charter 77 sought to promote a process of discussion between regime and society. But always a movement principally of intellectuals and subject to continuing harassment, Charter never developed mass roots and remained effectively isolated from the mass of the population. Despite the existence in Czechoslovakia of such organizations and of a 'parallel polis', autonomous social activity was less developed here than it was in Poland.

In Hungary, the post-1956 revolution evidence for the continuing salience of civil society pressures lies less in the development of opposition to the regime, because this was limited mainly to left wing intellectuals, many of whom left Hungary in the 1970s,[64] than in the emergence of a range of different sorts of civil organizations taking advantage of the generally more liberal atmosphere in Hungary than elsewhere. This does not mean that these intellectuals were not important. They were very influential in generating debate across the whole of Eastern Europe (and in the West) about the nature of Communism and were instrumental in keeping alive the notion of civil society in this region; a well-developed 'parallel polis' existed in Hungary. Unlike most other regimes in the region, the Hungarian regime recognized the legitimacy of the presence and open manifestation of group interests in the society and accepted that those interests could come into conflict with one another,[65] and it had legalized a private sphere of the economy. This means that a wide diversity of groups was encouraged to organize and play a part in Hungarian public life. The regime obviously did impose some limits on this, but by the 1980s the variety of autonomous organizations in Hungarian society was immense, although they were mostly weak and fragmented.

In the German Democratic Republic manifestations of worker opposition were vigorously put down by Soviet troops in 1953.

More important as cases of autonomous activity were the intellectuals and the church. There has been a continuing thread of dissident intellectual opinion in the GDR from shortly after the suppression of the workers' movement. Although this did not take an organizational form, the location of much of this criticism within the Marxist paradigm did give it a sense of a coherent debate, and it was instrumental in the emergence of the unofficial peace movement in 1981.[66] Also important in the foundation of this movement was the church. The German Evangelical Church was the only official organization in the GDR free from direct party control, and it was able to maintain its capacity to criticize general regime policies as well as simply defend its own institutional interests. The church took particular interest in the peace issue, criticizing what it saw as the regime's excessive militarization of German society.[67]

In Yugoslavia, as in Hungary, the authorities officially recognized the legitimacy of organized interests; indeed, the official ideology of self-managed Socialism assumed a degree of political pluralism, while the structuring of the Yugoslav federation made explicit provision for the organized representation of national interests. This means that there was generally a more liberal approach to the expression of critical opinion and informal discussion networks among intellectuals were prominent. Substantial press freedom provided a forum for the expression of a variety of heterodox views.[68] However, there were also limits to this (as the experience of Milovan Djilas showed) and the situation could vary from republic to republic. By the late 1980s Slovenia had, in the words of one author, 'developed a strong opposition movement and a true civil society made up of alternative movements, nationally-minded intellectuals, and a powerful youth movement.'[69] The other republics lagged behind Slovenia in terms of the growth of a civil society, but similar sorts of development did occur in Croatia and Serbia. The official ideology promoted an atmosphere which generally encouraged both the sort of freedom and discussion, within limits, that were not evident in many of the more hardline states.

None of the other countries was characterized by these sorts of manifestations of elements of a civil society. Although there were instances of opposition and dissent, they did not take the organized form evident in the countries discussed above, and in many cases this was not sustained over an extended period (although see the partial exception of the Soviet Union discussed below).[70] If we compare the countries which had the strongest elements of a civil society in the pre-Communist period with those in which autonomous social activity was strongest during the Communist period, the correspondence is striking. Of the five countries in each list, four are common: Hungary, Poland, Czechoslovakia and Germany/the GDR. In these cases it seems that while the Communist regime may have had some success in suppressing the elements of civil society it inherited, it certainly did not destroy that society. In contrast, the civil society was sufficiently robust to be able to withstand the regime. This robustness was especially marked in the cases of the GDR and Czechoslovakia where regime control has been characterized as being in the 'tight', and therefore most penetrative, category. The two countries that appear only on one list can be easily explained. The Soviet Union had elements of civil society emerging before the Communist revolution, but this found little reflection in activity during the Communist period.[71] This is principally because of the depth of the revolution the Communists imposed on the country, particularly in terms of agricultural collectivization and forced pace industrialization, and the political terror was far more extensive than anywhere else, with the result that the nascent civil society was destroyed. By the time the regime's rule began to be moderated in the 1950s and 1960s (and it thereby moved from being characterized by tight control to the medium category), in all parts of the Soviet Union except for the Baltic states the historical patterns of civil society were things to be read about in books; if they still resided in the interstices of the society, they were very weak. In Yugoslavia, where there had been little basis for civil society in the pre-Communist period, there were manifestations of autonomous social activity under Communist rule. This was a result of the direct sponsorship of the regime. To the extent that elements of civil society emerged in Yugoslav society, they emerged because the regime encouraged their development. Thus, rather than growing from pre-existing roots, the Yugoslav embryonic civil society was a product largely of state action.

Comparing the characteristics of regime control and the development of civil society, it is possible to plot the nine countries on a matrix. The civil society axis represents a combination of the pre-Communist history of civil society and the strength of the manifestations of civil society during the Communist period:

		Civil Society		
		Strong		Weak
	Tight	GDR		Romania
		Czechoslovakia		Albania
Regime control	Medium	Poland	USSR	Bulgaria
	Weak	Hungary	Yugoslavia	

One general characteristic of Communist development should be noted at this point. While the political regime of Communism, and especially its merging of the economic and political realms, was inherently antithetical to the development of a civil society (elements of civil society could develop only where the principles of the political regime were moderated), the economic and social changes which it encouraged did create the preconditions for such a development. Industrialization, urbanization and education were the keys here. The combination of these three factors produced in all of these countries a growing middle class whose consciousness of shared interests could only grow as communications and the media brought them even closer together. What inhibited the development of this potential into fully fledged civil societies, through the generation, development and interaction of autonomous associations, was political control. It was the control by the regimes which prevented the transformation of the potential for civil societies into actual civil societies throughout this region.

What does all of this mean for our understanding of the process of transition in these former Communist states? The course of the transition in each of these countries was fundamentally shaped by the sorts of historical factors discussed above, the nature of the society and the regime and the relationship between them. This history was not deterministic, but it did shape the alternatives that were possible and define the chief actors who were able to play a part in the transition. Of course, these structuring factors did not act in precisely the same way everywhere or have exactly the same effect, because contemporary actors were not the complete captives of this context; as the transition to democracy literature argues, élites did possess some freedom of room to manoeuvre, and the way they used this room could affect the course of subsequent development. Nevertheless, the structuring provided by recent history also created the context within which such manoeuvring took place. The effect of this context can be seen in the patterns of transition experienced by each of the former Communist countries.

The relationship between historical legacy and transition pattern is perhaps most starkly exposed in one of the cases of mass initiated change, Romania. Pre-Communist Romania had very little in the way of a civil society, it was characterized by very tight Communist regime control over society, the regime did not have influential reformist elements within it, and there was no pattern of organized autonomous social activity during the Communist period. This meant that there was no basis upon which organized opposition forces could rest, no leading organizations with which the regime could have opened negotiations, and no influential faction to press for such negotiations had a partner been available; therefore there could be no negotiated withdrawal, and mass demonstrations and rallies were the principal form of popular protest and the main dynamic of regime change. It is also reflected in the fact that the oppositionist élite which initially took over from Ceausescu came in part from among the popular opposition, but was principally spawned by that section of the regime élite which split from the dictator, the military.

The other four cases of mass initiated transition (Albania, Bulgaria, the GDR and Czechoslovakia) were also profoundly affected by their particular historical legacies. Pre-Communist society in both the GDR and Czechoslovakia had been characterized by the strong development of civil society, and this had continued to be manifested through organized autonomous social activity during the Communist period. What had held such development within bounds was the tightness of regime control. In Albania there was no basis for a pre-Communist civil society and little manifestation of such a development under Communism, with once again tight regime control restricting this. In Bulgaria the pre-Communist basis for civil society was also weak, and although it also did not appear during the Communist period, the more moderate control exercised by the regime meant that the potential for the development of a civil society was stronger in Bulgaria than it was in Albania. As a consequence principally of this tight control in the GDR and Czechoslovakia and of the weakness of the civil society base in Bulgaria and Albania (and in this case the tight control also), the transition was initiated not by interactions between reformist elements in the regime and opposition élites, but by the mass of the populace in the streets. The pressure they brought to bear created the opening which enabled the weaker opposition élites to come to the fore and, ultimately, through a process of discussion with newly strengthened reformist elements in the regime, achieve a negotiated withdrawal. The weaker position of the opposition élites in Albania compared with Czechoslovakia, the GDR and Bulgaria is reflected in the more drawn out nature of the transition in Tirana than in the other three capitals.

The apparent inconsistency in this comparison of mass-initiated change concerns Romania and Albania: both were characterized by tight regime control and weak development of civil society, yet the paths of regime change differed. This is explained chiefly by the nature of the respective regimes. Romania under Ceausescu was a personalist system, where the authority and power of the regime resided in one man, with little scope for the organization of alternative factions or groups. When the populace rose against him, the regime quickly fell because elements of the regime saw their interests to be best served by abandoning the leader and throwing in their lots with the opposition. By doing so, they choked off the possibility of further change based on the emergence of mass-based popular groups. In Albania, personalist rule had ended with the death of Enver Hoxha in 1985 at a time when the absence of popular protest enabled the regime to stabilize itself by consolidating a new leadership in power. Although the new leader, Ramiz Alia, was very powerful, he did not exercise the sort of close control which had characterized his predecessor; the élite was not monolithic. As a result, when popular protest mounted in 1990, the regime was better placed to be able to defend itself through negotiations. Also, it did not split in the same way that the Romanian regime did. The longer time the process took in Albania meant that there was greater scope for autonomous groups to emerge and play some part in the process than in Romania, where the post-Ceausescu process was much more managed by the newly emergent NSF leadership.

The single case of opposition élite initiated transformation was Poland, and this was the only country which shared a particular combination of qualities: strong pre-Communist basis for civil society, developed civil society manifestations during the Communist period, and moderate regime control. This combination meant that opposition élites were very well placed to take a leading part in the transition; they had an established organizational identity, a popular support base, and room within which to move to both maximize their support and increase the pressure upon the regime.

Through their mass support and strategic location, they were able to push the regime into concessions and negotiations.

In Hungary, the ruling élite, characterized by strong reformist elements, initiated change which opened the way for negotiations with opposition élites, leading to a negotiated transition. Hungary was characterized by the strong development of civil society in the pre-Communist period, considerable manifestations of it under Communism, and loose regime control. But Hungary differed from the other countries in which civil society elements developed strongly under Communism in that much of this development in Hungary did not take an anti-regime character. Because of the *modus vivendi* the regime had sought to establish with society, much of the autonomous organization which occurred was not characterized by an anti-regime impetus. There were certainly political opposition groups, but they were not so dominant as to define the character of the emergent civil society. It was therefore possible for the regime, when it decided to shift from a process of liberalization to democratization, to largely structure the initial stages of that and to define the conditions under which these early steps were taken. But the robustness of civil society soon ensured that regime control did not last long.

In Yugoslavia there was little history of pre-Communist civil society, some development of this under communism, and generally loose regime control. However, what prevented civil society groups from playing a leading role in a Yugoslav transition was the salience of the ethnic factor and the activities of ethnic élites. When unity at the centre disappeared, the running in structuring the agenda of change was taken out of the hands of civil society groups by the ethnic élites entrenched in positions of state power by the Yugoslav federal system. By using their positions of state power in the republics, ethnic élites were able to generate popular support and to use this to crack open the Yugoslav federal state. So, in the Yugoslav case, the balance between ethnic state élites and civil society groups was heavily weighted in favour of the former by the Yugoslav Communist political structure, which thereby enabled pressures for democratization within the federal state to be overwhelmed by disintegrative ethnic nationalism.

In the Soviet Union, too, the pressures for a Soviet democratization were derailed by the drive for independence by ethnic élites located in some of the republican governments. The early shoots of civil society which had been present during the pre-Communist period were extinguished in the first two decades of Communist rule, and even though there seemed to be some stirrings of this with the emergence of the dissident movement at the time when the regime's control became looser than it had been, the impetus for civil society remained very underdeveloped. As a result, the initiation of change came from reformist elements in the central regime élite, and opposition forces based in society were very slow to respond and gain momentum. When they did, the strongest form they took was national protest in some of the union republics, although a democratic opposition did take form in Moscow. However, real pressure was placed on the central élite only when democratic and nationalist opposition based in society allied itself with ethnic élites in the new republican governments, leading to the perception that democracy could be achieved only with the destruction of the federal Soviet state. Again, it was the political legacy from the Soviet period, in particular the combination of weak civil society forces and ethnic élites entrenched in the federal state structure, which was crucial.

It is thus apparent that the course of post-Communist transition can be understood fully only by taking into account the historical legacy which was present at that time. A focus purely upon the contemporary period and on élite action as advocated in the transition to democracy literature can enable a comparison of the individual cases, but it cannot provide either an adequate explanation of them or why they differ. Only if the legacy of the past is fed into the analysis can the different patterns of transition be understood and their outcomes appreciated. It is this past legacy that determined which actors were best placed to play a part in structuring the course of the transition. Was there a stable basis of autonomous group activity which could throw up popular leaderships to spearhead the struggle with the regime, or was such a basis absent? Were ethnic élites so powerful that they could cut across civil society forces? Was the regime of such a type that, under pressure, it was likely to split, and if so, how strong were reformist elements likely to be? These questions are crucial to an understanding of the post-Communist transitions, but they can only be answered by the longer-term comparative historical sociological analysis. An élite-focused study will not achieve this.

Similarly, the objections outlined at the start of this chapter fall away if the longer-term comparative historical sociological analysis is undertaken. Most of the objections relate to context, and to the complaint that the context is different: Communist regimes are more authoritarian, their political economy is different, their level of economic development is greater, they have a flatter social structure, they involved a question of identity, they were characterized by greater ethnic diversity, they were more affected by international influences, and the agenda of transition was different. But if we accept that these transitions can be understood only in terms of the broader context, these differences do not make the transitions necessarily qualitatively different from regime changes in Latin America and Southern Europe. Rather, the context is different, and therefore the options and alternatives open to the actors will be different and the strength of the various actors is also likely to be different. For example, the relative absence of pacts in Communist transitions is a direct reflection of the nature of the society and the general weakness of civil society forces.[72] Similarly, the other point of difference noted at the beginning, the perceived greater role of the masses, is also a reflection of the socio-historical legacy and the weakness of such forces. Once we accept that the key structuring principle in transition is the relationship between regime élites and civil society and that this can be understood only through a longer-term socio-historical analysis, not only is the difference between Communist and non-Communist transitions reduced, but also our understanding of non-Communist transitions is enhanced. It is only through this type of analysis that the weaknesses of a purely élite-focused approach can be overcome.

Conclusion: Towards Consolidation?

The course of democratic transition, ideally, gives way to the third stage in the process, democratic consolidation. Although there have been differing conceptions of consolidation depending upon what analysts saw to be its specific purpose, to prevent the decay or erosion back to authoritarian rule or to build a qualitatively better democratic system,[1] the basic understanding of what consolidation is about has been widely agreed. The notion of consolidation refers to the embedding of democratic procedures into the infrastructure as a whole so that that system is secure and is generally seen as the appropriate way of organizing political life. In the words of two scholars, a consolidated democracy is 'a regime that meets all the procedural criteria of democracy and also in which all politically significant groups accept established political institutions and adhere to democratic rules of the game.'[2] A regime is therefore said to be consolidated when it is seen as 'the only game in town',[3] when no alternative methods of organizing politics are seen as appropriate replacements of the democratic process. This does not mean that, once consolidated, a democracy will remain stable and firmly in place for ever. Like any regime, a consolidated democracy can break down, but it should be more immune from that process than an unconsolidated democracy would be.

There is no clear and unambiguous criterion for distinguishing between a consolidated and an unconsolidated regime. One measure that can be used is time: democratic regimes that have lasted for considerable periods of time are likely to be more consolidated than those in the first year of their birth, although even this statement must be qualified by recognition of the fact that some long-term regimes may be in decline while some newer ones may be securely established at an early stage in their lives. But in any case, there can be no rigid time period which enables distinction between a consolidated and unconsolidated state. Another measure that has been used has been that of two changes of government through the electoral process.[4] This has the advantage of being clear and relatively unambiguous, although it does encounter difficulties in cases where dominant parties continually win government through competitive elections, as in Mexico and India. It is the clarity of this as an indicator which has appealed to many students and encouraged them to use it as a rough guide to consolidation.

The value of this as an indicator of consolidation lies in the way in which it provides an institutional means of judging whether the essence of consolidation has been achieved, viz. whether political actors accept that this is the appropriate means of ordering political life and thereby accept the rules of the democratic political game as binding. This sort of acceptance, meaning that political actors acknowledge the normative force of democratic procedures and institutions rather than simply accepting them as temporary expedients until they need to overturn them in the pursuit of policy ends, constitutes an embedding of democratic principles into the collective consciousness of the system and thereby the effective institutionalization of that system. This notion of consolidation involving normative adherence to the procedures of democracy has generally been reflected in a scholarly focus upon institutional structures.

A large part of the writing on consolidation has taken the form of a discussion of the types of institutional structures which would best facilitate democratic development.[5] This was stimulated by the recognition that formal institutional structures play a significant role in shaping political life, and that the forms those institutions take (and any flaws in the rules whereby they function) can have a significant impact upon political outcomes. For example, Juan Linz has argued that presidentialism was likely to facilitate non-democratic outcomes because of the way in which fixed terms and the winner-takes-all nature of presidential elections produced rigidity in the political process, the weakness of adequate mechanisms for the representation of societal interests, authority divided between executive and legislature, and a fragmented party system, with the resultant stalemate combined with concentration of power increasing the likelihood of the resort to non-democratic means.[6] This stimulated a significant debate on the respective merits of presidential and parliamentary systems.[7] There has been a similar concern with other aspects of the institutional structure, including the electoral system[8] and political parties.[9]

Much of this literature is rich in insight and, by focusing upon the way in which institutional structures shape political outcomes, it brings to the forefront of our attention the importance of political institutions. But it is also an approach which concentrates on the activity of the élites and their role in crafting the institutional structure of the new regime.[10] If the institutions are so important in shaping political outcomes, then the design of those institutions themselves is crucial. And this is a task which is carried out by the élites. It is those élites who decide whether a presidential or parliamentary system will be established, what form of electoral system will be used (and thereby in part determining the contours of party conflict), and how the constitution will distribute authority between various institutional actors. In most cases these are all the subject of conscious political decisions taken by élites. This is the process of establishing the rules of the political game, of crafting the political system, and this is clearly crucial in determining whether the new system will have a democratic shape or not. This sort of focus on institutional design enables us to see whether the procedural minima for democracy have been established, or whether there remain significant limitations upon the operation of democratic institutions and processes; the continuing presence of tutelary or oversight powers exercised by a section of the old regime (usually the military), the designation of areas of public policy as outside the government's authority (again this has often involved military rights and prerogatives), and restrictions upon the electoral laws are frequent limitations imposed upon new regimes which should become evident through a focus on institutional design. It can, then, enable us to identify what has been called 'democracy with adjectives',[11] systems in which the full operation of democracy's procedural principles are limited in some way. But while a focus on institutional design can approach the procedural minima question, alone it is not enough.

The assumption behind much of this literature is that what is crucial is that élite political actors abide by democratic rules and procedures, and that over time this will lead to those rules and procedures becoming embedded in the collective consciousness of the system, including the mass of the population. Political actors will become habituated to shaping their actions to accord with those rules and procedures. There is merit in this argument. The more the system is seen to work, the stronger it will become, and thereby the less the likelihood that actors will seek to go outside it to achieve their ends. It will generate normative authority at all levels of society. This approach is valuable because it places the relationship between democratic procedures and political actors at the centre of attention. But the way in which the question is conceived is limiting because of its reliance upon a procedural definition of democracy. Providing there are regular, competitive, relatively fair elections based on wide suffrage which produce a government that then implements the policies it placed before the electorate, democracy is said to exist. This sort of procedurally minimalist definition clearly captures something which is essential for a democratic system to exist, but alone it is an unsatisfactory measure. In order to get a more satisfying conception of democracy, our gaze must be significantly broader than a narrow focus on political institutions and the élites which inhabit them.[12] To understand whether democracy is substantively, as opposed to simply procedurally, in existence, we need to look at the society more broadly within which the political institutions rest.

Two scholars who recognize that a purely procedural approach is unsatisfactory are Juan Linz and Alfred Stepan.[13] They define a consolidated democracy in terms of three elements:

1. Behaviourally, when no significant political groups seek to overthrow the democratic regime or secede from the state.
2. Attitudinally, when democratic procedures and institutions are viewed generally by the populace as the most appropriate means of governing collective life, and there is little support for alternatives.
3. Constitutionally, when political forces 'become subjected to, and habituated to, the resolution of conflict within the specific laws, procedures, and institutions sanctioned by the new democratic process.'

A democracy is deemed to be consolidated when these three elements are all present; 'with consolidation, democracy becomes routinized and deeply internalized in social, institutional, and even psychological life, as well as in calculations for achieving success.'[14] The advantage of this approach over a more narrowly procedural conception is that while acknowledging the importance of procedural elements, it also specifically recognizes that the mass of the populace have a part to play in a democratic polity. Given that intrinsic to the notion of democracy is that of popular participation and control, any attempt to discuss the stability or future of a democratic regime that ignored the popular role must fail to see a crucial dynamic of the regime and its functioning. It is not just élite actors who can disrupt democratic processes, but mass actors also. Not only Linz and Stepan acknowledge the importance of popular commitment to democratic values. Larry Diamond sees public opinion survey data as an important resource for establishing whether a democracy has become consolidated, arguing that what is necessary is a 'broad and deep legitimation' among the populace as well as the élites.[15] This is consistent with the arguments about the importance of culture, more particularly a democratic political culture, for the stability and durability of democracy[16] noted in Chapter 1. This is also consistent with arguments about the role of civil society in democratic consolidation.[17]

Recognition that the populace has a role in determining whether a democratic regime becomes consolidated or not, and thereby whether that regime breaks down and is transformed into one of an authoritarian disposition, is linked with the type of questions dealt with in Chapter 2, and especially that of regime performance. A regime that is functioning effectively is more likely to generate popular support than one which is not. At one level this means those institutions central to the procedural focus of much of the consolidation literature. If the populace is not convinced that those bodies at the top of the political structure are working in accord with the democratic principles their leaders espouse and are operating effectively, popular commitment to the regime is likely to erode. At another level it also refers to those institutions which link the populace with the political system more narrowly defined, the institutions of civil society. But it also refers to economic performance. A recent study has argued that while a range of factors are important in making a democracy more likely to survive, economic factors are the most important.[18] Among those economic factors are a society's affluence, economic growth with moderate inflation, and declining inequality. This combination of the short and longer-term results of government policy underpins regime stability. It is also consistent with the discussion of economic prerequisites in Chapter 1.

However, a focus on economic development may be misleading in terms of its perceived relationship with democracy if it ignores the potential political implications of the sort of inequality that often accompanies such development. This is not an argument about the formal equality of citizens that is central to the democratic ideal, although this is an important issue. Rather, it is about the way in which economic development does not share the benefits of that development equally throughout the society, and about the capacity of powerful economic interests to act in ways which undercut the meaning of the regime's procedural principles. The emergence of powerful economic interests can seriously compromise a regime's democratic credentials even if the basic procedural principles of democracy continue to be observed. Regular elections may be held, governments formally elected to power, representative institutions meet on a regular basis, and there may be broad-based popular support for these structures, but if powerful economic interests are able unduly to influence government and shape its decisions (and historically, powerful economic interests have usually been able to exercise significant influence on governments), the formal institutions may be a sham. This depends, in part, on how that influence is exercised. We can posit two major modes of operating for those with substantial resources who wish to further their interests in the political sphere: they can operate principally through the public structures and processes of civil society where major issues of concern are raised and openly discussed, or they can act through the private channels and personal contacts they possess with leading political actors. Where the economically powerful act principally through civil society channels and the formalized procedures of the society, democracy is more soundly based than when they operate through shadowy behind the scenes mechanisms out of public view. Under these latter circumstances, the capture of the political process by partial interests is more likely, and thereby aspirations for democratic rule undermined.

Civil society is important not only because it is the site within which many of the institutions through which democratic political actors act are located, but because it is the repository of the democratic values which underpin any sustained democratic structure. While élites may establish a procedural democracy, those institutions are unlikely to continue to function in a democratic fashion unless they are sustained by a culture in the society at large which supports those democratic principles. If the maintenance of the system is left to the preferences of the élites, the growth of popularly exclusionist politics is likely. In contrast, if the culture validates continuing popular involvement in the political process in a structured fashion through the institutions of civil society, and those institutions are well developed and able to influence political life, the domination of the system by élites (including economic élites) is less likely. What is crucial here is the activity of powerful institutions of civil society, such as political parties, labour unions and interest associations, which link élite politics with the populace and, by providing channels for popular participation and oversight, enable the realization of democratic values in political forms. In this way, while democratic structures may be created mainly through élite action and may be able to sustain themselves for some time, their consolidation is unlikely without more broadly-based support for democracy and the institutional channels through which that support can be acted out. This means that the prospects for democratic consolidation are strengthened by the growth and development of a powerful civil society, reflected in the presence of vigorous organizational vehicles for popular participation, an established arena for the public discussion and contestation of issues, and firm linkages between these and leading political actors.

So, fundamental for the issue of the future of a democratic system is this relationship between the political process, private interests and civil society. If the principal threads of that relationship are mediated through civil society, even though all private interests are not equal, the public mediation process should ensure some transparency and public oversight and therefore that the system does not come to be dominated by a few. If it does become thus dominated, whatever type of regime becomes consolidated will not be democratic in a substantive sense despite its being in accord with the procedural minima of democracy. Similarly, even if democratic structures are created principally as a result of élite action, their survival will ultimately depend upon them becoming embedded within a vigorous civil society embodying a culture of public involvement.

It is clear that civil society has a crucial part to play in the stabilization of a democratic system and therefore that a focus upon the élite crafting of institutions alone will be inadequate as a guide to democratic consolidation. This is consistent with the primary argument of this book, that civil society forces are intrinsic to the process of democratic transition. Such forces constitute major elements in the dynamic of democratic transition. They embody the threat which persuades a section of the ruling élite of the need for an opening to society in an attempt to stabilize the regime. They give the process of regime change a democratic orientation and keep that change moving in a democratic direction. They define the powerful interests in society with which the regime must come to terms, and thereby identify relevant negotiating partners for regime élites. And they provide the basic underpinning for the emergent democratic system. This means that civil society forces are fundamental for each stage of the process of regime change, from the onset of crisis to the stabilization of democracy. To fail to see their role and only to see that of the élites is to misunderstand this process. Where civil society forces are not developed, and political élites are freer to act of their own volition, the pattern of political change will be different and the outcome more likely to be some sort of restabilization of authoritarian rule. But where civil society forces do play a role along with regime élites and that process leads to a democratic outcome, this process is likely itself to constitute the transformation of those civil society forces into full-blown civil society. In this sense, civil society can be achieved only through the efforts of that society itself in pursuing democratic change. Civil society cannot be created from above, but must constitute itself through its own activity. After all, that is the essence of democracy.

Notes and References

Chapter 1   Democratization: Economic Prerequisites

1. Samuel P. Huntington, *The Third Wave. Democratization in the Late Twentieth Century* (Norman, University of Oklahoma Press, 1991).
2. Francis Fukuyama, *The End of History and the Last Man* (London, Penguin, 1992).
3. Huntington, pp. 13–26.
4. Huntington, p. 17. This is representative of the minimalist notion of democratization generally used in studies of this process, including in this book, viz. the change of regime from one functioning on the basis of non-democratic principles to one resting on democratic principles. This begs the important question of what is meant by democracy, and this is raised in the Conclusion.
5. It is not clear that the metaphor of the wave is completely satisfactory; waves tend to be regular in timing, there is often a certain uniformity both within and between waves, the effect of one wave is over-whelmed by the next (at least when the tide is coming in), and the notion of a wave lasting 100 years robs the metaphor of any meaning. The metaphor can obscure differences between the cases comprising the waves. For example, in the case of the decolonized states in the second wave, the crucial authorities were external, the colonial masters, and it was the disappearance of their will and capacity to maintain their rule in the colony which was essential rather than the breakdown of the local power structure. In the third wave cases (and those non-colonial second wave cases) it was the breakdown of the local authority structures which was important. Nevertheless, it has become established in the literature as a useful way of referring to the democratizations of the 1970s and 1980s, and will therefore be used in the subsequent discussion.
6. Gabriel A. Almond and Sidney Verba, *The Civic Culture: Political Attitudes and Democracy in Five Nations* (Boston, Little, Brown & Co., 1965).
7. Robert A. Dahl, *Polyarchy. Participation and Opposition* (New Haven, Yale University Press, 1971), Chapter 8.
8. See this discussed in Huntington, pp. 298–311.
9. See the discussion in Kenneth A. Bollen, 'Political Democracy and the Timing of Development', *American Sociological Review* ,44, 4, 1979, pp. 572–587. The reverse of this was the argument about the incompatibility of Roman Catholicism and democratic outcomes. For example, Howard Wiarda, 'Toward a Framework for the Study of

Political Change in the Iberic–Latin Tradition: The Corporative Model', *World Politics* 25, 2, January 1972, pp. 206–235.

10. Seymour Martin Lipset, 'Some Social Requisites of Democracy: Economic Development and Political Legitimacy', *American Political Science Review* 53, 1, March 1959, pp. 69–105.

11. For example, see the discussions in Seymour Martin Lipset, Kyoung-Ryung Soong and John Charles Torres, 'A Comparative Analysis of the Social Requisites of Democracy', *International Social Science Journal* 136, May 1993, pp. 155–175; Seymour Martin Lipset, 'The Social Requisites of Democracy Revisited', *American Sociological Review* 59, February 1994, pp. 1–22; Carlos H. Waisman, 'Capitalism, the Market, and Democracy', *American Behavioral Scientist* 35, 4/5, March/June 1992, pp. 500–516; Mick Moore, 'Democracy and Development in Cross-National Perspective: A New Look at the Statistics', *Democratization* 2, 2, Summer 1995, pp. 1–19.

12. Lipset, p. 75.

13. For example, see Larry Diamond, 'Economic Development and Democracy Reconsidered', *American Behavioral Scientist* 35, 4/5, March/June 1992, pp. 450–453.

14. See Diamond pp. 454–455; Samuel P. Huntington, 'Will More Countries Become Democratic?', *Political Science Quarterly*, 99, 2, Summer 1984, pp. 200–201; Huntington, Third Wave, pp. 59–64; Adam Przeworski and Fernando Limongi, 'Modernization: Theories and Facts', *World Politics* 49, 2, 1997, pp. 159–160. For Huntington, the range was defined as 'upper middle income'. For an argument that posits the occurrence of democracy when 'power resources have become so widely distributed that no group is any longer able to suppress its competitors or to maintain its hegemony', see Tatu Vanhanen, *Prospects of Democracy. A Study of 172 Countries* (London, Routledge, 1997). The quotation is from p. 5.

15. Diamond, p. 454.

16. Przeworski and Limongi, pp. 159–160.

17. To use another of Huntington's terms.

18. For some data, see Huntington, *Third Wave* ... p. 62.

19. See Huntington, 'Will More Countries ...' p. 199.

20. Huntington, *Third Wave* ... Chapter 2.

21. This is based on the discussion in Diamond, pp. 475–485, which is in turn based principally on Lipset.

22. This is based on Lipset's views about the political susceptibilities of the working class and the problems they can pose for democratic stability. In particular, see Seymour Martin Lipset, *Political Man* (London, Heinemann, 1960), Chapters 3 and 4.

23. Civil society is itself shaped by the course of economic development. The contours of the groups of which civil society consists (especially those related to employment), the improved educational levels which underpin increased popular involvement, and the development of a mass communications network which helps shape the public sphere, are all themselves directly shaped by the course of economic development.

24. Guillermo O'Donnell, Philippe C. Schmitter and Laurence Whitehead (eds.), *Transitions from Authoritarian Rule: Prospects for Democracy* (Baltimore, The Johns Hopkins University Press, 1986). See Chapter 3 for more details. Use of the term 'transition' has been criticized for its teleological overtones, but those working in the field have generally not seen the process as inevitably leading to democracy. The breakdown of an authoritarian regime may lead to its replacement by another authoritarian regime. A democratic regime established in the transition phase may not become consolidated. Indeed, a consolidated democratic regime may itself fall and be replaced by an authoritarian set of ruling arrangements.
25. Juan J. Linz and Alfred Stepan, *The Breakdown of Democratic Regimes* (Baltimore, The Johns Hopkins University Press, 1978).

Chapter 2   The Breakdown of Authoritarian Regimes

1. To use the language of Samuel P. Huntington, *The Third Wave. Democratization in the Late Twentieth Century* (Norman, University of Oklahoma Press, 1991).
2. For an attempt to schematize the transition in terms similar to this, see Robert H. Dix, 'The Breakdown of Authoritarian Regimes', *Western Political Quarterly* 35, 4, 1982, pp. 568–569.
3. The probability that a democratic regime would survive four or five consecutive years of negative growth was said to be 57 per cent and 50 per cent respectively. Juan J. Linz and Alfred Stepan, *Problems of Democratic Transition and Consolidation. Southern Europe, South America and Post-Communist Europe* (Baltimore, The Johns Hopkins University Press, 1996), p. 79, citing an unpublished study by Fernando Limongi and Adam Przeworski.
4. Stephen Haggard and Robert R. Kaufman, *The Political Economy of Democratic Transitions* (Princeton, Princeton University Press, 1995), pp. 33–36.
5. However, it is doubtful that anything can be read into these earlier bouts of economic difficulty, except perhaps that authoritarian regimes survived them, because all countries experience such periods at times.
6. Haggard and Kaufman, p. 46.
7. On economic crisis and the bureaucratic authoritarian regime, see David Collier (ed.), *The New Authoritarianism in Latin America* (Princeton, Princeton University Press, 1979).
8. Haggard and Kaufman, Chapter 2. These examples are discussed more fully in Chapter 5.
9. Manuel Antonio Garreton, 'The Political Evolution of the Chilean Military Regime and Problems in the Transition to Democracy', Guillermo O'Donnell, Philippe C. Schmitter and Laurence Whitehead (eds.), *Transitions from Authoritarian Rule: Latin America* (Baltimore, The Johns Hopkins University Press, 1986).

10.   For some figures, which are not wholly consistent, see Haggard and Kaufman pp. 34–35 and Luis Carlos Bresser Pereira, Jose Maria Maravall and Adam Przeworski, *Economic Reforms in New Democracies. A Social Democratic Approach* (Cambridge, Cambridge University Press, 1993), p. 37.

11.   This is argued at some length in Haggard and Kaufman, Part One.

12.   Amos Perlmutter, *Modern Authoritarianism. A Comparative Institutional Analysis* (New Haven, Yale University Press, 1981), p. 2.

13.   Haggard and Kaufman pp. 11–13.

14.   This did not apply to Eastern Europe and the former Soviet Union, but they were, chiefly for political reasons, still on the margins of the dynamic engine of global economic growth.

15.   Fernando H. Cardoso, 'Entrepreneurs and the Transition Process: The Brazilian Case', Guillermo O'Donnell, Philippe C. Schmitter and Laurence Whitehead (eds.), *Transitions from Authoritarian Rule. Comparative Perspectives* (Baltimore, The Johns Hopkins University Press, 1986), pp. 137–153.

16.   For one discussion of this, see Karen L. Remmer, 'Redemocratization and the Impact of Authoritarian Rule in Latin America', *Comparative Politics* 17, 3, April 1985, pp. 253–275.

17.   On Spain, see Jose Maria Maravall and Julian Santamaria, 'Political Change in Spain and the Prospects for Democracy', Guillermo O'Donnell, Philippe C. Schmitter and Laurence Whitehead (eds.), *Transitions from Authoritarian Rule: Southern Europe* (Baltimore, The Johns Hopkins University Press, 1986). On Greece, see P. Nikiforos Diamandouros, 'Regime Change and the Prospects for Democracy in Greece: 1974–1983', *Transitions … Southern Europe*; Howard R. Penniman (ed.), *Greece at the Polls. The National Elections of 1974 and 1977* (Washington, American Enterprise Institute for Public Policy Research, 1981); Linz and Stepan, Chapter 8. On Argentina, see Marcelo Cavarozzi, 'Political Cycles in Argentina since 1955', *Transitions … Latin America*. Also Roberto Aizcorbe, *Argentina. The Peronist Myth. An Essay on the Cultural Decay in Argentina After the Second World War* (Hicksville, Exposition Press, 1975).

18.   See Huntington, *Third Wave* … pp. 72–85.

19.   On this, see Laurence Whitehead, 'International Aspects of Democratization', Transitions … Comparative Perspectives, pp. 25–31.

20.   Francis Fukuyama, *The End of History and the Last Man* (London, Penguin, 1992).

21.   On this see Harvey Starr, 'Democratic Dominoes: Diffusion Approaches to the Spread of Democracy in the International System', *Journal of Conflict Resolution* 35, 2, June 1991, pp. 356–381.

22.   It may be that the experiences of Portugal and Spain stimulated pressures for democratization in the South American countries because of their common cultural ties and the important symbolic role that the European metropoles played in Ibero–American culture.

23.   For a brief discussion of some approaches to this see Diane Ethier, 'Introduction: Processes of Transition and Democratic Consolidation:

Theoretical Indicators', Diane Ethier (ed.), *Democratic Transition and Consolidation in Southern Europe, Latin America and Southeast Asia* (London, Macmillan, 1990), p. 9.

24. Guillermo O'Donnell, *Modernization and Bureaucratic-Authoritarianism: Studies in South American Politics* (Berkeley, Institute of International Studies, University of California, Berkeley, 1973). But see the discussion in Collier.

25. Karen L. Remmer, 'New Theoretical Perspectives on Democratization', *Comparative Politics* 28, 1, October 1995, p. 107.

26. Dix, pp. 563–566.

27. This is the distinction drawn by Perlmutter between autocracy and tyranny, which both refer to rule by a single individual, and authoritarianism which refers to 'a collective dictatorship, an oligarchy, or a military government.' Perlmutter, p. 1.

28. For a discussion of single party regimes, see Gary D. Wekkin *et al.* (eds.), *Building Democracy in One-Party Systems* (Westport, Praeger, 1993).

29. On military regimes, see Eric A. Nordlinger, *Soldiers in Politics. Military Coups and Governments* (Englewood Cliffs, Prentice Hall, 1977); and Amos Perlmutter, 'The Comparative Analysis of Military Regimes: Formations, Aspirations, and Achievements', *World Politics* xxxiii, 1, October 1980, pp. 96–120.

30. On the nature of the Spanish regime, see Juan J. Linz, 'An Authoritarian Regime: Spain', Erik Allardt and Stein Rokkan (eds.), *Mass Politics: Studies in Political Sociology* (New York, The Free Press, 1970). The military was clearly a subordinate element in Spain.

31. On bureaucratic authoritarian regimes, see Collier; and O'Donnell, *Modernization . . .*

32. Charles G. Gillespie, 'Uruguay's Transition from Collegial Military-Technocratic Rule', *Transitions ... Latin America*, p. 181.

33. Kenneth Maxwell, 'Regime Overthrow and the Prospects for Democratic Transition in Portugal', *Transitions ... Southern Europe*. Also Constantine P. Danopoulos, 'Democratization by Golpe: The Experience of Modern Portugal', Constantine P. Danopoulos (ed.), *Military Disengagement from Politics* (London, Routledge, 1988), p. 239.

34. There is not a large literature on this sort of regime, but for some discussion, see for example, Robert H. Jackson and Carl G. Rosberg, 'Personal Rule. Theory and Practice in Africa', *Comparative Politics* 16, 4, July 1984, pp. 421–442; Guenther Roth, 'Personal Rulership, Patrimonialism, and Empire Building in the New States', *World Politics* xx, 2, January 1968, pp. 194–206; Ann Ruth Willner, *The Spellbinders. Charismatic Political Leadership* (New Haven, Yale University Press, 1984).

35. In part this was agreed because of fears of the excessive politicization of the military that could result from a more institutional arrangement.

36. Huntington's 'reformists' and 'standpatters'. Huntington, p. 121.

37. Perhaps the military institution, especially when in power, is the best illustration of this sort of structure.

38. See the discussion in Adam Przeworski, 'Some Problems in the Study of the Transition to Democracy', *Transitions ... Comparative Perspectives*.
39. Przeworski, 'Some Problems ...', pp. 50–3.
40. Diamandouros, p. 147.
41. On the difference between social and political revolution and their effects, see Theda Skocpol, *States and Social Revolution. A Comparative Analysis of France, Russia and China* (Cambridge, Cambridge University Press, 1979).

Chapter 3   Elites and Transition

1.   Dankwart A. Rustow, 'Transitions to Democracy. Toward a Dynamic Model', *Comparative Politics* 2, 3, April 1970, pp. 337–363.
2.   Rustow, p. 353.
3.   Rustow, p. 355.
4.   Rustow, p. 356.
5.   Guillermo O'Donnell, Philippe C. Schmitter and Laurence Whitehead (eds.), *Transitions from Authoritarian Rule: Southern Europe* (Baltimore, The Johns Hopkins University Press, 1986), *Transitions from Authoritarian Rule: Latin America* (Baltimore, The Johns Hopkins University Press, 1986), *Transitions from Authoritarian Rule: Comparative Perspectives* (Baltimore, The Johns Hopkins University Press, 1986), and Guillermo O'Donnell and Philippe C. Schmitter (eds.), *Transitions from Authoritarian Rule: Tentative Conclusions about Uncertain Democracies* (Baltimore, The Johns Hopkins University Press, 1986). All four volumes have also been published in a consolidated version, Guillermo O'Donnell, Philippe C. Schmitter and Laurence Whitehead (eds.), *Transitions from Authoritarian Rule: Prospects for Democracy* (Baltimore, The Johns Hopkins University Press, 1986). Henceforth all references will be to the separate volumes.
6.   *Transitions ... Tentative Conclusions*, p. 6.
7.   *Transitions ... Tentative Conclusions*, p. 3.
8.   *Transitions ... Tentative Conclusions*, pp. 5 and 4 respectively.
9.   *Transitions ... Tentative Conclusions*, p. 19.
10. *Transitions ... Tentative Conclusions*, pp. 28–31, 37 and 38.
11. Theorization has been attempted using game theory and, within the confines of this approach, has had some success. See Gretchen Casper and Michelle M. Taylor, *Negotiating Democracy. Transitions from Authoritarian Rule* (Pittsburgh, University of Pittsburgh Press, 1996). See below.
12. *Transitions ... Tentative Conclusions*, p. 7.
13. Luciano Martins, 'The Liberalization of Authoritarian Rule in Brazil', *Transitions ... Latin America*, p. 88.
14. Samuel P. Huntington, *The Third Wave. Democratization in the Late Twentieth Century* (Norman, University of Oklahoma Press, 1991), p. 9.

15. It is also more useful than the discussion in Linz and Stepan, who give examples of liberalization without actually defining it. Juan J. Linz and Alfred Stepan, *Problems of Democratic Transition and Consolidation. Southern Europe, South America, and Post-Communist Europe* (Baltimore, The Johns Hopkins University Press, 1996), p. 3.

16. See the discussion in Adam Przeworski, 'Democracy as a contingent outcome of conflicts', Jon Elster and Rune Slagstad (eds.), *Constitutionalism and Democracy* (Cambridge, Cambridge University Press, 1988), p. 61. Also Adam Przeworski, *Democracy and the Market. Political and Economic Reform in Eastern Europe and Latin America* (Cambridge, Cambridge University Press, 1991), pp. 54–66.

17. Enrique A. Baloyra, 'Democratic Transition in Comparative Perspective', Enrique A. Baloyra (ed.), *Comparing New Democracies. Transition and Consolidation in Mediterranean Europe and the Southern Cone* (Boulder, Westview Press, 1987), pp. 40–42.

18. For the argument that what is central is negotiation between regime 'Defender' and regime 'Challenger' with the 'Mass Public' playing a mediating role, see Casper and Taylor.

19. *Transitions ... Tentative Conclusions*, p. 37. For Friedheim, a pact is 'an open-ended bargaining process rather than a formal contract.' Daniel V. Friedheim, 'Bringing Society Back into Democratic Transition Theory after 1989: Pact Making and Regime Collapse', *East European Politics and Societies* 7, 3, Fall 1993, p. 491

20. *Transitions ... Tentative Conclusions*, p. 38. On pacts also see Charles Guy Gillespie, *Negotiating Democracy. Politicians and Generals in Uruguay* (Cambridge, Cambridge University Press, 1991), Chapter 8.

21. *Transitions ... Tentative Conclusions*, p. 38.

22. *Transitions ... Tentative Conclusions*, pp. 39–47.

23. Huntington, p. 165.

24. Huntington, p. 166.

25. Terry Lynn Karl, 'Dilemmas of Democratization in Latin America', *Comparative Politics*, 23, 1, October 1990.

26. Karl 'Dilemmas ...', p. 11.

27. Samuel P. Huntington, 'How Countries Democratize', *Political Science Quarterly* 106, 4, 1991–92, p. 584.

28. Huntington, *Third Wave ...* , p. 169.

29. Huntington, *Third Wave ...* , p. 169.

30. For one discussion of these, see Robert H. Dix, 'The Breakdown of Authoritarian Regimes', *Western Political Quarterly* 35, 4, 1982, pp. 567–568.

31. Huntington, *Third Wave ...* , p. 171.

32. For a discussion of the conservatizing effects of pact-making in Brazil, see Frances Hagopian, "Democracy by Undemocratic Means'? Elites, Political Pacts, and Regime Transition in Brazil', *Comparative Political Studies* 23, 2, July 1990, pp. 147–170.

33. O'Donnell, 'Introduction to the Latin American Cases', *Transitions ... Latin America*, pp. 12–13.

34. For example, see the comments in Diane Ethier, 'Introduction:

Processes of Transition and Democratic Consolidation: Theoretical Indicators', Diane Ethier (ed.), *Democratic Transition and Consolidation in Southern Europe, Latin America and Southeast Asia* (London, Macmillan, 1990), p. 11.

35. Ethier, 'Introduction', p. 11.

36. This is a principal element of the argument in Casper and Taylor. But here the population is considered as an undifferentiated mass, with no account taken of how popular opinion is manifested or the relationship between élites and mass.

37. Huntington, *Third Wave* ... , p. 146. The total of 33 comes from p. 14.

38. e.g. John Keane, *Democracy and Civil Society* (London, Verso, 1988) and John Keane (ed.), *Civil Society and the State* (London, Verso, 1988).

39. According to Weigle and Butterfield, civil society is 'the independent self-organization of society, the constituent parts of which voluntarily engage in public activity to pursue individual, group, or national interests within the context of a legally defined state-society relationship.' Marcia A. Weigle and Jim Butterfield, 'Civil Society in Reforming Communist Regimes. The Logic of Emergence', *Comparative Politics* 25, 1 October 1992, p. 3. The strength of this definition lies in its acknowledgement of the importance of state recognition of a sphere of autonomous social activity, but its weakness is the view that that sphere must be legally defined. While formal, legal definition may strengthen social autonomy, to demand that this always be present seems unnecessarily restrictive.

40. For one argument in relation to ex-Communist states, see Baohui Zhang, 'Corporatism, Totalitarianism, and Transitions to Democracy', *Comparative Political Studies* 27, 1, April 1994, pp. 108–136. Also see below. The church can be a significant actor in the revival of civil society. Poland is an excellent example. For a discussion of its role in Brazil, see Andrew Hurrell, 'The International Dimensions of Democratization in Latin America: The Case of Brazil', Laurence Whitehead (ed), *The International Dimensions of Democratization. Europe and the Americas* (Oxford, Oxford University Press, 1996), pp. 153–157.

41. Philippe C. Schmitter, 'An Introduction to Southern European Transitions from Authoritarian Rule: Italy, Greece, Portugal, Spain and Turkey', *Transitions ... Southern Europe*, p. 7.

42. For one argument that this hierarchy of causes is not as clear cut as the transition school has suggested, but which indirectly shows the difficulty of saying much meaningful about the effect of international factors (i.e. either statements at a high level of generality or the identification of specific influences in particular cases), see Geoffrey Pridham, 'International Influences and Democratic Transition: Problems of Theory and Practice in Linkage Politics', Geoffrey Pridham (ed.), *Encouraging Democracy. The International Context of Regime Transition in Southern Europe* (Leicester, Leicester University Press, 1991), pp. 1–30.

43. Alfred Stepan, 'Paths toward Redemocratization: Theoretical and

Comparative Considerations', *Transitions ... Comparative Perspectives*, pp. 64–84. Also see Laurence Whitehead, 'Democracy by Convergence and Southern Europe: a Comparative Politics Perspective', Pridham, *Encouraging Democracy*, pp. 45–61, esp. pp. 46–48.

44. The restoration of democratic rule in countries liberated from the Nazis, such as Netherlands, France and Belgium, would be variants on this theme. Decolonization has also been significant, and may be seen as a variant of this theme.

45. For a discussion of US attempts to promote democracy in the Caribbean basin, see Laurence Whitehead, 'The Imposition of Democracy: The Caribbean', Whitehead, *International Dimensions ...*, pp. 59–92.

46. Transition studies frequently note the role of the oil price shock of the early 1970s in fostering regime change, but this is rarely linked to a broader structural view of the international economy. For example, see Alfred Tovias, 'The International Context of Democratic Transition', *West European Politics* 7, 2, April 1984, pp. 158–171.

47. For a discussion of Nicaragua, see Whitehead, 'Imposition ...', pp. 77–83.

48. For an interesting argument, see Whitehead, 'Democracy by Convergence', pp. 50–52.

49. For a survey of Central America which notes the US role, see Dietrich Rueschemeyer, Evelyne Huber Stephens and John D. Stephens, *Capitalist Development and Democracy* (Cambridge, Polity Press, 1992), Chapter 6. Also see Whitehead, 'Imposition ...'. For one discussion of Greece in these terms, see Susannah Verney and Theodore Couloumbis, 'State-International Systems Interaction and the Greek Transition to Democracy in the mid-1970s', Pridham, *Encouraging Democracy ...* , pp. 109–110. Also see below.

50. For a study of the US use of human rights in Latin America, see Kathryn Sikkink, 'The Effectiveness of US Human Rights Policy, 1973–1980', Whitehead, *International Dimensions ...* , pp. 93–124.

51. See the discussion in Thomas Carothers, 'The Resurgence of United States Political Development Assistance to Latin America in the 1980s', Whitehead, *International Dimensions ...* , pp. 125–145.

52. See Whitehead, 'Imposition ...', pp. 77–83.

53. An example of a party is the Portuguese Socialist Party which had operated from Toulouse in France before the fall of the Caetano regime.

54. For a discussion of the role of the EC, see Geoffrey Pridham, 'The Politics of the European Community, Transnational Networks and Democratic Transition in Southern Europe', Pridham, *Encouraging Democracy* ... , pp. 212–245. On Greece, see Basilios Tsingos, 'Underwriting Democracy: The European Community and Greece', Whitehead, *International Dimensions ...* , pp. 315–355, who sees the EC as having been much less activist in pressing democracy on Greece than other authors. He is particularly critical of Verney and Couloumbis (fn.58). Such conditionality, the attachment of specific

conditions to the distribution of benefits, has been a common practice
of such bodies as the IMF, although these are not usually specifically
democratic in form.

55. Laurence Whitehead, 'International Aspects of Democratization',
    Transitions ... Comparative Perspectives, pp. 25–31. For a broader dis-
    cussion, see Wolf Grabendorff, 'International Support for Democracy
    in Contemporary Latin America: The Role of the Party Internationals',
    Whitehead, *International Dimensions ...* , pp. 201–226.
56. For one study, see Michael Pinto-Duschinsky, 'International Political
    Finance: The Konrad Adenauer Foundation and Latin America',
    Whitehead, *International Dimensions ...* , pp. 227–255.
57. For one discussion of the role of the church, see Huntington, *Third
    Wave ...* , pp. 72–85.
58. For one discussion of this see Harvey Starr, 'Democratic Dominoes.
    Diffusion Approaches to the Spread of Democracy in the International
    System', *Journal of Conflict Resolution* 35, 2, June 1991, pp.
    356–381. Also see Laurence Whitehead, 'Three International
    Dimensions of Democratization', Whitehead, *International
    Dimensions ...* , pp. 5–8. A list of possible cases of contagion will be
    found on p. 5.
59. Whitehead, 'Three International Dimensions ...', pp. 21–22.
60. Huntington, *Third Wave ...* , p. 103.
61. Philippe C. Schmitter, 'The International Context of Contemporary
    Democratization', *Stanford Journal of International Affairs* 2, 1993,
    pp. 19–22. A longer form of this paper will be found in Whitehead,
    International Dimensions ... , pp. 26–54.
62. Donald Share, 'Transitions to Democracy and Transition Through
    Transaction', *Comparative Political Studies* 19, 4, January 1987, p. 540.
63. O'Donnell, 'Introduction', *Transitions ... Latin America*, p. 5.
64. Donald Share and Scott Mainwaring, 'Transitions Through
    Transaction: Democratization in Brazil and Spain', Wayne A. Selcher
    (ed.), *Political Liberalization in Brazil. Dynamics, Dilemmas and
    Future Prospects* (Boulder, Westview Press, 1985), pp. 178–179.
65. Huntington, *Third Wave ...* , pp. 113–114. For another schema see
    Baloyra, pp. 10–18..
66. In his discussion of paths of redemocratization, Alfred Stepan identi-
    fies three variants of foreign intervention: (1) A functioning democ-
    racy that was conquered in war is restored after the conqueror is
    defeated by external force, e.g. Netherlands 1945; (2) The conqueror
    of a democracy is defeated by external force and a new democratic
    regime put in place, e.g. France 1945; (3) Democratic powers defeat
    an authoritarian regime and play a major part in the installation of a
    democratic regime e.g. West Germany 1945. Alfred Stepan, 'Paths
    toward Redemocratization: Theoretical and Comparative
    Considerations', *Transitions ... Comparative Perspectives*, pp. 66–72.
67. Huntington, *Third Wave ...* , p. 114.
68. In a later article, Donald Share, while acknowledging that the élite
    participated in the process, seemed less sure that they should initiate
    or lead it. Share, 'Transitions to Democracy ... ', pp. 529–531.

69. Juan J. Linz, 'Crisis, Breakdown and Reequilibrium', Juan J. Linz and Alfred Stepan (eds), *The Breakdown of Democratic Regimes* (Baltimore, The Johns Hopkins University Press, 1978), p. 35. Huntington, *Third Wave* ... , p. 114. It is also called transition by transaction by Diane Ethier. See Ethier, 'Introduction', p. 8.
70. He saw this type of transition as usually being fostered by a major institutional power-holder in the regime which came to believe that their long-term interests would be better served by a shift toward democracy than maintenance of the status quo. Such a path leaves the way open for elements within the regime to seek to tailor the process in such a way as to protect their core interests. As examples, he cites Spain where the process was initiated by a civilian or civilianized political leadership, Brazil where it was partly a case of initiation by 'military as government', and Greece (1973) and Portugal (1974) where it was initiated by the 'military as institution.' Stepan, p. 72.
71. Huntington, *Third Wave* ... , pp. 127–141.
72. Share and Mainwaring, pp. 178–179. However in Share's article, extrication has a different meaning; it 'occurs when authoritarian regimes experience a sudden loss of legitimacy, and abruptly hand power over to the democratic opposition.' Share, 'Transitions to Democracy ... ', p. 531.
73. Ethier, p. 8, who also emphasizes how the regime has only a tenuous control over the process because of the relative importance of opposition movements. Stepan's notion of 'party pact' comes closest to this type of transition. He sees it as involving the construction of an oppositional pact to defeat the regime and lay the basis for democracy, and cites Colombia and Venezuela in 1958 as examples. Stepan, pp. 79–81.
74. Huntington did not include Bolivia in this category, but this is how it has been seen by Share and Mainwaring.
75. Huntington, *Third Wave* ... , pp. 152–153.
76. He saw four sub-types of this: revolution, coup, collapse and extrication. Share, 'Transitions to Democracy ... , p. 531.
77. Stepan had three equivalents of this: (1) 'Society-led regime termination', taking the form of diffuse protests, e.g. Greece in 1973, Argentina after the Cordoba revolt in 1969 and Peru after the general strike of July 1977 had elements of this; (2) 'Organized violent revolt coordinated by democratic reformist parties', e.g. Costa Rica 1948 and Venezuela 1958 approximated this; (3) Marxist-led revolutionary war, of which there are no examples. Stepan, pp. 78–84.
78. Huntington, *Third Wave* ... , pp. 142–149.
79. Huntington, *Third Wave* ... , p. 115.
80. For example, see Karl, 'Dilemmas ... '; and Casper and Taylor.
81. Linz and Stepan.
82. For example, Karl, 'Dilemmas ... ', p. 1.
83. Rustow, pp. 350–352.
84. Linz and Stepan, p. 7.
85. Linz and Stepan, p. 7.
86. For example, Richard Snyder, 'Explaining Transitions from

254 Notes and References

Neopatrimonial Dictatorships', *Comparative Politics* 24, 4, July 1992,
pp. 379–399; Stephen Haggard and Robert R. Kaufman, *The Political
Economy of Democratic Transitions* (Princeton, Princeton University
Press, 1995).
87. This is discussed in Linz and Stepan, Chapter 3, and is well summarized on pp. 44–45.
88. Linz and Stepan, p. 42.
89. Juan J. Linz, 'An Authoritarian Regime: Spain', Erik Allardt and Stein
Rokkan (eds.), *Mass Politics: Studies in Political Sociology* (New
York, The Free Press, 1970). This conception provides the basis upon
which the whole typology has been constructed.
90. This is discussed in Linz and Stepan, Chapter.4, esp. pp. 57–60.
91. Although if society is as flattened as Linz and Stepan imply, it is difficult to see how meaningful elections would be.
92. Linz and Stepan do not explain the relationship between early and late
on the one hand, and early, frozen and mature post-totalitarian
regimes on the other.
93. Linz and Stepan, Chapter 5. The reference is on p. 66.

Chapter 4   Beyond the Elites?

1. Luciano Martins, 'The "Liberalization" of Authoritarian Rule in
Brazil' and Terry Lynn Karl, 'Petroleum and Political Pacts: The
Transition to Democracy in Venezuela', Guillermo O'Donnell,
Philippe C. Schmitter and Laurence Whitehead, *Transitions from
Authoritarian Rule: Latin America* (Baltimore, The Johns Hopkins
University Press, 1986).
2. Terry Lynn Karl, 'Dilemmas of Democratization in Latin America',
Comparative Politics 23, 1, October 1990, p. 6.
3. Guillermo O'Donnell and Philippe C. Schmitter, *Transitions from
Authoritarian Rule. Tentative Conclusions about Uncertain
Democracies* (Baltimore, The Johns Hopkins University Press, 1986),
p. 3.
4. *Transitions ... Tentative Conclusions*, p. 5.
5. The most explicit in this is the work of Adam Przeworski.
6. *Transitions ... Tentative Conclusions*.
7. For example, according to Huntington, 'democratic regimes that last
have seldom, if ever, been instituted by mass popular action.' Samuel
P. Huntington, 'Will More Countries Become Democratic?', *Political
Science Quarterly* 99, 2, 1984, p. 212.
8. One attempt to theorize transition using game theory does build in a
role for the mass of the population, but this is only in a subsidiary
capacity, as giving support usually to the regime challengers. In this
view, what is crucial is the positions of the regime defenders and challengers, and the willingness and capacity of the defenders to defy or
even suppress the popular view. But this élite-focused approach con-
centrating on élite preferences eschews consideration of the relative

unity and power of the respective élites, any connections between élites and mass, and the way that the mass make their preferences known. Gretchen Casper and Michelle M. Taylor, *Negotiating Democracy. Transitions from Authoritarian Rule* (Pittsburgh, University of Pittsburgh Press, 1996).

9. *Transitions from Authoritarian Rule ...*
10. Enrique A. Baloyra (ed.), *Comparing New Democracies. Transition and Consolidation in Mediterranean Europe and the Southern Cone* (Boulder, Westview Press, 1987).
11. As one student has argued, to say that democratization began with division inside an authoritarian regime is not to say very much because such divisions 'are presumably ubiquitous and not readily identified as significant apart from the phenomenon they are intended to explain.' Karen L. Remmer, 'New Theoretical Perspectives on Democratization', *Comparative Politics* 28, 1, October 1995, p. 107.
12. Although there have been cases when political élites not under any pressure from the populace embarked on a course of liberalization in an attempt to improve the performance of the regime. Gorbachev's USSR is a good case in point.
13. Fernando H. Cardoso, 'Entrepreneurs and the Transition Process: The Brazilian Case', Guillermo O'Donnell, Philippe C. Schmitter and Laurence Whitehead (eds), *Transitions from Authoritarian Rule. Comparative Perspectives* (Baltimore, The Johns Hopkins University Press, 1986), pp. 137–153.
14. Kenneth Maxwell, 'Regime Overthrow and the Prospects for Democratic Transition in Portugal', Guillermo O'Donnell, Philippe C. Schmitter and Laurence Whitehead (eds.), *Transitions from Authoritarian Rule. Southern Europe* (Baltimore, The Johns Hopkins University Press, 1986).
15. This point is made in Daniel H. Levine, 'Paradigm Lost: Dependence to Democracy', *World Politics* 40, 3, April 1988, p. 390.
16. For example, see note 7 above.
17. Linz and Stepan do talk about the deepening of democracy, meaning the quality of it, but this is not part of their definition, nor is it discussed in their analysis. Juan J. Linz and Alfred Stepan, *Problems of Democratic Transition and Consolidation. Southern Europe, South America, and Post-Communist Europe* (Baltimore, The Johns Hopkins University Press, 1996), p. 457.
18. See Levine, p. 385.
19. Levine, p. 394.
20. See Adam Przeworski, 'Democracy as a Contingent Outcome of Conflicts', Jon Elster and Rune Slagstad (eds.), *Constitutionalism and Democracy* (Cambridge, Cambridge University Press, 1988).
21. Even the most sophisticated structural accounts of change are unsatisfactory unless they give due weight to the activity of political actors. For example, see Theda Skocpol, *States and Social Revolutions. A Comparative Analysis of France, Russia and China* (Cambridge, Cambridge University Press, 1979).
22. Karl, 'Dilemmas ...', p. 6.

23. Klaus Nielsen, Bob Jessop and Jerzy Hausner, 'Institutional Change in Post-Socialism', Jerzy Hausner, Bob Jessop and Klaus Nielson (eds.), *Strategic Choice and Path Dependency in Post-Socialism. Institutional Dynamics in the Transformation Process* (Aldershot, Edward Elgar, 1995), p. 6. The determinative orientation of these authors' view of path dependency is reflected in the fact that they contrast this with a notion of path shaping, whereby forces can intervene at certain conjunctures to eliminate constraints and launch development onto a new path. pp. 6–7.

24. Nielsen *et al*, p. 6.

25. For discussion of this issue, see the classic accounts in Eric A. Nordlinger, *Soldiers in Politics: Military Coups and Governments* (Englewood Cliffs, Prentice Hall, 1977) Chapter 4, and S.E. Finer, *The Man on Horseback. The Role of the Military in Politics* (Harmondsworth, Penguin, 1975) Chapter 11.

26. For a discussion which focuses upon the relationship between the military and the ruler, see Richard Snyder, 'Explaining Transitions from Neopatrimonial Dictatorships', *Comparative Politics* 24, 4, July 1992, pp. 379–399.

27. Adam Przeworski, 'The Games of Transition', Scott Mainwaring, Guillermo O'Donnell and J. Samuel Valenzuela (eds.), *Issues in Democratic Consolidation. The New South American Democracies in Comparative Perspective* (Notre Dame, University of Notre Dame Press, 1992), p. 117.

28. Terry Lynn Karl and Philippe C. Schmitter, 'Modes of Transition in Latin America, Southern and Eastern Europe', *International Social Science Journal* 128, May 1991, p. 272.

29. See the argument in Karen L. Remmer, 'Redemocratization and the Impact of Authoritarian Rule in Latin America', *Comparative Politics* 17, 3, April 1985, pp. 253–275.

30. Baohui Zhang, 'Corporatism, Totalitarianism, and Transitions to Democracy', *Comparative Political Studies* 27, 1, April 1994, pp. 108–136.

31. Zhang, p. 122.

32. To quote the titles of two very influential books. William McNeill, *The Rise of the West. A History of the Human Community* (Chicago, The University of Chicago Press, 1963) and E. L. Jones, *The European Miracle. Environments, Economies and Geopolitics in the History of Europe and Asia* (Cambridge, Cambridge University Press, 1981).

33. Barrington Moore Jr, *Social Origins of Dictatorship and Democracy. Lord and Peasant in the Making of the Modern World* (Harmondsworth, Penguin, 1969, originally published in 1966).

34. Moore, p. viii.

35. Moore, p. 414.

36. For one discussion substantially in these terms, see Lester M. Salamon, 'Comparative History and the Theory of Modernization', *World Politics* 23, 1, October 1970, pp. 97–98.

37. For a good short discussion, upon which the following rests, see

Ronald P. Dore, 'Making Sense of History', *Archives européennes de sociologie* X, 1969, p. 297.

38. Discussion will not embrace the fourth path, which does not lead to the same sort of political outcome as those with which Moore is most concerned.

39. Moore, p. 434 cf Theda Skocpol, 'A critical review of Barrington Moore's *Social Origins of Dictatorship and Democracy*', *Politics and Society* 4, 1, 1973, pp. 14–16.

40. Although there were many times when perceived interests did not coincide, e.g. the cases of emancipation and the Stolypin reforms in Russia were instances when the state sought to alter existing power arrangements in the countryside.

41. Moore, p. 418.

42. As well as those used in the following discussion, see J. V. Femia, 'Barrington Moore and the Preconditions for Democracy', *British Journal of Political Science* 2, 1, 1972; Stanley Rothman, 'Barrington Moore and the Dialectics of Revolution: An Essay Review', *American Political Science Review* 64, 1, March 1970; Jonathan Tumin, 'The Theory of Democratic Development', *Theory and Society* 11, 2, 1982; Ton Zwaan, 'One Step Forward, Two Steps Back. Tumin's Theory of Democratic Development: A Comment', *Theory and Society* 11, 2, 1982; Brian M. Downing, 'Constitutionalism, Warfare, and Political Change in Early Modern Europe', *Theory and Society* 17, 7, 1988. For a discussion of the critics see Jonathan M. Wiener, 'The Barrington Moore Thesis and Its Critics', *Theory and Society* 2, 1975.

43. For example, Dore, pp. 298–99.

44. Indeed, this general point applies to all of the class actors in Moore's analysis.

45. For one critic who makes much of the difficulty of measuring the strength of what she calls the 'bourgeois impulse', see Skocpol.

46. See the discussion in Ralf Dahrendorf, *Society and Democracy in Germany* (Garden City, Doubleday, 1969), Chapters 3 and 4.

47. Zwaan, p. 173.

48. Timothy A. Tilton, 'The Social Origins of Liberal Democracy: The Swedish Case', *American Political Science Review* 68, 2, June 1974 and Francis G. Castles, 'Barrington Moore's Thesis and Swedish Political Development', *Government and Opposition* 8, 3, Summer 1973.

49. Tilton and Castles.

50. Castles, p. 330.

51. Tilton, p. 569.

52. The absence of a standing army, and therefore of the possibility of repression, may also have been significant. Tilton, p. 568.

53. Goran Therborn, 'The Rule of Capital and the Rise of Democracy', *New Left Review* 103, May–June 1977.

54. Moore, pp. 30–32.

55. For example, see the argument in Perry Anderson, *Lineages of the Absolutist State* (London, Verso, 1979, originally published 1974).

56. See Moore, p. 214 and the discussion by Skocpol, p. 29.

57.   Therborn, pp. 21–23; Michael Mann, 'War and Social Theory: into Battle with Classes, Nations and States', Michael Mann, *States, War and Capitalism. Studies in Political Sociology* (Oxford, Blackwell, 1988), pp. 158–159 and Michael Howard 'War and the Nation State', *Daedalus* 108, 1979.

58.   Moore, p. 414.

59.   This is a more useful way of approaching this question than Skocpol's insistence upon notions of state autonomy. The latter may be reduced to an issue of differences in historical interpretation between Moore and Skocpol on particular periods, because an assumption about the possibility of state autonomy seems to underpin much of Moore's analysis.

60.   Dietrich Rueschemeyer, Evelyne Huber Stephens and John D. Stephens, *Capitalist Development and Democracy* (Cambridge, Polity, 1992). For an earlier version, see John D. Stephens, 'Democratic Transition and Breakdown in Western Europe, 1870–1939: A Test of the Moore Thesis', *American Journal of Sociology* 94, 5, March 1989.

61.   Rueschemeyer, Stephens and Stephens, p. 77.

62.   The working class was not always the main actor. In the agrarian democracies of Switzerland and Norway, the working class was politically included and democracy was established by peasant–urban middle class coalitions before the working class became a significant political actor. Stephens, pp. 1032 and 1035.

63.   Also see the discussion in Chapter 3 above.

64.   Rueschemeyer *et al*, pp. 80–81.

65.   Kurth argues that the bourgeoisie need not be subordinated to agrarian classes in order for this alliance to come about. He argues that the economic situation of that class, or of segments of it, the need to maintain control over the working class, and the role of the state in industrialization, logically leads the bourgeoisie to alliance with a similarly-placed class in the rural area. James R. Kurth, 'Industrial Change and Political Change: A European Perspective', David Collier (ed.), *The New Authoritarianism in Latin America* (Princeton, Princeton University Press, 1979).

66.   Stephens, p. 1038.

67.   Rueschemeyer *et al*, p. 83.

68.   Karl and Schmitter, p. 271. Examples cited of countries where these did not exist are respectively Venezuela and Chile, and Greece, northern Italy, Argentina and Uruguay.

69.   See the argument in Robert M. Fishman, 'Rethinking State and Regime: Southern Europe's Transition to Democracy', *World Politics* 42, 3, April 1990, pp. 422–440.

70.   And an interim government to administer the transition is unlikely.

71.   This sort of schema also enables us to place classic types of regimes in comparative positions along these axes, and thereby to generalize about their propensity to experience democratic transition. Classic totalitarianism: high regime unity and atomized society. Military regime: usually high unity (especially if it is a Linz/Stepan hierar-

chical military regime, less so for a non-hierarchical regime) and society with some civil society elements. One man leadership: usually high unity but with high potentiality to disintegrate, and society with some civil society elements. Bureaucratic authoritarianism: segmentary regime, emergent civil society. Traditional authoritarianism: segmentary regime, weak beginnings of civil society.

Chapter 5   Transition and Civil Society

1. Samuel P. Huntington, *The Third Wave. Democratization in the Late Twentieth Century* (Norman, University of Oklahoma Press, 1991), p. 114.
2. Juan J. Linz and Alfred Stepan, *Problems of Democratic Transition and Consolidation. Southern Europe, South America, and Post-Communist Europe* (Baltimore, The Johns Hopkins University Press, 1996) p. 88.
3. David Gilmour, *The Transformation of Spain. From Franco to the Constitutional Monarchy* (London, Quartet Books, 1985), p. 23.
4. Gilmour, pp. 59–65.
5. For an excellent discussion of this, see Raymond Carr and Juan Pablo Fusi, *Spain. Dictatorship to Democracy* (London, Allen and Unwin, 1981).
6. For a study which uses public opinion data from the period leading up to the transition, see Rafael Lopez-Pintor, 'Mass and Elite Perspectives in the Process of Transition to Democracy', Enrique A. Baloyra (ed.), *Comparing New Democracies. Transition and Consolidation in Mediterranean Europe and the Southern Cone* (Boulder, Westview Press, 1987).
7. Gilmour, p. 92.
8. Gilmour, pp. 54–59.
9. See Carr and Fusi, Chapter 9.
10. Paul Preston, *The Triumph of Democracy in Spain* (London, Methuen, 1986), p. 18.
11. For a discussion of the background to local nationalism in Catalonia and the Basque lands, see Gilmour, Chapter 6.
12. Preston, p. 51.
13. Jose Maria Maravall and Julian Santamaria, 'Political Change in Spain and the Prospects for Democracy', Guillermo O'Donnell, Philippe C. Schmitter and Laurence Whitehead (eds.), *Transitions from Authoritarian Rule. Southern Europe* (Baltimore, The Johns Hopkins University Press, 1986), p. 82.
14. Which also stimulated the emergence among young officers of the Union Militar Democratica (UMD), an organization favouring the establishment of a democratic system of government and political independence of the military. Charles Powell, 'International Aspects of Democratization; The Case of Spain', Laurence Whitehead (ed.), *The International Dimensions of Democratization. Europe and the*

Americas (Oxford, Oxford University Press, 1996), p. 287. See pp. 287–289 for the broader effects on developments in Spain of the Portuguese experience.

15. Gilmour, p. 139.
16. For the argument that, in principle, the king had three options, to seek to preserve the essence of the existing regime, to initiate change from within the regime, or to seek a 'democratic rupture', see Kenneth Medhurst, 'Spain's Evolutionary Pathway from Dictatorship to Democracy', *West European Politics* 7, 2, April 1984, pp. 32–33. On US support for the king, see Jonathan Story and Benny Pollack, 'Spain's Transition: Domestic and External Linkages', Geoffrey Pridham, *Encouraging Democracy. The International Context of Regime Transition in Southern Europe* (Leicester, Leicester University Press, 1991), pp. 131–132.
17. Gilmour, p. 145.
18. Preston, pp. 95–96.
19. The Law for Political Reform involved popular sovereignty, universal suffrage, recognition of political pluralism, the abolition of the Franquist Cortes, *Movimiento* and National Council, elections for a bicameral legislature, and codification of the position of the king. Gilmour, p. 158.
20. Carr and Fusi, p. xiii.
21. Also potentially significant was Suarez's unrivalled access to public opinion polling results and his consequent ability to read the political landscape better than his opponents. Medhurst, p. 36.
22. Preston, pp. 113–114.
23. Maravall and Santamaria, p. 85.
24. Maravall and Santamaria, p. 88.
25. Preston, p. 138. Also see the discussion in Gilmour, pp. 194–202.
26. For an analysis which focuses upon the 1977, 1979 and 1982 elections, see Mario Casiagli, 'Spain: Parties and Party System in the Transition', *West European Politics* 7, 2, April 1984.
27. Although Linz and Stepan argue that the problem of 'stateness', or national unity (and specifically the Basque problem) had still to be resolved before the transition could be classed as ended. Linz and Stepan, pp. 99–107.
28. With some assistance from abroad, especially Western Europe. See Powell.
29. In the terminology of Linz and Stepan, p. 166.
30. For an argument that this reflected the military's identification with Western values, see Andrew Hurrell, 'The International Dimensions of Democratization in Latin America. The Case of Brazil', Whitehead, International Dimensions, p. 158. Also see Alfred Stepan, *Rethinking Military Politics. Brazil and the Southern Cone* (Princeton, Princeton University Press, 1988), Chapters 5 and 6.
31. On these issues see Stepan, *Rethinking*, Chapter 2 and pp. 33–35.
32. Stephen Haggard and Robert R. Kaufman, *The Political Economy of Democratic Transitions* (Princeton, Princeton University Press, 1995), p. 72.

33. Stepan, *Rethinking* ... , p. 37.
34. Stepan, *Rethinking* ... , p. 40.
35. Luciano Martins, 'The "Liberalization" of Authoritarian Rule in Brazil', Guillermo O'Donnell, Philippe C. Schmitter and Laurence Whitehead (eds.), *Transitions from Authoritarian Rule. Latin America* (Baltimore, The Johns Hopkins University Press, 1986), p. 83.
36. Martins, p. 90.
37. Fernando H. Cardoso, 'Entrepreneurs and the Transition Process: The Brazilian Case', Guillermo O'Donnell, Philippe C. Schmitter and Laurence Whitehead (eds.), *Transitions from Authoritarian Rule. Comparative Perspectives* (Baltimore, The Johns Hopkins University Press, 1986), pp. 137–153.
38. Stepan, *Rethinking* ... , p. 56.
39. Although there had been pressures for some time from within the business community favouring a form of liberalization. See the general discussion in Cardoso and Haggard and Kaufman, pp. 58–59.
40. Haggard and Kaufman, p. 62.
41. Stepan, *Rethinking* ... , pp. 57–59 and 65.
42. Linz and Stepan, pp. 168–169.
43. On the Pinochet regime, see Arturo Valenzuela, 'The Military in Power. The Consolidation of One-Man Rule', Paul W. Drake and Ivan Jaksic (eds.), *The Struggle for Democracy in Chile* (Lincoln, University of Nebraska Press, 1995) and J. Samuel Valenzuela and Arturo Valenzuela, *Military Rule in Chile. Dictatorships and Oppositions* (Baltimore, The Johns Hopkins University Press, 1986).
44. Paul W. Drake and Ivan Jaksic, 'Introduction: Transformation and Transition in Chile, 1982–1990', Drake and Jaksic, p. 5.
45. Drake and Jaksic, 'Introduction', p. 5.
46. Drake and Jaksic, 'Introduction', p. 6.
47. Alan Angell, 'International Support for the Chilean Opposition, 1973–1989: Political Parties and the Role of Exiles', Whitehead, *International Dimensions* ... , pp. 175–200.
48. See the discussion in Guillermo Campero, 'Entrepreneurs Under the Military Regime', Drake and Jaksic, pp. 134–139.
49. Borzutzky cites work by Valenzuela and Valenzuela that argues that parties were able to maintain their identity and autonomy despite regime repression and that 'limiting organizational and electoral activities, rather than undermining politics, freezes the positions of recognized leaders and shifts party activities to other outlets in civil society.' Silvia T. Borzutzky, 'The Pinochet Regime: Crisis and Consolidation', James M. Malloy and Mitchell A. Seligson (eds.), *Authoritarians and Democrats. Regime Transition in Latin America* (Pittsburgh, University of Pittsburgh Press, 1987), p. 80. Also see Manuel Antonio Garreton, 'The Political Opposition and the Party System Under the Military Regime', Drake and Jaksic.
50. Borzutzky, p. 83.
51. Augusto Varas, 'The Crisis of Legitimacy of Military Rule in the 1980s', Drake and Jaksic, p. 84.
52. Garreton, pp. 227–228.

53. For a discussion of this, see Linz and Stepan, pp. 207–210.
54. For one discussion, see Herbert S. Klein, *Bolivia. The Evolution of a Multi-Ethnic Society* (New York, Oxford University Press, 1992), p. 246–247.
55. For this characterization of the military, see Robert Pinkney, *Right-Wing Military Government* (Boston, Twayne Pubs, 1990), p. 84.
56. Eduardo A. Gamarra, 'Bolivia: Disengagement and Democratization', Constantine P. Danopoulos (ed.), *Military Disengagement from Politics* (London, Routledge, 1988), p. 52–53.
57. Laurence Whitehead, 'Bolivia's Failed Democratization, 1977–1980', *Transitions ... Latin America*, pp. 56–57.
58. Gamarra, p. 55–56.
59. Klein, pp. 256–257.
60. Haggard and Kaufman, p. 65.
61. Whitehead, 'Bolivia's ... ', p. 62.
62. For details on these, see Gamarra, pp. 65–72.
63. Whitehead, 'Bolivia's ... ', p. 63.
64. For some details, see Whitehead, 'Bolivia's ... ', p. 65.
65. Whitehead, 'Bolivia's ... ', p. 67.
66. For an analysis which focuses upon the quasi-presidential and party structures, see Luis E. Gonzalez, *Political Structures and Democracy in Uruguay* (Notre Dame, University of Notre Dame Press, 1991).
67. Charles Guy Gillespie, *Negotiating Democracy. Politicians and Generals in Uruguay* (Cambridge, Cambridge University Press, 1991), p. 56.
68. Pinkney, p. 62.
69. Gillespie, *Negotiating ...* , p. 50.
70. Gillespie, *Negotiating ...* , p. 62.
71. Gillespie, *Negotiating ...* , p. 71.
72. Linz and Stepan, p. 153.
73. Gillespie, *Negotiating ...* , pp. 174–175.
74. Charles G. Gillespie, 'Uruguay's Transition from Collegial Military-Technocratic Rule', *Transitions ... Latin America*, p. 183.
75. For some figures, see Gillespie, 'Uruguay's ... ', p. 184.
76. Haggard and Kaufman, p. 71.
77. Gillespie, *Negotiating ...* , p. 131.
78. Gillespie, *Negotiating ...* , pp. 144–145.
79. Linz and Stepan, pp. 154–155.
80. Robin Luckham, 'Faustian Bargains: Democratic Control over Military and Security Establishments', Robin Luckham and Gordon White (eds.), *Democratization in the South. The Jagged Wave* (Manchester, Manchester University Press, 1996), p. 130.
81. Luckham, p. 134.
82. Sung-Joo Han, 'South Korea: Politics in Transition ', Larry Diamond, Juan J. Linz and Seymour Martin Lipset (eds.), *Democracy in Developing Countries. Volume 3. Asia* (Boulder, Lynne Rienner, 1989), p. 280.
83. For some figures on opposition support, see James Cotton, 'From Authoritarianism to Democracy in South Korea', James Cotton (ed.),

Korea Under Roh Tae-woo. Democratization, Northern Policy and Inter-Korean Relations (Canberra, Allen and Unwin, 1993), p. 30.

84. Gordon White, 'Civil Society, Democratization and Development', Luckham and White, p. 196.
85. For one discussion, see David Potter, 'Democratization at the Same Time in South Korea and Taiwan', David Potter, David Goldblatt, Margaret Kiloh and Paul Lewis (eds.), *Democratization* (Cambridge, Polity Press, 1997), pp. 230–231.
86. Cotton, p. 30.
87. This continued into 1986 when there were at least 1700 protest demonstrations. White, p. 194.
88. Even when Kim Young Sam had formerly advocated a parliamentary system for Korea. Han, p. 285.
89. Cotton, p. 31.
90. Okonogi Masao, 'South Korea's Experiment in Democracy', Cotton, p. 9.
91. Potter, p. 228; Cotton, p. 32; Han, p. 287.
92. Masao, p. 12.
93. Cotton, p. 33–34.
94. Constantine P. Danopoulos, 'Democratization by Golpe: The Experience of Modern Portugal', Constantine P. Danopoulos (ed.), *Military Disengagement from Politics* (London, Routledge, 1988), p. 234.
95. Hugo Gil Ferreira and Michael W. Marshall, *Portugal's Revolution: Ten Years On* (Cambridge, Cambridge University Press, 1986), p. 254.
96. Kenneth Maxwell, *The Making of Portuguese Democracy* (Cambridge, Cambridge University Press, 1995, p. 58.
97. For a discussion of the parties' emergence, see Walter C. Opello Jr, 'Portugal: A Case Study of International Determinants of Regime Transition', Pridham, *Encouraging Democracy* ... , p. 86.
98. Kenneth Maxwell, 'Regime Overthrow and the Prospects for Democratic Transition in Portugal', *Transitions ... Southern Europe*, p. 120.
99. Maxwell, *Making* ... , p. 86.
100. According to Opello, these were organized by leftist groups, but COPCON refused to dismantle them. Opello, p. 92.
101. Although Gomes was not himself a radical, taking pains to assure the US that Portugal would adopt a Western liberal democratic system. Opello, p. 94.
102. Maxwell, *Making* ... , p. 110.
103. For its text, see Ferreira and Marshall pp. 256–262. For discussion, Maxwell, *Making* ... , p. 112.
104. Support from Western sources worried about the possibility of radicalism in Portugal had been flowing to some of these parties, especially the PSP, for some time. At this time, Soviet support for the PCP was limited to material assistance; Moscow sought to rein in the ambitions of the Portuguese Communists so as not to endanger détente. Opello, pp. 88–89.

105.   Linz and Stepan, p. 122.
106.   For the text see Ferreira and Marshall, pp. 263–268.
107.   For a discussion of the political parties and subsequent elections, see J. R. Lewis and A. M. Williams, 'Social Cleavages and Electoral Performance: The Social Basis of Portuguese Parties, 1976–83', *West European Politics* 7, 2, April 1984.
108.   Constantine P. Danopoulos, 'Farewell to Man on Horseback: Intervention and Civilian Supremacy in Modern Greece', Constantine P. Danopoulos, *From Military to Civilian Rule* (London, Routledge, 1992), pp. 42–43.
109.   Danopoulos, p. 44–45.
110.   For a balanced view which sees international factors as secondary to domestic in structuring the Greek transition, see Basilios Tsingos, 'Underwriting Democracy: The European Community and Greece', Whitehead, *International Dimensions ...* , pp. 315–355.
111.   This follows Danopoulos, pp. 45–46.
112.   Linz and Stepan, p. 132.
113.   This goes some way toward explaining why there was no military reaction to the trial and sentencing of many officers accused of crimes in 1975. Linz and Stepan, p. 132.
114.   Linz and Stepan, pp. 190–191.
115.   For a discussion of Galtieri's strategy, see James W. McGuire, 'Interim Government and Democratic Consolidation: Argentina in Comparative Perspective', Yossi Shain and Juan J. Linz (eds.), *Between States. Interim Governments and Democratic Transitions* (Cambridge, Cambridge University Press, 1995), pp. 187–188.
116.   Cited in McGuire, p. 188.
117.   For some details about these documents, see McGuire, pp. 188–189.
118.   Enrique A. Baloyra, 'Democratic Transition in Comparative Perspective', Enrique A. Baloyra (ed.), *Comparing New Democracies. Transition and Consolidation in Mediterranean Europe and the Southern Cone* (Boulder, Westview Press, 1987), p. 24.
119.   Linz and Stepan, p. 193.
120.   McGuire, pp. 189–190.

Chapter 6   Transition and the Collapse of Communism

1.   For example, Juan J. Linz and Alfred Stepan, *Problems of Democratic Transition and Consolidation. Southern Europe, South America and Post-Communist Europe* (Baltimore, The Johns Hopkins University Press, 1996); Russell Bova, 'Political Dynamics of the Post-Communist Transition. A Comparative Perspective', *World Politics* 44, 1, October 1991, pp. 113–138. For an explicit argument about both the validity and value of applying the transition methodology to the post-Communist transition, see Philippe C. Schmitter with Terry Lynn Karl, 'The Conceptual Travels of

Transitologists and Consolidologists: How Far to the East Should They Attempt to Go?', *Slavic Review* 53, 1, Spring 1994, pp. 173–185. This prompted a vigorous, if not very satisfying, exchange: Valerie Bunce, 'Should Transitologists Be Grounded?', *Slavic Review* 54, 1, Spring 1995, pp. 111–127; Terry Lynn Karl and Philippe C. Schmitter, 'From an Iron Curtain to a Paper Curtain: Grounding Transitologists or Students of Postcommunism?', *Slavic Review* 54, 4, Winter 1995, pp. 965–978 and Valerie Bunce, 'Paper Curtains and Paper Tigers', *Slavic Review* 54, 4, Winter 1995, pp. 979–987.

2. This list is my own rendering of similar points made by other authors. See Bunce, 'Transitologists ... ', pp. 119–123; Sarah Meiklejohn Terry, 'Thinking About Post–communist Transitions: How Different Are They?', *Slavic Review* 52, 2, Summer 1993, pp. 333–337.

3. In addition, for the Slovaks the Czechs may have appeared as oppressors while in the former Yugoslavia it was the Serbs who were given this guise.

4. Terry, p. 334.

5. For a discussion of the nature, importance and role of Round Table talks in Eastern Europe generally, see Helga A. Welsh, 'Political Transition Processes in Central and Eastern Europe', *Comparative Politics* 26, 4, July 1994, pp. 383–388.

6. For details of the agreements, see Keith Crawford, *East Central European Politics Today* (Manchester, Manchester University Press, 1996), p. 60.

7. In contrast to Poland where the Round Table resulted in an agreement on power sharing, in Hungary the opposition eschewed this course and went straight to competitive elections.

8. Crawford, pp. 63–64.

9. Developments in the republican capitals were crucial for structuring the overall course of events in Yugoslavia, but they will not be discussed in detail here. However, in some areas, in particular Slovenia, autonomous popular forces played a major role in shaping developments. For studies which pay attention to republican developments, see Misha Glenny, *The Rebirth of History. Eastern Europe in the Age of Democracy* (Harmondsworth, Penguin, 1990) and Laura Silber and Allan Little, *The Death of Yugoslavia* (Harmondsworth, Penguin, 1995).

10. For one discussion of developments in Slovenia, see Tomaz Mastnak, 'Civil Society in Slovenia: From Opposition to Power', *Studies in Comparative Communism* XXIII, 3/4, Autumn/Winter 1990, pp. 305–317.

11. McSweeney and Tempest argue that there was a distinctive East European path of transition characterized by dependence on the relaxation of foreign control and the opposition of crowds on the streets, but this level of generality obscures the important differences that did exist between countries. Dean McSweeney and Clive Tempest, 'The Political Science of Democratic Transition in Eastern Europe', *Political Studies* xli, 3, September 1993, p. 417.

12. For other discussions, see Welsh, pp. 379–394; Ekiert offers a tripar-

tite analysis:
(a) where political society is stronger and pragmatic/reformist elements in the party–state are more influential, the result will be negotiated openings, as in Poland and Hungary;
(b where political society is weaker and pragmatic/reformist elements in the party–state are ineffective, the result will be popular upsurge, as in the GDR and Czechoslovakia;
(c) where political society and pragmatic/reformist elements are both absent, the result is revolutionary upheaval, as in Rumania.
Grzegorz Ekiert, 'Democratization Processes in East Central Europe: A Theoretical Reconsideration', *British Journal of Political Science* 21, 3, 1991, p. 307.

13. There is an immense amount of material on each of these regimes. The references cited in the following footnotes are only a very few of these which have been particularly useful.

14. On Ceausescu's power and the regime he ran, see Edward Behr, *'Kiss the Hand You Cannot Bite'. The Rise and Fall of the Ceausescus* (Harmondsworth, Penguin, 1991) and Michael Shafir, *Romania. Politics, Economics and Society* (London, Frances Pinter, 1985), esp. Chapter 6.

15. On the Czechoslovak party, see Zdenek Suda, *Zealots and Rebels. A History of the Ruling Communist Party of Czechoslovakia* (Stanford, Hoover Institution Press, 1980).

16. On the policy of 'normalization' see Milan Simechka, *The Restoration of Order. The Normalization of Czechoslovakia 1969–1976* (London, Verso, 1984).

17. For a survey of the GDR, see David Childs, *The GDR: Moscow's German Ally* (London, Allen and Unwin, 1983).

18. See Nicholas C. Pano, 'Albania', Teresa Rakowska-Harmstone (ed.), *Communism in Eastern Europe* (Bloomington, Indiana University Press, 1984).

19. Joseph Rothschild, *Return to Diversity. A Political History of East Central Europe Since World War II* (Oxford, Oxford University Press, 1993), p. 254.

20. On Hungary, see Rudolf L. Tokes, *Hungary's Negotiated Revolution. Economic Reform, Social Change and Political Succession, 1957–1990* (Cambridge, Cambridge University Press, 1996); Bennett Kovrig, *Communism in Hungary. From Kun to Kadar* (Stanford, Hoover Institution Press, 1979).

21. For studies of Yugoslav reformism, see Paul Shoup, 'Crisis and Reform in Yugoslavia', *Daedalus* 79, Spring 1989, pp. 129–145; Denison Rusinow, *The Yugoslav Experiment 1948–1974* (Berkeley, University of California, 1977); April Carter, *Democratic Reform in Yugoslavia: The Changing Role of the Party* (Princeton, Princeton University Press, 1982).

22. See the survey of the Polish experience in Andrzej Korbonski, 'Poland', Rakowska-Harmstone.

23. For a paper which addresses this theme, see Stephen F. Cohen, 'The Friends and Foes of Change: Reformism and Conservatism in the

Soviet Union', and comments by T. H. Rigby, S. Frederick Starr, Frederick Barghoorn and George Breslauer, and Cohen's response, *Slavic Review* 38, 2, June 1979, pp. 187–223.

24. For a history of the Bulgarian Communist Party, see John D. Bekk, *The Bulgarian Communist Party from Blagoev to Zhivkov* (Stanford, Hoover Institution Press, 1986).

25. This distinction is similar to that drawn by Marcia A. Weigle and Jim Butterfield, 'Civil Society in Reforming Communist Regimes. The Logic of Emergence', *Comparative Politics* 25, 1, October 1992, p. 1. Also see the discussion by Ekiert which distinguishes between 'domestic society' which is 'the domain of purposeful action restricted to the private sphere and organized in terms of material needs and self-interests' and 'political society' which 'embraces the entirety of voluntary associations and social movements in an active political community.' Ekiert, p. 300.

26. For characterizations of these regimes, see Hugh Seton-Watson, *Eastern Europe Between the Wars, 1918–1941* (London, Cambridge University Press, 1945); Antony Polonsky, *The Little Dictators. The History of Eastern Europe since 1918* (London, Routledge & Kegan Paul, 1975); Joseph Rothschild, *East Central Europe between the Two World Wars* (Seattle, University of Washington Press, 1974); Gregory M. Luebbert, *Liberalism, Fascism, or Social Democracy. Social Classes and the Political Origins of Regimes in Interwar Europe* (Oxford, Oxford University Press, 1991), pp. 260–263.

27. Politically this was often manifested through a government party operating in a pseudo–parliamentary system.

28. On state primacy, see the classic Perry Anderson, *Lineages of the Absolutist State* (London, New Left Books, 1974); also the stimulating George Schopflin, 'The Political Traditions of Eastern Europe', *Daedalus* 119, Winter 1990, esp. pp. 61–65.

29. Crawford, p. 17.

30. Schopflin, p. 65.

31. Figures for agriculture (which include significant numbers of landless rural labourers in Hungary and Poland) come from Joni Lovenduski and Jean Woodall, *Politics and Society in Eastern Europe* (London, Macmillan, 1987), p. 32. The average in Western Europe at this time was about 20 per cent. For industry they come from Polonsky, p. 175.

32. As Lovenduski and Woodall argue, many areas lacked 'an enterprising middle class of townspeople anxious for economic progress. The peasantry, overwhelmingly the largest class, lacked the skills, capital and legal freedoms to become entrepreneurs, whilst the landowning aristocracy saw no need to augment or risk its wealth.' p. 29.

33. The broader ethnic divisions were also a major handicap to such a sense of society developing.

34. For an argument applied to most of the region which explains this urban migration of the gentry in terms of their inability to prosper in international competition, see Andrew C. Janos, 'The Politics of Backwardness in Continental Europe, 1780–1945', *World Politics* xli, 3, April 1989, pp. 331–335.

35. Rothschild, *East Central Europe* ... , p. 28.
36. Lovenduski and Woodall, p. 34. Although there were regional variations within Poland. See Rothschild, pp. 29–31.
37. In Schopflin's term, state administration was subject to 'colonization' by the gentry. Schopflin, p. 70.
38. Rothschild, *East Central Europe* ... , pp. 190–191.
39. This was a long-term process, being based on a textile industry which went back to the sixteenth century.
40. For some details, see Gale Stokes, 'The Social Origins of East European Politics', Daniel Chirot (ed.), *The Origins of Backwardness in Eastern Europe. Economics and Politics from the Middle Ages Until the Early Twentieth Century* (Berkeley, University of California Press, 1989), pp. 217–218.
41. Luebbert, p. 291. On the divisions within the working class based on ethnicity, region and political outlook, see Luebbert, pp. 293–294.
42. Cited in Lovenduski and Woodall, p. 36.
43. There is a good discussion of some of this in Rothschild, *East Central Europe* ...
44. As a class these had been destroyed by the Turks.
45. Rothschild, *East Central Europe* ... , p. 289.
46. Rothschild, *East Central Europe* ... , p. 321.
47. As in Serbia, this had been destroyed by the Turks.
48. Rothschild, *East Central Europe* ... , p. 323.
49. Rothschild, *East Central Europe* ... , p. 359.
50. Rothschild, *East Central Europe* ... , p. 360.
51. The sketches are incomplete in the sense that they downplay two extremely important types of division in this region, ethnic identification and religion. If anyone were seeking to understand the course of development in this region in the inter-war period, due concern would need to be paid to these two dimensions of social structure. However, the present analysis seeks not to explain that course of development, but to identify the existence or otherwise of the sort of bourgeois arena of organizations and ideas essential to the generation of the sort of autonomous social activity with which we are concerned. For some figures on ethnic minorities, see Luebbert, p. 260.
52. Although the Polish political and intellectual élite and bourgeoisie were decimated during World War II to a far greater extent than anywhere else in the region. Ekiert, p. 302.
53. For a discussion of this in relation to political parties, see Karen L. Remmer, 'Redemocratization and the Impact of Authoritarian Rule in Latin America', *Comparative Politics* 17, 3, April 1985, pp. 253–275.
54. This is linked to the earlier discussion of the levels of control the different regimes exercised. But whereas the former discussion focused upon regime capacity, this one concerns the capacity of the society to throw up autonomous social organizations in spite of regime pressure. For some discussions of the development of civil society under Communism, see for example, Zbigniew Rau (ed.), *The Reemergence of Civil Society in Eastern Europe and the Soviet Union* (Boulder, Westview Press, 1991); Chandran Kukathas, David W. Lovell and

William Maley (eds.), *The Transition from Socialism. State and Civil Society in the USSR* (Melbourne, Longman Cheshire, 1991); Robert F. Miller (ed.), *The Developments of Civil Society in Communist Systems* (Sydney, Allen and Unwin, 1992).

55. For the argument that this was related to the twin crises of Communist regimes, their inability to inculcate the population with Communist values and modes of participation, and the inability to meet popular material expectations, see Weigle and Butterfield.

56. For an argument that the West, especially through the CSCE process, helped stimulate the development of civil society forces, see Laurence Whitehead, 'Democracy and Decolonization: East-Central Europe', Laurence Whitehead (ed.), *The International Dimensions of Democratization. Europe and the Americas* (Oxford, Oxford University Press, 1996) pp. 376–379. For a discussion of what is termed 'weak society' in Bulgaria and 'strong society' in Hungary, Poland and Yugoslavia, see Sabrina P. Ramet, *Social Currents in Eastern Europe. The Sources and Meaning of the Great Transformation* (Durham, Duke University Press, 1991).

57. On Polish intellectuals in politics, see Jacques Rupnik, 'Dissent in Poland, 1968–78: the End of Revisionism and the Rebirth of Civil Society', Rudolf L. Tokes (ed.), *Opposition in Eastern Europe* (London, Macmillan, 1979).

58. Michael Bernhard, 'Civil Society and Democratic Transition in East Central Europe', *Political Science Quarterly* 108, 2, Summer 1993, p. 313.

59. See Michael Bernhard, *The Origins of Democratization in Poland: Workers, Intellectuals, and Oppositional Politics, 1976–1980* (New York, Columbia University Press, 1993).

60. On worker organization, see Jadwiga Staniszkis, *Poland's Self-Limiting Revolution* (Princeton, Princeton University Press, 1984); Neal Ascherson, *The Polish August. What Happened in Poland* (Harmondsworth, Penguin, 1981).

61. On the church, see Suzanne Hruby, 'The Church in Poland and its Political Influence', *Journal of International Affairs* 36, 2, 1982–83, pp. 317–328.

62. On the 'Prague Spring' see H. G. Skilling, *Czechoslovakia's Interrupted Revolution* (Princeton, Princeton University Press, 1976).

63. On Charter 77 and VONS see H. G. Skilling, 'Independent Currents in Czechoslovakia', *Problems of Communism* 34, 1, January–February 1985, pp. 32–49; H. G. Skilling, *Charter 77 and Human Rights in Czechoslovakia* (London, Allen and Unwin, 1981); and H. G. Skilling, *Samizdat and an Independent Society in Central and Eastern Europe* (Columbus, Ohio State University Press, 1989).

64. On these intellectuals, see Rudolf L. Tokes, 'Hungarian Reform Imperatives', *Problems of Communism* 33, 5, September–October 1984, pp. 1–23;. Tokes, *Negotiated Revolution*, Chapter 4; and George Schopflin, 'Opposition and Para-Opposition: Critical Currents in Hungary, 1968–1978', in Tokes, *Opposition*.

65. See the quotation from Poszgay cited in M. Huber and H-G. Heinrich,

'Hungary – Quiet Progress?', Leslie Holmes (ed.), *The Withering Away of the State?* (London, Sage, 1981), p. 154.

66. For a discussion of this intellectual dissent, see Leslie Holmes, *Politics in the Communist World* (Oxford, Clarendon Press, 1986) pp. 258–262 and Pedro Ramet, 'Disaffection and Dissent in East Germany', *World Politics* 35, 1, October 1984, pp. 85–111; also see Vladimir Tismaneanu, 'Nascent Civil Society in the German Democratic Republic', *Problems of Communism* 38, 2/3, March/June 1989, pp. 90–111; and Werner Volkmer, 'East Germany: Dissenting Views during the Last Decade', in Tokes, *Opposition*.

67. On the church, see Pedro Ramet, 'Church and Peace in the GDR', *Problems of Communism* 33, 4, July–August 1984, pp. 44–57; and Stephen Bowers, 'Private Institutions in Service to the State: The German Democratic Republic's Church in Socialism', *East European Quarterly* xvi, 1, 1982; and Joyce Marie Mushaben, 'Swords to Plowshares: The Church, The State, and the East German Peace Movement', *Studies in Comparative Communism* XVII, 2, Summer 1984, pp. 123–135.

68. Shoup, pp. 137–138.

69. Shoup, p. 141. Also see Mastnak.

70. This activity in Czechoslovakia was not sustained over a long continuous period either, but the scale of organization especially in 1968 outweighs this objection.

71. Some might object that this is wrong because of the dissident movement which emerged in the 1960s and was stamped out at the beginning of the 1980s. But this was always very restricted in the numbers of people it embraced, it had few links into the society at large, and unlike the Hungarian, German and Yugoslav cases discussed above, it was not accompanied by any other organized manifestation of a potential civil society. For arguments about civil society in the Soviet Union, see S. Frederick Starr, 'Soviet Union: A Civil Society', *Foreign Policy* 70, Spring 1988, pp. 26–41; T. H. Rigby, 'The USSR: End of a Long, Dark Night?', Miller; Geoffrey Hosking, *The Awakening of the Soviet Union* (London, Heinemann, 1990), Chapter 4.

72. For a similar point, see Baohui Zhang, 'Corporatism, Totalitarianism, and Transitions to Democracy', *Comparative Political Studies*, 27, 1, April 1994, pp. 108–136.

Conclusion

1. For a discussion of this, see Andreas Schedler, 'What is Democratic Consolidation?', *The Journal of Democracy* 9, 2, 1988, pp. 91–107.

2. John Higley and Richard Gunther (eds.), *Elites and Democratic Consolidation in Latin America and Eastern Europe* (Cambridge, Cambridge University Press, 1992) p. 3.

3. Juan J. Linz, 'Transitions to Democracy', *The Washington Quarterly*

13, 3, Summer 1990, p. 156. Also see Richard Gunther, P. Nikiforos Diamandouros and Hans-Jurgen Puhle (eds.), *The Politics of Democratic Consolidation. Southern Europe in Comparative Perspective* (Baltimore, The Johns Hopkins University Press, 1995), pp. 5–10.

4. Samuel P. Huntington, *The Third Wave. Democratization in the Late Twentieth Century* (Norman, University of Oklahoma Press, 1991), p. 267.

5. Although, as Guillermo O'Donnell points out, this has focused on formal rules and ignored the importance of informal rules. Guillermo O'Donnell, 'Illusions About Consolidation', *Journal of Democracy* 7, 2, April 1996, pp. 34–51. This provoked comment and a response, *Journal of Democracy* 7, 4, October 1996, pp. 150–168. For an alternative view of consolidation, which does take in broader issues, see Adrian Leftwich, 'From Democratization to Democratic Consolidation', David Potter, David Goldblatt, Margaret Kiloh and Paul Lewis (eds.), *Democratization* (Cambridge, Polity Press, 1997), pp. 524–532.

6. Juan Linz, 'The Perils of Presidentialism', *The Journal of Democracy* 1, 1, Winter 1990, pp. 51–69.

7. For some interventions in this debate, see Arend Lijphart (ed.), *Parliamentary versus Presidential Government* (Oxford, Oxford University Press, 1992); Juan J. Linz and Arturo Valenzuela (eds.), *The Failure of Presidential Democracy: Comparative Perspectives* (Baltimore, The Johns Hopkins University Press, 1994); M. Shugart and J. Carey, *Presidents and Assemblies: Constitutional Design and Electoral Dynamics* (Cambridge, Cambridge University Press, 1992); Alfred Stepan and Cindy Skach, 'Constitutional Frameworks and Democratic Consolidation: Parliamentarianism and Presidentialism', *World Politics* 46, 1, October 1993, pp. 1–22; Scott Mainwaring, 'Presidentialism, Multipartism, and Democracy: The Difficult Combination', *Comparative Political Studies* 26, 2, 1993, pp. 198–228; Arend Lijphart, 'Constitutional Choices for New Democracies', Larry Diamond and Marc F. Plattner (eds.), *The Global Resurgence of Democracy* (Baltimore, The Johns Hopkins University Press, 1993); Arend Lijphart and Carlos H. Waisman (eds.), *Institutional Design in New Democracies. Eastern Europe and Latin America* (Boulder, Westview Press, 1996).

8. For example, Andre Blais and Stephane Dion, 'Electoral Systems and the Consolidation of Democracies', Diane Ethier (ed.), *Democratic Transition and Consolidation in Southern Europe, Latin America and Southeast Asia* (London, Macmillan, 1990).

9. For example, Alex MacLeod, 'The Parties and Consolidation of Democracy in Portugal: The Emergence of a Dominant Two-Party System', Ethier; Renato R. Boschi, 'Social Movements, Party Systems and Democratic Consolidation: Brazil, Uruguay and Argentina', Ethier; Scott Mainwaring and Timothy R. Scully (eds.), *Building Democratic Institutions. Party Systems in Latin America* (Stanford, Stanford University Press, 1995); Geoffrey Pridham and

Paul G. Lewis (eds.), *Stabilising Fragile Democracies. Comparing New Party Systems in Southern and Eastern Europe* (London, Routledge, 1996).

10. For an explicit case, see Juan Linz and Alfred Stepan, 'Political Crafting of Democratic Consolidation or Destruction: Europe and South American Comparisons', Robert A. Pastor (ed.), *Democracy in the Americas. Stopping the Pendulum* (New York, Holmes and Meier, 1989).

11. David Collier and Steven Levitsky, 'Democracy with Adjectives: Conceptual Innovation in Comparative Research', *World Politics* 49, 3, April 1997, pp. 430–451. Also see J. Samuel Valenzuela, 'Democratic Consolidation in Post-Transitional Settings: Notion, Process and Facilitating Conditions', Scott Mainwaring, Guillermo O'Donnell and J. Samuel Valenzuela (eds.), *Issues in Democratic Consolidation: The New South American Democracies in Comparative Perspective* (Notre Dame, University of Notre Dame Press, 1992), pp. 62–70.

12. For the argument that in discussing consolidation, the definition of democracy should be related to minimal conditions because no democracy can ever achieve the ideal that is associated with maximalist conditions, see Valenzuela, pp. 59–60.

13. Juan J. Linz and Alfred Stepan, *Problems of Democratic Transition and Consolidation. Southern Europe, South America, and Post-Communist Europe* (Baltimore, The Johns Hopkins University Press, 1996), pp. 5–6.

14. Linz and Stepan, *Problems ... ,* p. 5.

15. Larry Diamond, 'Introduction: In Search of Consolidation', Larry Diamond, Marc F. Plattner, Yun-han Chu and Hung-mao Tien (eds.), *Consolidating the Third Wave Democracies. Themes and Perspectives* (Baltimore, The Johns Hopkins University Press, 1997), p. xix.

16. For example, Gabriel A. Almond and Sidney Verba, *The Civic Culture: Political Attitudes and Democracy in Five Nations* (Boston, Little Brown and Co., 1965); Robert A. Dahl, *Polyarchy: Participation and Opposition* (New Haven, Yale University Press, 1971), pp. 124–162; Roland Pennock, *Democratic Political Theory* (Princeton, Princeton University Press, 1979); Larry Diamond (ed.), *Political Culture and Democracy in Developing Countries* (Boulder, Lynne Rienner, 1993).

17. For example, Larry Diamond, 'Toward Democratic Consolidation', *Journal of Democracy* 5, 3, July 1994, pp. 4–17; and Diamond, 'Introduction ... ', pp. xxx–xxxii.

18. Adam Przeworski, Michael Alvarez, Jose Antonio Cheibub and Fernando Limongi, 'What Makes Democracies Endure?', *Journal of Democracy* 7, 1, January 1996, pp. 39–55. As well as the economic factors noted above, the authors identified a democratic structure, favourable international climate, and parliamentary institutions.

Bibliography

This bibliography includes only works referred to in the notes of this book.

Aizcorbe, Roberto, *Argentina. The Peronist Myth. An Essay on the Cultural Decay in Argentina After the Second World War* (Hicksville, Exposition Press, 1975).

Almond, Gabriel A. and Verba, Sidney, *The Civic Culture: Political Attitudes and Democracy in Five Nations* (Boston, Little, Brown & Co., 1965).

Anderson, Perry, *Lineages of the Absolutist State* (London, Verso, 1979).

Angell, Alan, 'International Support for the Chilean Opposition, 1973–1989: Political Parties and the Role of Exiles', Whitehead, *International Dimensions*.

Ascherson, Neal, *The Polish August. What Happened in Poland* (Harmondsworth, Penguin, 1981).

Baloyra, Enrique A. (ed.), *Comparing New Democracies. Transition and Consolidation in Mediterranean Europe and the Southern Cone* (Boulder, Westview Press, 1987).

Baloyra, Enrique A., 'Democratic Transition in Comparative Perspective', Baloyra.

Behr, Edward, *'Kiss the Hand You Cannot Bite'. The Rise and Fall of the Ceausescus* (Harmondsworth, Penguin, 1991).

Bekk, John D., *The Bulgarian Communist Party from Blagoev to Zhivkov* (Stanford, Hoover Institution Press, 1986).

Bernhard, Michael, 'Civil Society and Democratic Transition in East Central Europe', *Political Science Quarterly* 108, 2, Summer 1993.

Bernhard, Michael, *The Origins of Democratization in Poland: Workers, Intellectuals, and Oppositional Politics, 1976–1980* (New York, Columbia University Press, 1993).

Blais, Andre and Dion, Stephane, 'Electoral Systems and the Consolidation of Democracies', Ethier.

Bollen, Kenneth A., 'Political Democracy and the Timing of Development', *American Sociological Review* 44, 4, 1979.

Borzutsky, Silvia, 'The Pinochet Regime: Crisis and Consolidation', James M. Malloy and Mitchell A. Seligson (eds.), *Authoritarians and Democrats. Regime Transition in Latin America* (Pittsburgh, University of Pittsburgh Press, 1987).

Boschi, Renato R., 'Social Movements, Party Systems and Democratic Consolidation: Brazil, Uruguay and Argentina', Ethier.

Bova, Russell, 'Political Dynamics of the Post-Communist Transition. A Comparative Perspective', *World Politics* 44, 1, October 1991.

Bowers, Stephen, 'Private Institutions in Service to the State: The German Democratic Republic's Church in Socialism', *East European Quarterly* xvi, 1, 1982.

Bunce, Valerie, 'Paper Curtains and Paper Tigers', *Slavic Review* 54, 4, Winter 1995.

Bunce, Valerie, 'Should Transitologists Be Grounded?', *Slavic Review* 54, 1, Spring 1995.

Campero, Guillermo, 'Entrepreneurs Under the Military Regime', Drake and Jaksic.

Cardoso, Fernando H., 'Entrepreneurs and the Transition Process: The Brazilian Case', O'Donnell *et al*, *Transitions ... Comparative Perspectives*.

Carothers, Thomas, 'The Resurgence of United States Political Development Assistance to Latin America in the 1980s', Whitehead, *International Dimensions*.

Carr, Raymond and Fusi, Juan Pablo, *Spain. Dictatorship to Monarchy* (London, Allen and Unwin, 1981).

Carter, April, *Democratic Reform in Yugoslavia: The Changing Role of the Party* (Princeton, Princeton University Press, 1982).

Casiagli, Mario, 'Spain: Parties and Party System in the Transition', *West European Politics* 7, 2, April 1984.

Casper, Gretchen and Taylor, Michelle M., *Negotiating Democracy. Transitions from Authoritarian Rule* (Pittsburgh, University of Pittsburgh Press, 1996).

Castles, Francis G., 'Barrington Moore's Thesis and Swedish Political Development', *Government and Opposition* 8, 3, Summer 1973.

Cavarozzi, Marcelo, 'Political Cycles in Argentina since 1955', O'Donnell *et al.*, *Transitions ... Latin America*.

Childs, David, *The GDR: Moscow's German Ally* (London, Allen and Unwin, 1983).

Cohen, Stephen F., 'The Friends and Foes of Change: Reformism and Conservatism in the Soviet Union', *Slavic Review* 38, 2, June 1979.

Collier, David (ed.), *The New Authoritarianism in Latin America* (Princeton, Princeton University Press, 1979).

Collier, David and Levitsky, Steven, 'Democracy with Adjectives: Conceptual Innovation in Comparative Research', *World Politics* 49, 3, April 1997.

Crawford, Keith, *East Central European Politics Today* (Manchester, Manchester University Press, 1996).

Dahl, Robert A., *Polyarchy. Participation and Opposition* (New Haven, Yale University Press, 1971).

Dahrendorf, Ralf, *Society and Democracy in Germany* (Garden City, Doubleday, 1969).

Danopoulos, Constantine P., 'Democratization by Golpe: The Experience of Modern Portugal', Danopoulos, *Military Disengagement*.

Danopoulos, Constantine P., 'Farewell to Man on Horseback: Intervention and Civilian Supremacy in Modern Greece', Constantine P. Danopoulos (ed.), *From Military to Civilian Rule* (London, Routledge, 1992).

Danopoulos, Constantine P. (ed.), *Military Disengagement from Politics* (London, Routledge, 1988).

Diamandouros, P. Nikiforos, 'Regime Change and the Prospects for Democracy in Greece: 1974–1983', O'Donnell *et al.*, *Transitions ... Southern Europe.*

Diamond, Larry, 'Economic Development and Democracy Reconsidered', *American Behavioral Scientist* 35, 4/5, March/June 1992.

Diamond, Larry, 'Introduction: In Search of Consolidation', Larry Diamond, Marc F. Plattner, Yun-han Chu and Hung-mao Tien (eds.), *Consolidating the Third Wave Democracies. Themes and Perspectives* (Baltimore, The Johns Hopkins University Press, 1997).

Diamond, Larry, *Political Culture and Democracy in Developing Countries* (Boulder, Lynne Rienner, 1993).

Dix, Robert H., 'The Breakdown of Authoritarian Regimes', *Western Political Quarterly* 35, 4, 1982.

Dore, Ronald P., 'Making Sense of History', *Archives europeenes de sociologie* X, 1969.

Downing, Brian M., 'Constitutionalism, Warfare, and Political Change in Early Modern Europe', *Theory and Society* 17, 7, 1988.

Drake Paul W. and Jaksic, Ivan, 'Introduction: Transformation and Transition in Chile, 1982–1990', Drake and Jaksic.

Drake, Paul W. and Jaksic, Ivan (eds.), *The Struggle for Democracy in Chile* (Lincoln, University of Nebraska Press, 1995).

Ekiert, Grzegorz, 'Democratization Processes in East Central Europe: A Theoretical Reconsideration', *British Journal of Political Science* 21, 3, 1991.

Ethier, Diane, 'Introduction: Processes of Transition and Democratic Consolidation: Theoretical Indicators', Ethier.

Ethier, Diane (ed.), *Democratic Transition and Consolidation in Southern Europe, Latin America and Southeast Asia* (London, Macmillan, 1990).

Femia, J. V., 'Barrington Moore and the Preconditions for Democracy', *British Journal of Political Science* 2, 1, 1972.

Ferreira, Hugo Gil and Marshall, Michael W., *Portugal's Revolution: Ten Years On* (Cambridge, Cambridge University Press, 1986).

Finer, S. E., *The Man on Horseback. The Role of the Military in Politics* (Harmondsworth, Penguin, 1975).

Fishman, Robert M., 'Rethinking State and Regime: Southern Europe's Transition to Democracy', *World Politics* 42, 3, April 1990.

Friedheim, Daniel V., 'Bringing Society Back into Democratic Transition Theory after 1989: Pact Making and Regime Collapse', *East European Politics and Societies* 7, 3, Fall, 1993.

Fukuyama, Francis, *The End of History and the Last Man* (London, Penguin, 1992).

Gamarra, Eduardo A., 'Bolivia: Disengagement and Democratisation', Danopoulos.

Garreton, Manuel Antonia, 'The Political Evolution of the Chilean Military Regime and Problems in the Transition to Democracy', O'Donnell *et al.*, *Transitions ... Latin America.*

Garreton, Manuel Antonio, 'The Political Opposition and the Party System Under the Military Regime', Drake and Jaksic.

Gillespie, Charles G., 'Uruguay's Transition from Collegial Military–Technocratic Rule', O'Donnell *et al.*, *Transitions ... Latin America.*

Gillespie, Charles Guy, *Negotiating Democracy. Politicians and Generals in Uruguay* (Cambridge, Cambridge University Press, 1991).

Gilmour, David, *The Transformation of Spain. From Franco to the Constitutional Monarchy* (London, Quartet Books, 1985).

Glenny, Misha, *The Rebirth of History. Eastern Europe in the Age of Democracy* (Harmondsworth, Penguin, 1990).

Gonzalez, Luis E., *Political Structures and Democracy in Uruguay* (Notre Dame, University of Notre Dame Press, 1991).

Grabendorff, Wolf, 'International Support for Democracy in Contemporary Latin America: The Role of the Party Internationals', Whitehead, *International Dimensions.*

Gunther, Richard, Diamandouros, P. Nikiforos and Puhle, Hans-Jurgen (eds.), *The Politics of Democratic Consolidation. Southern Europe in Comparative Perspective* (Baltimore, The Johns Hopkins University Press, 1995).

Haggard, Stephen and Kaufman, Robert R., *The Political Economy of Democratic Transitions* (Princeton, Princeton University Press, 1995).

Hagopian, Frances, ''Democracy by Undemocratic Means'? Elites, Political Pacts, and Regime Transition in Brazil', *Comparative Political Studies* 23, 2, July 1990.

Hausner, Jerzy, Jessop, Bob and Nielsen, Klaus (eds.), *Strategic Choice and Path Dependency in Post-Socialism. Institutional Dynamics in the Transformation Process* (Aldershot, Edward Elgar, 1995).

Higley, John and Gunther, Richard (eds.), *Elites and Democratic Consolidation in Latin America and Eastern Europe* (Cambridge, Cambridge University Press, 1992).

Holmes, Leslie, *Politics in the Communist World* (Oxford, Clarendon Press, 1986).

Hosking, Geoffrey, *The Awakening of the Soviet Union* (London, Heinemann, 1990).

Hruby, Suzanne, 'The Church in Poland and Its Political Influence', *Journal of International Affairs* 36, 2, 1982–83.

Huber, M. and Heinrich, H-G, 'Hungary – Quiet Progress?', Leslie Holmes (ed.), *The Withering Away of the State?* (London, Sage, 1981).

Huntington, Samuel P., 'How Countries Democratize', *Political Science Quarterly* 106, 4, 1991–92.

Huntington, Samuel P., *The Third Wave. Democratization in the Late Twentieth Century* (Norman, University of Oklahoma Press, 1991).

Huntington, Samuel P., 'Will More Countries Become Democratic?, *Political Science Quarterly* 99, 2, Summer 1984.

Hurrell, Andrew, 'The International Dimensions of Democratization in Latin America: The Case of Brazil', Whitehead, *International Dimensions.*

Jackson, Robert H. and Rosberg, Carl G., 'Personal Rule. Theory and Practice in Africa', *Comparative Politics* 16, 4, July 1984.

Janos, Andrew C., 'The Politics of Backwardness in Continental Europe, 1780–1945', *World Politics* xli, 3, April 1989.

Jones, E. L., *The European Miracle. Environments, Economies and Geopolitics in the History of Europe and Asia* (Cambridge, Cambridge University Press, 1981).

Karl, Terry Lynn, 'Dilemmas of Democratization in Latin America', *Comparative Politics* 23, 1, October 1990.

Karl, Terry Lynn, 'Petroleum and Political Pacts: The Transition to Democracy in Venezuela', O'Donnell *et al.*, *Transitions ... Latin America*.

Karl, Terry Lynn and Schmitter, Philippe C., 'From an Iron Curtain to a Paper Curtain: Grounding Transitologists or Students of Postcommunism?', *Slavic Review* 54, 4, Winter 1995.

Karl, Terry Lynn and Schmitter, Philippe C., 'Modes of Transition in Latin America, Southern and Eastern Europe', *International Social Science Journal* 128, May 1991.

Keane, John, *Civil Society and the State* (London, Verso, 1988),

Keane, John, *Democracy and Civil Society* (London, Verso, 1988).

Klein, Herbert S., *Bolivia. The Evolution of a Multi-Ethnic Society* (New York, Oxford University Press, 1992).

Korbonski, Andrzej, 'Poland', Teresa Rakowska-Harmstone (ed.) *Communism in Eastern Europe* (Bloomington, Indiana University Press, 1984).

Kovrig, Bennett, *Communism in Hungary. From Kun to Kadar* (Stanford, Hoover Institution Press, 1979).

Kukathas, Chandran, Lovell, David W. and Maley, William (eds.), *The Transition from Socialism. State and Civil Society in the USSR* (Melbourne, Longman Cheshire, 1991).

Kurth, James R., 'Industrial Change and Political Change: A European Perspective', Collier.

Leftwich, Adrian, 'From Democratization to Democratic Consolidation', David Potter, David Goldblatt, Margaret Kiloh and Paul Lewis (eds.), *Democratization* (Cambridge, Polity Press, 1997).

Levine, Daniel H., 'Paradigm Lost: Dependence to Democracy', *World Politics* 40, 3, April 1988.

Lewis, J. R. and Williams, A. M., 'Social Cleavages and Electoral Performance: The Social Basis of Portuguese Parties, 1976–83', *West European Politics* 7, 2, April 1984.

Lijphart, Arend, 'Constitutional Choices for New Democracies', Larry Diamond and Marc F. Plattner (eds.), *The Global Resurgence of Democracy* (Baltimore, The Johns Hopkins University Press, 1993).

Lijphart, Arend (ed.), *Parliamentary versus Presidential Government* (Oxford, Oxford University Press, 1992).

Lijphart, Arend and Waisman, Carlos H. (eds.), *Institutional Design in New Democracies. Eastern Europe and Latin America* (Boulder, Westview Press, 1996).

Linz, Juan J., 'An Authoritarian Regime: Spain', Erik Allardt and Stein Rokkan (eds.), *Mass Politics: Studies in Political Sociology* (New York, The Free Press, 1970).

Linz, Juan J., 'Crisis, Breakdown and Reequilibrium', Linz and Stepan (1978).

Linz, Juan J., 'The Perils of Presidentialism', *The Journal of Democracy* 1, 1, Winter 1990.

Linz, Juan J., 'Transitions to Democracy', *The Washington Quarterly* 13, 3, Summer 1990.

Linz, Juan J. and Stepan, Alfred, 'Political Crafting of Democratic Consolidation or Destruction: Europe and South American Comparisons', Robert A. Pastor (ed.), *Democracy in the Americas. Stopping the Pendulum* (New York, Holmes and Meier, 1989).

Linz, Juan J. and Stepan, Alfred, *Problems of Democratic Transition and Consolidation. Southern Europe, South America and Post-Communist Europe* (Baltimore, The Johns Hopkins University Press, 1996).

Linz, Juan J. and Stepan, Alfred, *The Breakdown of Democratic Regimes* (Baltimore, The Johns Hopkins University Press, 1978).

Linz, Juan J. and Valenzuela, Arturo (eds.), *The Failure of Presidential Democracy: Comparative Perspectives* (Baltimore, The Johns Hopkins University Press, 1994).

Lipset, Seymour Martin, 'Some Social Requisites of Democracy: Economic Development and Political Legitimacy', *American Political Science Review* 53, 1, March 1959.

Lipset, Seymour Martin, 'The Social Requisites of Democracy Revisited', *American Sociological Review* 59, February 1994.

Lipset, Seymour M., Soong, Kyoung-Ryung and Torres, John C. 'A Comparative Analysis of the Social Requisites of Democracy', *International Social Science Journal* 136, May 1993.

Lopez-Pintor, Rafael, 'Mass and Elite Perspectives in the Process of Transition to Democracy', Baloyra.

Lovenduski, Joni and Woodall, Jean, *Politics and Society in Eastern Europe* (London, Macmillan, 1987).

Luebbert, Gregory M., *Liberalism, Fascism, or Social Democracy. Social Classes and the Political Origins of Regimes in Interwar Europe* (Oxford, Oxford University Press, 1991).

Lyrintzis, Christos, 'Political Parties in Post-Junta Greece: A Case of "Bureaucratic Clientelism"', *West European Politics* 7, 2, April 1984.

MacLeod, Alex, 'The Parties and Consolidation of Democracy in Portugal: The Emergence of a Dominant Two-Party System', Ethier.

Mainwaring, Scott, 'Presidentialism, Multipartism, and Democracy: The Difficult Combination', *Comparative Political Studies* 26, 2, 1993.

Mainwaring, Scott, O'Donnell, Guillermo and Valenzuela, J. Samuel (eds.), *Issues in Democratic Consolidation. The New South American Democracies in Comparative Perspective* (Notre Dame, University of Notre Dame Press, 1992).

Mainwaring, Scott and Scully, Timothy R. (eds.). *Building Democratic Institutions. Party Systems in Latin America* (Stanford, Stanford University Press, 1995).

Mann, Michael, 'War and Social Theory: into Battle with Classes, Nations and States', Michael Mann, *States, War and Capitalism. Studies in Political Sociology* (Oxford, Blackwell, 1988).

Maravall, Jose M. and Santamaria, Julian, 'Political Change in Spain and the Prospects for Democracy', O'Donnell *et al.*, *Transitions ... Southern Europe*.

Martins, Luciano, 'The "Liberalization" of Authoritarian Rule in Brazil', O'Donnell *et al.*, *Transitions ... Latin America*.

Mastnak, Tomaz, 'Civil Society in Slovenia: From Opposition to Power', *Studies in Comparative Communism* XXIII, 3/4, Autumn/Winter 1990.

Maxwell, Kenneth, 'Regime Overthrow and the Prospects for Democratic Transition in Portugal', O'Donnell *et al.*, *Transitions ... Southern Europe*.

Maxwell, Kenneth, *The Making of Portuguese Democracy* (Cambridge, Cambridge University Press, 1995).

McGuire, James W., 'Interim Government and Democratic Consolidation: Argentina in Comparative Perspective', Yossi Shain and Juan J. Linz (eds.), *Between States. Interim Governments and Democratic Transitions* (Cambridge, Cambridge University Press, 1995).

McNeill, William, *The Rise of the West. A History of the Human Community* (Chicago, The University of Chicago Press, 1963).

McSweeney, Dean and Tempest, Clive, 'The Political Science of Democratic Transition in Eastern Europe', *Political Studies* xli, 3, September 1993.

Medhurst, Kenneth, 'Spain's Evolutionary Pathway from Dictatorship to Democracy', *West European Politics* 7, 2, April 1984.

Miller, Robert F. (ed.), *The Developments of Civil Society in Communist Systems* (Sydney, Allen and Unwin, 1992).

Moore Jr., Barrington, *Social Origins of Dictatorship and Democracy. Lord and Peasant in the Making of the Modern World* (Harmondsworth, Penguin, 1969).

Moore, Mick, 'Democracy and Development in Cross-National Perspective: A New Look at the Statistics', *Democratization* 2, 2, Summer 1995.

Mushaben, Joyce M. 'Swords to Plowshares: The Church, The State, and the East German Peace Movement', *Studies in Comparative Communism* xvii, 2, Summer 1984.

Nielsen, Klaus, Jessop, Bob and Hausner, Jerzy, 'Institutional Change in Post-Socialism', Hausner *et al.*

Nordlinger, Eric A., *Soldiers in Politics. Military Coups and Governments* (Englewood Cliffs, Prentice Hall, 1977).

O'Donnell, Guillermo, 'Illusions About Consolidation', *The Journal of Democracy* 7, 2, April 1996.

O'Donnell, Guillermo, 'Introduction', O'Donnell *et al.*, *Transitions ... Latin America*.

O'Donnell, Guillermo, *Modernization and Bureaucratic-Authoritarianism: Studies in South American Politics* (Berkeley, Institute of International Studies, University of California, Berkeley, 1973).

O'Donnell, Guillermo and Schmitter, Philippe C., *Transitions from Authoritarian Rule: Tentative Conclusions About Uncertain Democracies* (Baltimore, The Johns Hopkins University Press, 1986).

O'Donnell, Guillermo, Schmitter, Philippe C. and Whitehead, Laurence (eds.), *Transitions from Authoritarian Rule: Prospects for Democracy* (Baltimore, The Johns Hopkins University Press, 1986).

O'Donnell, Guillermo, Schmitter, Philippe C. and Whitehead, Laurence (eds.), *Transitions from Authoritarian Rule: Comparative Perspectives* (Baltimore, The Johns Hopkins University Press, 1986).

O'Donnell, Guillermo, Schmitter, Philippe C. and Whitehead, Laurence (eds.), *Transitions from Authoritarian Rule: Latin America* (Baltimore, The Johns Hopkins University Press, 1986).

O'Donnell, Guillermo, Schmitter, Philippe C. and Whitehead, Laurence (eds.), *Transitions from Authoritarian Rule: Southern Europe* (Baltimore, The Johns Hopkins University Press, 1986).

Opello Jr., Walter C., 'Portugal: A Case Study of International Determinants of Regime Transition', Pridham.

Pano, Nicholas C., 'Albania', Teresa Rakowska-Harmstone (ed.), *Communism in Eastern Europe* (Bloomington, Indiana University Press, 1984).

Payne, Stanley G., *The Franco Regime 1936–1975* (Madison, The University of Wisconsin Press, 1987).

Penniman, Howard R. (ed.), *Greece at the Polls. The National Elections of 1974 and 1977* (Washington, American Enterprise Institute for Public Policy Research, 1981).

Pennock, Roland, *Democratic Political Theory* (Princeton, Princeton University Press, 1979).

Pereira, Luis C. B., Maravall, Jose M. and Przeworski, Adam, *Economic Reforms in New Democracies. A Social Democratic Approach* (Cambridge, Cambridge University Press, 1993).

Perlmutter, Amos, *Modern Authoritarianism. A Comparative Institutional Analysis* (New Haven, Yale University Press, 1981).

Perlmutter, Amos, 'The Comparative Analysis of Military Regimes: Formations, Aspirations, and Achievements', *World Politics* xxxiii, 1, October 1980.

Pinkney, Robert, *Right-Wing Military Government* (Boston, Twayne Publishers, 1990).

Pinto-Duschinsky, Michael, 'International Political Finance: The Konrad Adenauer Foundation and Latin America', Whitehead, *International Dimensions*.

Polonsky, Antony, *The Little Dictators. The History of Eastern Europe since 1918* (London, Routledge and Kegan Paul, 1975).

Powell, Charles, 'International Aspects of Democratization; The Case of Spain', Whitehead, *International Dimensions*.

Preston, Paul, *The Triumph of Democracy in Spain* (London, Methuen, 1986).

Pridham, Geoffrey, 'International Influences and Democratic Transition: Problems of Theory and Practice in Linkage Politics', Pridham.

Pridham, Geoffrey (ed.), *Encouraging Democracy. The International Context of Regime Transition in Southern Europe* (Leicester, Leicester University Press, 1991).

Pridham, Geoffrey, 'The Politics of the European Community, Transnational Networks and Democratic Transition in Southern Europe', Pridham.

Pridham, Geoffrey and Lewis, Paul G. (eds.), *Stabilising Fragile Democracies. Comparing New Party Systems in Southern and Eastern Europe* (London, Routledge, 1996).

Przeworski, Adam, *Democracy and the Market. Political and Economic Reform in Eastern Europe and Latin America* (Cambridge, Cambridge University Press, 1991).

Przeworski, Adam, 'Democracy as a Contingent Outcome of Conflicts', Jon Elster and Rune Slagstad (eds.), *Constitutionalism and Democracy* (Cambridge, Cambridge University Press, 1986).

Przeworski, Adam, 'Some Problems in the Study of the Transition to Democracy', O'Donnell *et al.*, *Transitions ... Comparative Perspectives.*

Przeworski, Adam, 'The Games of Transition', Mainwaring *et al.*

Przeworski, Adam, Alvarez, Michael, Cheibub, Jose A. and Limongi, Fernando, 'What Makes Democracies Endure?', *The Journal of Democracy* 7, 1, January 1996.

Przeworski, Adam and Limongi, Fernando, 'Modernization: Theories and Facts', *World Politics* 49, 2, 1997.

Ramet, Pedro, 'Church and Peace in the GDR', *Problems of Communism* 33, 4, July–August 1984.

Ramet, Pedro, 'Disaffection and Dissent in East Germany', *World Politics* 35, 1, October 1984.

Ramet, Sabrina P., *Social Currents in Eastern Europe. The Sources and Meaning of the Great Transformation* (Durham, Duke University Press, 1991).

Rau, Zbigniew (ed.), *The Reemergence of Civil Society in Eastern Europe and the Soviet Union* (Boulder, Westview Press, 1991).

Remmer, Karen L., 'New Theoretical Perspectives on Democratization', *Comparative Politics* 28, 1, October 1995.

Remmer, Karen L., 'Redemocratization and the Impact of Authoritarian Rule in Latin America', *Comparative Politics* 17, 3, April 1985.

Rigby, T. H., 'The USSR: End of a Long, Dark, Night?', Miller.

Roth, Guenther, 'Personal Rulership, Patrimonialism, and Empire Building in the New States', *World Politics* xx, 2, January 1968.

Rothman, Stanley, 'Barrington Moore and the Dialectics of Revolution: An Essay Review', *American Political Science Review* 64, 1, March 1970.

Rothschild, Joseph, *East Central Europe Between the Two World Wars* (Seattle, University of Washington Press, 1974).

Rothschild, Joseph, *Return to Diversity. A Political History of East Central Europe Since World War II* (Oxford, Oxford University Press, 1993.

Rueschemeyer, Dietrich, Stephens, Evelyne H. and Stephens, John, *Capitalist Development and Democracy* (Cambridge, Polity Press, 1992).

Rupnik, Jacques, 'Dissent in Poland, 1968–78: the End of Revisionism and the Rebirth of Civil Society', Rudolf L. Tokes (ed.), *Opposition in Eastern Europe* (London, Macmillan, 1979).

Rusinow, Denison, *The Yugoslav Experiment 1948–1974* (Berkeley, University of California Press, 1977).

Rustow, Dankwart A., 'Transitions to Democracy. Toward a Dynamic Model', *Comparative Politics* 2, 3, April 1970.

Salamon, Lester M., 'Comparative History and the Theory of Modernization', *World Politics* 23, 1, October 1970.

Schedler, Andreas, 'What is Democratic Consolidation?', *The Journal of Democracy* 9, 2, 1988.

Schmitter, Philippe C., 'An Introduction to Southern European Transitions from Authoritarian Rule: Italy, Greece, Portugal, Spain and Turkey', O'Donnell *et al.*, *Transitions ... Southern Europe*.

Schmitter, Philippe C., 'The International Context of Contemporary Democratization', *Stanford Journal of International Affairs* 2, 1993.

Schmitter, Philippe C. and Karl, Terry Lynn, 'The Conceptual Travels of Transitologists and Consolidologists: How Far to the East Should They Attempt to Go?', *Slavic Review*, 53, 1, Spring 1994.

Schopflin, George, 'Opposition and Para-Opposition: Critical Currents in Hungary, 1968–1978', Rudolf L. Tokes (ed.), *Opposition in Eastern Europe* (London, Macmillan, 1979).

Schopflin, George, 'The Political Traditions of Eastern Europe', *Daedalus*, 119, Winter 1990.

Selcher, Wayne A. (ed.), *Political Liberalization in Brazil. Dynamics, Dilemmas and Future Prospects* (Boulder, Westview Press, 1985).

Seton-Watson, Hugh, *Eastern Europe Between the Wars, 1918–1941* (London, Cambridge University Press, 1945).

Shafir, Michael, *Romania. Politics, Economics and Society* (London, Frances Pinter, 1985).

Share, Donald, 'Transitions to Democracy and Transition through Transaction', *Comparative Political Studies* 19, 4, January 1987.

Share, Donald and Mainwaring, Scott, 'Transitions Through Transaction: Democratization in Brazil and Spain', Selcher.

Shoup, Paul, 'Crisis and Reform in Yugoslavia', *Daedalus* 79, Spring 1989.

Shugart, M. and Carey J., *Presidents and Assemblies: Constitutional Design and Electoral Dynamics* (Cambridge, Cambridge University Press, 1992).

Sikkink, Kathryn, 'The Effectiveness of US Human Rights Policy, 1973–1980', Whitehead, *International Dimensions*.

Silber, Laura and Little, Allan, *The Death of Yugoslavia* (Harmondsworth, Penguin, 1995).

Simechka, Milan, *The Restoration of Order. The Normalization of Czechoslovakia 1969–1976* (London, Verso, 1984).

Skilling, H. Gordon, *Charter 77 and Human Rights in Czechoslovakia* (London, Allen and Unwin, 1981).

Skilling, H. Gordon, *Czechoslovakia's Interrupted Revolution* (Princeton, Princeton University Press, 1976).

Skilling, H. Gordon, 'Independent Currents in Czechoslovakia', *Problems of Communism* 34, 1, January–February 1985.

Skilling, H. Gordon, *Samizdat and an Independent Society in Central and Eastern Europe* (Columbus, Ohio State University Press, 1989).

Skocpol, Theda, 'A Critical Review of Barrington Moore's *Social Origins of Dictatorship and Democracy*', *Politics and Society* 4, 1, 1973.

Skocpol, Theda, *States and Social Revolution. A Comparative Analysis of France, Russia and China* (Cambridge, Cambridge University Press, 1979).

Snyder, Richard, 'Explaining Transitions from Neopatrimonial Dictatorships', *Comparative Politics* 24, 4, July 1992.

Staniszkis, Jadwiga, *Poland's Self-Limiting Revolution* (Princeton, Princeton University Press, 1984).

Starr, Harvey,'Democratic Dominoes: Diffusion Approaches to the Spread of Democracy in the International System', *Journal of Conflict Resolution* 35, 2, June 1991.

Starr, S. Frederick, 'Soviet Union: A Civil Society', *Foreign Policy* 70, Spring, 1988.

Stepan, Alfred, 'Paths Toward Redemocratization: Theoretical and Comparative Considerations', O'Donnell *et al.*, *Transitions … Comparative Perspectives*.

Stepan, Alfred, *Rethinking Military Politics. Brazil and the Southern Cone* (Princeton, Princeton University Press, 1988).

Stepan, Alfred and Skach, Cindy, 'Constitutional Frameworks and Democratic Consolidation: Parliamentarianism and Presidentialism', *World Politics* 46, 1, October 1993.

Stephens, John D., 'Democratic Transition and Breakdown in Western Europe, 1870–1939: A Test of the Moore Thesis', *American Journal of Sociology* 94, 5, March 1989.

Stokes, Gale, 'The Social Origins of East European Politics', Daniel Chirot (ed.), *The Origins of Backwardness in Eastern Europe. Economics and Politics from the Middle Ages Until the Early Twentieth Century* (Berkeley, University of California Press, 1989).

Story, Jonathan and Pollack, Benny, 'Spain's Transition: Domestic and External Linkages', Pridham.

Suda, Zdenek, *Zealots and Rebels. A History of the Ruling Communist Party of Czechoslovakia* (Stanford, Hoover Institution Press, 1980).

Terry, Sarah M., 'Thinking About Post-communist Transitions: How Different Are They?', *Slavic Review* 52, 2, Summer 1993.

Therborn, Goran, 'The Rule of Capital and the Rise of Democracy', *New Left Review* 103, May–June 1977.

Tilton, Timothy A., 'The Social Origins of Liberal Democracy: The Swedish Case', *American Political Science Review* 68, 2, June 1974.

Tismaneanu, Vladimir, 'Nascent Civil Society in the German Democratic Republic', *Problems of Communism* 38, 2/3, March/June 1989.

Tokes, Rudolf L., 'Hungarian Reform Initiatives', *Problems of Communism* 33, 5, September–October 1984.

Tokes, Rudolf L., *Hungary's Negotiated Revolution. Economic Reform, Social Change and Political Succession, 1957–1990* (Cambridge, Cambridge University Press, 1996).

Tovias, Alfred, 'The International Context of Democratic Transition', *West European Politics* 7, 2, April 1984.

Tsingos, Basilios, 'Underwriting Democracy: The European Community and Greece', Whitehead, *International Dimensions*.

Tumin, Jonathan, 'The Theory of Democratic Development', *Theory and Society* 11, 2, 1982.

Valenzuela, Arturo, 'The Military in Power. The Consolidation of One-Man Rule', Drake and Jaksic.

Valenzuela, J. Samuel, 'Democratic Consolidation in Post-Transitional Settings: Notion, Process and Facilitating Conditions', Mainwaring, O'Donnell and Valenzuela.

Valenzuela, J. Samuel and Valenzuela, Arturo, *Military Rule in Chile. Dictatorships and Oppositions* (Baltimore, The Johns Hopkins University Press, 1986).

Vanhanen, Tatu, *Prospects of Democracy. A Study of 172 Countries* (London, Routledge, 1997).

Varas, Augusto, 'The Crisis of Legitimacy of Military Rule in the 1980s', Drake and Jaksic.

Verney, Susannah and Couloumbis, Theodore, 'State-international Systems Interaction and the Greek Transition to Democracy in the mid-1970s', Pridham.

Volkmer, Werner, 'East Germany: Dissenting Views During the Last Decade', Rudolf L. Tokes (ed.), *Opposition in Eastern Europe* (London, Macmillan, 1979).

Waisman, Carlos H., 'Capitalism, the Market and Democracy', *American Behavioral Scientist* 35, 4/5 March/June 1992.

Weigle, Marcia A. and Butterfield, Jim, 'Civil Society in Reforming Communist Regimes. The Logic of Emergence', *Comparative Politics* 25, 1 October 1992.

Welsh, Helga A., 'Political Transition Processes in Central and Eastern Europe', *Comparative Politics* 26, 4, July 1994.

Wekkin, Gary D. *et al.* (eds.), *Building Democracy in One-Party Systems* (Westport, Praeger, 1993).

Whitehead, Laurence, 'Bolivia's Failed Revolution', O'Donnell *et al.*, *Transitions ... Latin America*.

Whitehead, Laurence, 'Democracy and Decolonization: East Central Europe', Whitehead.

Whitehead, Laurence, 'Democracy by Convergence and Southern Europe: a Comparative Politics Perspective', Pridham.

Whitehead, Laurence, 'International Aspects of Democratization', O'Donnell *et al.*, *Transitions ... Comparative Perspectives*.

Whitehead, Laurence, 'The Imposition of Democracy: The Caribbean', Whitehead.

Whitehead, Laurence (ed.), *The International Dimensions of Democratization. Europe and the Americas* (Oxford, Oxford University Press, 1996).

Wiarda, Howard, 'Toward a Framework for the Study of Political Change in the Iberic–Latin Tradition: The Corporative Model', *World Politics* 25, 2, January 1972.

Wiener, Jonathan M., 'The Barrington Moore Thesis and Its Critics', *Theory and Society* 2, 1975.

Willner, Ann R., *The Spellbinders. Charismatic Political Leadership* (New Haven, Yale University Press, 1984).

Zhang, Baohui, 'Corporatism, Totalitarianism, and Transitions to Democracy', *Comparative Political Studies* 27, 1, April 1994.

Zwaan, Ton, 'One Step Forward, Two Steps Back. Tumin's Theory of Democratic Development: A Comment', *Theory and Society* 11, 2, 1982.

Index

Rueschemeyer, Dietrich *et al.*
106–14, 118
Russia 222–3

Soviet Union 1, 17, 22, 23, 84, 176,
191, 193, 194, 205, 208–10,
211, 212, 213, 214, 215, 216,
217, 227, 228, 229, 232–3
Spain 1, 21, 24, 25–6, 28, 53, 55,
56, 58, 64, 66, 67, 68, 92, 93,
128–36, 162, 173, 176, 179,
182, 183

transition 1, 8–9, 43–79, 80–95,
124–7, 174–88, 189–211,
229–34, 245, 254–5, 258–9,
265–6
literature 7, 8, 43–79, 80–95,
212
through extrication 69–70, 127,
145–60, 174

through replacement 70–1, 127,
160–74
through transaction 68–9,
124–7, 128–45, 174

Uruguay 2, 26, 54, 55, 58, 64, 66,
69, 93, 150–6, 171, 172–3, 176,
178, 179, 184–5
USA 19, 23, 24, 63, 64, 160

war 8, 18, 19, 74, 100
waves of democratization 1–2, 8,
20, 21, 243
working class 4, 16–18, 104,
108–13, 115–16, 129, 142–3,
145, 147, 148, 159, 161, 163,
165, 217–23, 224–5, 258

Yugoslavia 24, 27, 191, 205–6,
211, 213, 214, 215, 216, 217,
218, 221, 227, 228, 229, 232